# BENDING OUR REALITY

# BENDING OUR REALITY

### Viviana Escobar

**MANA UNIVERSAL**
PUBLISHING

Library of Congress Control Number: 2023915543
ISBN: 979-8-9996596-0-6
Published by Mana Universal

# BENDING OUR REALITY

How to Easily Develop Your Emotional Intelligence
and Physical Well-being through Breathwork Technology
and Lifestyle Hacks

Author & Creatrix
**Viviana Escobar**

Illustrations & Co-creation of The Mana Breathwork Universe
**Joaquin *"Espinacas"* Astelarra**

Foreword
**Carolina Escobar**

Photography
**Santiago Vasquez**

Design
**Viviana Escobar**
**Joaquin Astelarra**
**Carlos Mendoza**
**Oscar Ruiz**

This book is the result of extensive research,
my personal experience, and the experiences of the masters,
teachers, and students who've impacted
my journey.

In loving memory of Leonard Orr
& Mango Eterno

## Dedicated to

The ones before me, the ones with me, and the ones to come.

My beloved family, who have always supported
and encouraged me on my journey.

My dedicated teachers, who have imparted their wisdom
and guidance.

And my darling students,
who've shown me just as much as I've shown them.

May this book serve as a reminder of the power of breath,
mindfulness, and connection to self and others.

# Table of Contents

# Disclaimer

Before you delve into the breathwork practices or apply the concepts mentioned in this book, we request you read this disclaimer meticulously. Your usage of this book implies your acceptance and agreement with the stipulations detailed below.

Personal Accountability: This book's author is not a licensed healthcare expert or therapist. The material offered in this book is primarily educational. We underscore that any engagement in the breathwork practices or application of ideas articulated in this book is purely at your discretion and risk.

Individual Variability: Everyone's physical and mental makeup is distinct. The techniques and exercises expounded in this book may not align with everyone's requirements. Hence, it is paramount to seek advice from a competent healthcare expert before you embark on any new fitness or wellness routine, including breathwork.

Health Concerns: Breathwork exercises often encompass deep breathing and might trigger physical and emotional reactions. If you suffer from preexisting medical conditions, including but not limited to, asthma, cardiovascular issues, hypertension, or any respiratory disorders, or if you are pregnant, we strongly urge you to confer with your healthcare provider prior to experimenting with any breathwork methods.

Emotional and Psychological Implications: Breathwork sessions can occasionally awaken intense emotions or bring to light buried memories. If you have a past of trauma or mental health challenges, or if you are presently in therapy, it is crucial to check with your therapist or mental health professional before initiating any breathwork practices elucidated in this book.

Liability Release: The author and publisher of this book absolve themselves of any liability for direct, indirect, or consequential loss or harm incurred by any individual as a consequence of the use of the techniques, practices, or ideas portrayed in this book. By utilizing this book, you consent to absolve the author, publisher, and any affiliated parties of any liability, including, but not limited to, injuries, illnesses, or other adverse impacts that may emerge from the implementation of the information contained in this book.

Author's Stance: The techniques, practices, and viewpoints expressed in this book reflect the author's perspectives alone. They are not designed to supplant professional medical counsel or direction. The author advises you to exercise personal discernment and prudence while leveraging the information provided.

By persisting with the use of this book, you acknowledge that you have read, comprehended, and accepted the above disclaimer. Should you disagree with any component of this disclaimer, we recommend that you desist from using this book or incorporating the breathwork practices detailed within it.

# Foreword

People usually consider walking on water or in thin air a miracle. But I think the real miracle is not to walk either on water or in thin air, but to walk on earth. Every day we are engaged in a miracle which we don't even recognize: a blue sky, white clouds, green leaves, the black, curious eyes of a child—our own two eyes. All is a miracle.

- Thich Nhat Hanh

My sister Viviana's life has always been marked by a profound curiosity about human consciousness. From an early age, I witnessed her mind ignite with wonder at the mysteries of existence, reaching for questions others might not have dared to ask. Even then, it was clear to me that her path—through the study of conscious breathing and the deep connection between body, mind, and soul—would become a journey of healing and transformation.

Over the years, Viviana has encountered life's miracles in her own unique way, always guided by the unwavering light of resilience. Bending Our Reality is more than a book; it is the embodiment of a life lived with purpose. It stands as a testament to the courage it takes to transcend pain and fear, and as an open invitation to explore the vast universe that resides within each of us.

As a psychologist specializing in human behavior, I have observed how Viviana has transformed her understanding of conscious breathing into a powerful instrument for inner growth.

It is not merely about the act of breathing—it is about awakening to each inhale and exhale, and discovering how every breath brings us closer to the essence of who we truly are.

This book is not simply a guide; it is a key—a gentle yet profound call to unlock the most authentic version of ourselves. Every page bears the imprint of Viviana's lived experience: her insight, her strength, and her boundless compassion.

I am pleased to offer this foreword as a witness to her path of transformation. I believe that within these pages, every reader will find not only inspiration, but a mirror—a reflection of their own potential and truth.

- Carolina Escobar L.

Psychologist · Psychometrician · Data Scientist

MSc. in Methodology of Behavioral and Health Sciences

## Preface
## Living a Joyful Life

I'm excited for your willingness to go on this journey with me and, through it, become more of who you are, for that is what life and these writings are all about.

Together, we will explore the idea of living a joyful and more authentic life. We will dive deep into the power of breathwork and self-love. Because unlike anything else, there is infinite power waiting in our breath. Resting in the space between our inhale and exhale. Accessible in the space between our thoughts. It is the source of all creation within ourselves; all humans have it, and we are all made of it. It is always available, but we keep looking outside ourselves.

For generations, we've been in the pursuit of happiness, creating and improving upon supportive societal structures, but have you noticed that the old systems and agreements are starting to fall apart? And as we move into this new world, we can no longer count on the social contracts that used to sustain us. So, instead of relying upon institutions, we are invited to rely upon ourselves moving toward the kind of sovereignty necessary to evolve.

We have been taught to run worldwide, prove our worth no matter what, and strive for something constantly. We have been conditioned to chase a million goals, or the next amazing one, rather than appreciating the one happening right now, being present in our presence, and sensing it deeply, and now is the time to change that.

As human beings, we share this unique ability to change everything in a heartbeat.

We can go beyond our minds, beliefs, and concepts with one breath. When we consciously take a deep breath, pause, and become aware of the now, we expand it, and the present moment contains everything that has ever happened as well as all our potential futures. It is the seed of all that it is and a point of acceptance, surrender, and inspiration. In the now, we connect to a power greater than everything we ever thought possible; we become the actual creators of our lives.

From there, we can see what we couldn't see before. From there, we are in the frequency of infinite possibilities, and we can become anything, discover the most profound wisdom, and overcome everything. For every question ever asked, there is an answer. For every step in our paths, there will be guidance. There is awakening. There is no separation, just oneness—everything connected in all ways—a step out of polarity into a new dimension.

The more time we spend in that frequency of possibilities, the more infinite we will realize we are. We start remembering who we are and align as we express our true authentic selves.

Gradually, our fears fade away, and peaceful, joyful excitement replaces them. The tension becomes a calm smile. Our smiles become appreciation that embraces our soul and nurtures our heart until it opens up fully and never loses sight of its actual and infinite nature. I feel your desire to evolve, and I connect to it.

Are you ready to take a leap? To see beyond the veil? To overcome the fears and doubts that hold you back?

Inspiration (n.)

The immediate influence of a God, is from Old French inspiration, "inhaling, breathing in; inspiration," from Late Latin inspirationem (nominative inspiratio), noun of action from the past participle stem of Latin inspirare "blow into, breathe upon," figuratively "inspire, excite, inflame," + spirare "to breathe."

# CHAPTER 1
# Awakening Is Not Linear

# When We Surrender, We Are Reborn into an Extraordinary Life

Awakening at dawn on a hot summer morning in Los Angeles back in 2002, I found myself gripped by a pain so severe, movement felt insurmountable.

This sharp pain, originating from my lumbar spine and radiating down to my lower extremities, rendered me immobile. In an instant, I found myself swallowed by a tempest of emotions, sensing the enclosing walls tightening as though entrapped within a progressively constricting tunnel.

As I struggled to comprehend my surroundings, I found myself asking, "What is happening to me? Where is Adrian?" Even through the haze of sleepiness, the thoughts in my mind revolved around locating my child. He was upstairs, but my ever-watchful maternal instinct remained focused on my seven-year-old son, because only a few months had passed since our relocation to the United States.

I was transported in an ambulance to a nearby hospital where I immediately underwent spinal surgery. After the procedure, I started experiencing high levels of pain in my right ankle and foot. The doctors were perplexed by my symptoms, unable to clarify not only the root cause of my pain but also the emergence of new, troubling symptoms.

As time wore on, I became painfully aware that they were essentially in the dark about my condition. My ensuing months were spent in a disconcerting cycle of frequent emergency room visits and medical appointments, all in a quest for a precise diagnosis. One physician even raised the alarming possibility of amputating my leg.

The pain was so intense that I was relegated to a mostly horizontal existence, spending the majority of each day lying down. My mobility was so impaired that I was forced to navigate my world in a wheelchair. For me, this was devastating.

My medications were so strong that their side effects, combined with my symptoms, didn't allow me to function. I lived with the highest pain levels and narcotics effects and couldn't see a way out.

After a while, the warrior in me gave up, and I began to experience deep grief. My dreams were gone, along with everything I was. I was experiencing the loss of my identity, personality, financial stability, my first marriage, my profession, and my independence, and seeing the awful consequences of my condition on my son's life. It was in a constant state of physical and emotional pain. It broke me into pieces.

I felt akin to a dim light, struggling to sustain its luminescence. If I were a bulb, I'd have been one stuck on a fading dimmer switch, straining to hold on to that glow, that spark of energy that said, "Hey, I'm still here, you know." I could feel the urge to flicker out, taking up more space in my chest every passing day, like some cosmic tenant that had overstayed its welcome.

In the quiet hours of the night, when the world withdrew into its dreams and stars stood as silent sentinels in the expansive sky, I found myself in solitary contemplation, the bitter anticipation of my end looming—a distinctive flavor on my tongue. It held a familiar sense, similar to the taste of aged wine—layered with undertones of fear and a hint of solace.

Balancing on life's precipice, the veil separating existence from oblivion seemed almost translucent, the lure of the beyond unnervingly persuasive. Yet, every time I thought giving up was my only choice, there arose within me a stately presence—a resilient ember that rejected these thoughts.

I experienced the dizzy dance of joy and sorrow, love and loss, and found it was the joy and love that I couldn't bring myself to abandon. The end, I decided, could wait.

With the arrival of winter, the festive glow of holiday lights began to flicker all around us, illuminating our every step.

One evening, while we were decorating the Christmas tree, the enticing aroma of cinnamon, pumpkin, and cardamom awakened my senses, compelling me to take a deep, life-affirming breath.

That inhalation was the very essence of life itself. I recall a fleeting moment of absolute lucidity amidst the fog of a morphine-induced disorientation, and my child's eyes mirroring the festive lights. I could sense my own heartbeat resounding once more. His innocent eyes were the embodiment of purity and goodness. Have you ever experienced it? Have you ever discerned love reflected in another's gaze? Have you ever pinpointed the precise instant when you comprehend, from your core, that you are capable of choice?

In these moments, we realize that we can choose the kind of life we want to live, and no matter how distracted we are, these moments will find us.

## Life Is About Choices

After a year, my treating doctors gave me a new diagnosis, a condition that medicine didn't understand well: Complex Regional Pain Syndrome (CRPS). Back then, it used to be called Reflex Sympathetic Dystrophy Syndrome.

CRPS is a form of pain that can affect an arm or a leg and other parts of the body. Its development is caused by an injury to or difference in the peripheral and central nervous systems. It can also appear after surgery or stroke and can progress to more disabling signs and symptoms.

Usually, it starts in one limb. The pain is overwhelming and stays at high levels along with other symptoms in the affected limb, like noticeable changes in temperature, nails, skin, bone density, and muscle mass; hypersensitivity to cold and touch; continuous burning or throbbing pain; changes in skin color, ranging from white and blotchy to red or blue; and severe swelling and weakness.

CRPS can spread to other areas in the body, such as the opposite limb. It is not transmissible directly from one person to another, but it's considered by some doctors to be irreversible. Its diagnosis is similar to saying, "Hey, you have a short circuit, but sorry, we don't know how to fix it."

I was determined to survive the excruciating pain and symptoms. I went from a wheelchair to relying on a cane and then gradually back on my two feet, walking with mild effort. The pain in my spine and foot was more manageable but still present enough to keep me researching.

Throughout the subsequent years, I found myself in survival mode, oscillating between debilitating flare-ups of CRPS and temporary bouts of recovery. Despite consulting with numerous experts, I found their predictions confusing and their treatment plans ineffective. Occasionally, their approaches even inflicted severe harm.

Further complicating my health were three serious car accidents that occurred over the years, each exacerbating my spine's condition.

It was during the time I was working alongside doctors that the third car accident took place. By then, the accumulation of injuries on my spine was so substantial that I began to perceive the situation as more than just a mere physical event. Could this be a reflection of past traumas? Could it be tied to a previous life, or was it the manifestation of some negative energy I was clinging onto?

I decided to shift my focus inward, seeking answers from within instead of relying on external sources. This marked the onset of a profound journey of self-discovery. Synchronously, the Yoga Path of the Audible Life Stream Lineage crossed my way, introducing me to the benefits of a plant-based diet and reminding me of my connection with the transformative power of meditation, a technique I learned as a child. A sense of familiarity began to resurface, akin to a long-forgotten sensation of returning to a place I didn't know existed. I could see how I was craving to feel my heart full, my soul seen, and my body loved.

## Ancestral Echoes

Since my childhood in Colombia, I have had mystical conversations with my elders, recognized that we all have exceptional gifts, and have known how to direct that energy. I had the natural aptitude for seeing and listening to what others couldn't see. When I was seven months old, my young mother would see me speaking with spirits. I started talking before I began to walk. I would spend hours communicating with the spirits with my voice and hand gestures.

As I grew, she thought I had a great imagination and, on many occasions, that something was wrong with me. Too often, children with psychic abilities are prescribed medication and even taken to mental facilities. I grew up believing something was off with me, and I enjoyed the 'band-aid' approach to my treatment and the pills' effects.

During my spine surgery recovery in California, I went to every church, temple, and school of thought I could find. I read philosophy and listened to masters and teachers from different doctrines and disciplines. But I kept feeling there was so much more beyond these structures. I decided to return to my birth country and reconnect with my roots to ask all who had been before me.

I embarked on a journey to the vibrant landscapes of my Colombia, immersing myself in the wisdom of Taita Ruben, a divine mentor hailing from the Inga tribe. Throughout this year of discovery, I navigated a myriad of profound, soul-stirring encounters under the guidance of sacred plant medicine.

The yagé and other plants offered an extraordinary journey that took me into realms of deep transformation. This immersive experience served as a catalyst for healing, touching the very core of my physical, mental, emotional, and spiritual existence. It was intense, yet in its intensity, I found a depth of healing that was profoundly transformative.

Sacred plants are nature's generous gift, best appreciated when you're guided by an experienced "Wisdom Keeper"—someone who's skilled and pure at heart. When you approach these wonders with a kind of humble respect, a liberated mind, and an accepting heart, you enter a whole new realm of understanding.

Over a fascinating passage, I communed with these plants more than twenty times, immersing myself in their soothing wisdom. In my last "Pinta," I received a profound message: my journey with the plants was complete for now. It was a breath-amplifying moment.

This led me on a dive within, navigating through my fragmented self. Slowly, I began to reassemble the pieces of my own being. My psychic abilities, once dormant, resurfaced, much like a forgotten melody suddenly playing again.

The sense of déjà vu was like a familiar knowing. I observed a significant improvement in my physical health, a bonus that came hand-in-hand with my inner growth. Above all, I awakened to my profound connection to Source Energy, the life-sustaining force that powers the universe. That awareness was both grounding and empowering, anchoring my experiences into a reality I had never dreamed possible.

The pain led me to study with the Taitas, deepening my understanding of how interconnected the body, mind, and energy are.

I learned how unresolved energy causes dysregulation in the nervous system and how much support nature provides.

Finally, I was feeling strong and more like myself. I wanted to do it all! So in the fall of 2007, I returned to Los Angeles as a single mother, healthy and full of life.

A new passion for life enveloped me, pushing me to engage in every activity I'd long denied myself. My world revolved around the pivot of affirmation, ambition, the elegance of a pair of stilettos, a cascade of achievements, and a burning desire to match the zeal of my peers.

However, after a few years, my body bore the brunt of this whirlwind pace, signaling me of wear and tear. Stubbornly, I chose to ignore the pleas of my own body.

Gradually, a certain dependency grew within me—a dependency on anything that could numb the pain, silence my body's protests, and veil my raw emotions. I sought solace in anything that would perpetuate the waning euphoria of divine oneness and the exhilarating rush of primal energy.

And why shouldn't I? The allure of feeling invincible amidst the turmoil was an illusion too tantalizing to resist. I fell into the rhythm of 'conditioning,' letting it dictate the beats of my life.

As 2014 wound down, after an intense few years of turbocharged performance and an escalating reliance on prescription drugs, I landed back in the cold, clinical world of a hospital. My reality had morphed into a glaring reflection of my inner turmoil—a relentless tide of bottled-up emotions, an assortment of traumas, and a mind that had lost its ability to quiet down.

Upon leaving the hospital, I had a breakdown. I couldn't do it anymore. The pain was back. I was experiencing various spine and health complications and had up to twenty panic attacks daily. By then, I was running two companies, had a very active social life, and was successfully fulfilling all my responsibilities, or that's what my anxiety believed.

A few months later, in the spring of 2015, I went to pick up my mother at the Los Angeles International Airport, and in one of those beautiful moments where all is aligned, a man stood next to my mother at the curb, waiting for his ride. When I exited the car to welcome my mom with a hug, I saw him looking at me with his sage, six-color eyes, extremely familiar face, and I-know-you vibe.

## Have We Been Here Before?

Instantly, a bond was formed. Joaquin was on a journey accompanied by his friends Leonard Orr and Egbert Sukop. They introduced me to Rebirthing Breathwork.

Joaquin led me through my first session, a deep dive into the inner self, just before leaving for the East Coast for a while.

Egbert remained with us, and became our teacher, and in the following ten days, Adrian and I immersed ourselves in daily breathwork sessions. Our Valley Village apartment began to pulse with newfound energy. It was as though it had become a vortex.

On the third day, I called my assistant to let her know I was taking time off without any logical explanation. I couldn't express with words what was going on. It was unfathomable. We gave away most of the objects in our place during the next few days, including our beds. Not too many things seemed necessary to keep. We rearranged what was left. It was like we were all floating in space with nothing to stop us, just in a loving and supporting free fall. I had profound insights and understanding, regressions, downloads, DNA activations, released birth trauma, generational trauma, and all types of trauma. Dopamine, serotonin, endorphins, oxytocin—my body was being hijacked with all kinds of feel-good hormones.

The process of energy breathing is a profound experience, and it can shake you from the core of your being in just a few days or even in one session. A good facilitator can be a mirror of our true path in life.

In my sessions, paradigms shifted for me; my whole perception shifted and turned again and again. I let go of the need to solve it all mentally, and I discovered my innate inner technology to make the right decisions at the right time. My mind's eye was wide open. I synced with my infinite intelligence; I felt the creative energy flowing through me and to me. All the answers were in front of me. All the possibilities, pure LOVE energy, felt almost tangible. By observing my breath, I was reborn.

## A New Way

We are multidimensional beings living a physical experience.

Of all the therapies I tried, breathwork was the one that genuinely gave me the ability to naturally initiate the shift. It transformed me so profoundly that healing was just a natural consequence.

Our suffering intuitively guides us to heal ancient wounds and to awaken to our life's purpose. Now, I was the expansion of consciousness and breathwork, my bridge to Source. The torch was lit, and I was eager to go deeper into this (old) new lifestyle.

In the summer of 2015, Joaquin and I planned to deepen our connection. Although we had shared a kiss before, this was to be the first time we would truly immerse ourselves in each other's company.

That same summer, we participated in the SierraVille Annual Rebirthing Training with Leonard Orr, known as "The Father of Breathwork," whom I had met earlier in Los Angeles.

Later in the fall, my son Adrian journeyed to Leonard's home in Virginia to study breathwork under both his and Egbert's mentorship. Over the following years, Joaquin and I remained focused on expanding our knowledge and assisting Leonard with his Conscious Energy Breathing training in both Los Angeles and Ojai. Leonard departed from this realm in Asheville, NC, on September 5, 2019. He left behind a treasure trove of knowledge in his books for all his students worldwide.

After his passing, we continued our studies and collaborations with world-renowned researchers, doctors, spiritual teachers, and other masters of breathwork. We created a library of healing modalities, each contributing to our growth. As a result of these experiments, Joaquin and I developed a comprehensive practice based on self-observation and breath mastery for exploring consciousness. I believe this represents the evolution of what we learned from many worldwide, adapted to our experiences and those of our students in a new world and new thought paradigm.

We have shared "The Mana Breathwork Universe" through conferences, seminars, webinars, workshops, retreats, and individual and group sessions, reaching students all around the globe.

Many of the tools we currently use are this book's roots, which you will inherit in the upcoming chapters.

## Incorporating Energy Breathing into Our Lives

"As we change, our world changes as well."
- Mana Breathwork

This book introduces the art of generating self-healing and transformation through higher states of consciousness, using our breath.

Breathing signifies our entrance into this world and punctuates our departure. It is the first act we perform when we are born, and the last one we perform when we leave this world. 'Energy Breathing' is the art of moving energy as well as air.

This practice harmonizes the movement of both energy and air because our breath isn't merely a physiological function. It is a powerful force with the capacity to shape our reality.

Conscious Energy Breathing consists of oscillatory motions. It is conscious because we focus just on our breathing, and it is circular because we merge the inhale and exhale, and then the exhale with the inhale, avoiding any gaps between them. It is continuous because we breathe for long periods of time.

It is perhaps the most valuable technique that humans can master. It allows you to recover your repressed ability to breathe freely and release old unhelpful breathing patterns and restrictions accumulated since the beginning of your life due to negative thoughts, stress, fear, trauma, anxiety, habits, posture, and other factors.

It operates at a gentle yet profound level and is used to shift your body's nervous system from a state of tension to one of relaxation.

Many of today's illnesses are caused or worsened by stress, dysfunctional breathing, or unbalanced oxygenation. Breathing is the essence of health and the key to your longevity.

The connected, coherent, slow, and rhythmic breathing helps you react to external circumstances with peace, and responding differently over and over is the beginning of creating new patterns and a new lifestyle.

It's a simple yet powerful approach that allows you to take charge of your own learning and healing process because it's not a series of passive treatments but an active exploration that changes how you think and respond to life. How we inhale represents our capacity to receive, and how we exhale means our ability to let go.

We can pinpoint every person's challenges just by observing how they breathe.

We all have a deep desire to unearth our true selves. This true self is hidden beneath layers of conditioning, traumas, and limiting beliefs, waiting for us to listen to it. As a matter of fact, it is always there shouting for attention, and it wants to be found. When we are open to seeing who we really are in these higher states, we gain access to sources of bliss, fulfillment, and resilience. We recover our strength to live passionately and fearlessly and find our voice. This High Vibration state of being is not a degree we can obtain and embody for life to come. Enlightenment is a constant process, a daily event. Breathing is the bridge to the present moment and the gate to Infinite Intelligence. The path to constant alignment.

The Mana Breathwork Universe is the way we observe ourselves, and it is a daily practice rather than a path to particular accomplishments. The method consists of specific curated techniques involving our breath and the spiritual use of our mind and body. Mana Breathwork is a practice of observation. A vessel to keep us on the path. The path of less resistance, more allowance, and more enjoyment. It is a practice to empower our life and help us navigate life's contrasts.


## Reborn


I was reborn in 2015. I felt renovated, and even though my life had changed completely, I realized something else was creating this miracle. But what?

*There is something greater than our practices, relationships, and conditions, and even more significant than our purpose. It is that we are co-creators, and we are constantly manifesting something.*

We don't have to learn how to create or manifest; this is automatic and already integrated into us, but we have forgotten. What's important is how we become more aware of how we do it so we can manifest what we prefer instead of manifesting our unconscious beliefs.

The key lies in understanding a simple yet powerful concept: learning to tune our own 'energy' to match that of our dreams and wishes. Many of us tend to think that our desires are like exotic birds, attracted from far-off places. When we let go of something, we imagine it flying away from us to somewhere else, disappearing from our world.

But that's not quite how it works. Our desires don't zip off to some distant location or zip in from outer space. Instead, they behave more like chameleons, shifting and adjusting within the colorful landscape of our own life's energy.

We don't have to pull things out of thin air with our thoughts because everything we ever need or want is right here, waiting in our 'quantum field.'

Our potential, our passions, our wealth, and our health—they're all part of this field. Just as all lands are linked by the seven seas, and all regions are united under one sky, we too are woven together by this invisible web of energy.

All we have to do is calibrate with this frequency to allow these desires to manifest in our reality, and the breath is the most practical tool for this.

All our potential futures, pasts, and everything within our reach are contained in the present moment. Breathing serves as a bridge that connects us to a state of consciousness where we are in tune with this very moment.

Love in all its expressions, joy, happiness, creativity, passion, wholeness, and freedom are different ways of expressing the vibration of our authentic self.

Our frequency is that resonant energy, that vibration that is unique to us, that identifies us as a unique aspect and, at the same time, as part of the whole.

We can apply that characteristic frequency to what gives us tremendous excitement or joy without expectation or assumption about the outcome but rather to allow synchronicity to present the opportunities within. When we allow joy to be our guide, we discover that it can function as the driving force, the organizing principle, and the thread leading to all other expressions of love.

It is also like the mirror that will reveal to us what is out of alignment with that frequency so that we can identify it and align ourselves again, expanding our life in that way.

As we allow ourselves to behave in this way, we will notice that our life will become an explosion of synchronicities, and magical things will begin to happen around us because magic is the very nature of existence. Miracles are the natural order of things, not the exception.

So the way this attraction and manifestation works is to recognize that we are already emitting; we are already radiating a vibration in alignment with our higher self, and that vibration is already doing its best to attract everything that is representative of that frequency.

Often our minds become a whirlwind of uncertainties and "what ifs." They can spin uncontrollably from one concern to another like a rabid storm.

One moment you're worried about an impending work deadline, the next, you're contemplating a recent argument with a friend; then, suddenly, you're questioning your career trajectory or the future of the world's environment.

This unchecked mental spiral can feel overwhelming and distressing. But the key to transforming these ideas into a source of inspiration lies in our perspective.

By reframing these thoughts and focusing on solutions rather than problems, we can harness this energy and channel it into constructive avenues. A work deadline becomes an opportunity to demonstrate skills and dedication, a disagreement with a friend transforms into a moment for personal growth and improved communication, and career worries turn into motivation for acquiring new knowledge and skills. In this way, we can convert the seemingly chaotic thoughts that our minds conjure into catalysts for positive action and inspiration.

We do this through our breath. Each inspiration has rebirth, creation, awakening, transmutation, and transformation.

Our perception and reality can change in the beat of our hearts because our reality mirrors our thoughts and emotions. And by observing it, we can discover what patterns we have created based on limiting beliefs.

When we have dense thoughts, we can observe them and ask, how does this thought make me feel? Is this thought true? How would I feel right now if I redirected my attention? Why am I attached to this thought?

Take a deep breath and replace it with a thought that gives you butterflies or, in other words, that activates your heart and solar plexus. It can be the image of a loved one or a situation. Take one breath, ten times as if you are breathing through the heart while focusing on the positive.

If it is challenging to think about something else, take a break, change the activity, even for a few minutes, or if you have more time, take a bath, a walk, or nap.

There is no point in denying resistance; you can observe it and, gently and without judgment, take baby steps to change it.

The ups and downs and the polarity can help us to expand. We come to this world to learn through changes, and contrasts can be a creative opportunity. The truth often lies in the grey. We do not need to stay in the drama of the situation or the hype of the emotion. Nor fall into the demand and blame when we live in situations that we do not want.

Life can be easy when we allow our blessings to manifest. There is no lack of anything because everything is already in our quantum field.

Imagine elements of a specific frequency eager to enter our lives, yet being held back. Our own beliefs stand guard at the door, inadvertently keeping out what we most desire. It's not about mastering a mysterious law of attraction; it's about becoming skilled conductors of our own energy symphony, orchestrating a harmonious exchange between us and the universe.

Our very being hums with a unique frequency, tuned to bring certain experiences into our lives. Yet, there are vibrations that discord with our tune. We often hold onto these out of habit, fear, or misunderstanding, marring our melody. That's where the art of exhalation comes in—it's a purging process, a letting go of dissonant vibrations that no longer serve our song.

On the flip side, inhalation is the act of welcoming in—inviting the resonant melodies that are waiting, ready to join our symphony.

Breathwork is a potent part of the process, yet it extends beyond mere respiratory rhythms. This practice invites us on a process of self-discovery, nudging us to be genuinely ourselves, live fully in the present, and honor the unique vibration that is our own. By doing this, we create a harmonious resonance that allows elements in tune with us to manifest physically in our lives, turning our world into a symphony of experiences that truly resonate with who we are.

How can we put these concepts into daily practice?

Learning to breathe consciously and live in a state of appreciation is a good start. Knowing that happiness is a choice and love is a decision will give you freedom. You are not condemned to anything genetically or energetically; you are not your circumstances or possessions.

Your life is a new canvas, and one of the results of acting from a state of love and appreciation is the increased positive synchronicity, where everything happens at the right time, and when it is not like that, we must have faith and trust in our path because we made our soul agreements long before coming to this planet to experience these lessons.

Our life's purpose lies in the joy of knowing ourselves, others, and the impact we have on others, allowing ourselves to surprise ourselves.

So by now, you should be asking yourself, but how? Well, you can begin by giving yourself a chance to live your life from an authentic zone. Begin by surrendering to what it is and raising your frequency; the rest will follow.

Authenticity is about presence, living in the moment with conviction and confidence, and staying true to the spirit. You always have a choice. Fear or love. Being happy is a choice, self-love and appreciation are a choice, and kindness is a choice. So is the way we treat our body, see ourselves, and interact with others, our thoughts, words, emotions, and actions. All count, and they are all equally important in mastering our energy.

We have little control over external circumstances, but how we feel and what we choose to do with them is all on us. We must feel joy; it is our birthright, and we must return to that joyful state every time we drift from it because that's how we raise our frequency, through an elevated emotion. And it is from there we want to create our reality, not from the lower frequencies.

The truth can be a catalyst, beautiful truth, painful truth, chaotic truth, genuine hardship, challenges, life contrast, the high and low, the deep and shallow, all.

Even then, we have resources like the elements to clean our energy and help understand nature's laws through these human occurrences. The fire to burn what's irrelevant, the breath to move it, the tears to water it, the earth to root us like tall trees, and space as luminous emptiness, which is the basis of higher spiritual experiences.

In these pages, we will go over ideas and practices that will invite you to question everything you perceive, see and feel. That will clear your mind and allow you to become the joyful, flexible, and resilient superhuman that you were born to be.

## R34ll t Y

Los Angeles is not a cliché; it is a vortex. Maybe because we are standing over a vast and misunderstood oceanic crust of alternating magnetic polarity, there is a unique energy here.

People can live their highest joy and consequently experience the life they designed, a more accessible life. I see it all around me.

There are humans from all over the world, all cultures, sharing ideas. It is a big soup of good intentions, and a beautiful city filled with magic. Or that's what I CHOOSE to see?

You can use your time on earth in blaming, complaining, and bouncing against every living being, society, and environment, or you can create and attract what you want. For the world to change we have to change as well.

Bending our reality is calibrating the perception of everything we experience. But to exercise the ability to do so and be a conduit of a supreme force, we need to be clear. And for that we use practices like cleaning our physical body, emotional body, and energy body.

Maybe my words are relatable, or perhaps it's unreal to imagine constantly feeling at peace, and that's okay because there is no such thing as permanence.

Even the highest living masters go to the most extreme challenges with health, relationships, finances, etc., and feel what they need to feel. We need to release the ideas around punishment or the demands for perfect success.

Everyone is learning a lesson, and emotions are part of the human experience—it's not about pretending that loss, pain, sadness, fear, etc. are not there.

The game is about transforming those emotions and the thoughts that create them into something that matches our highest self.

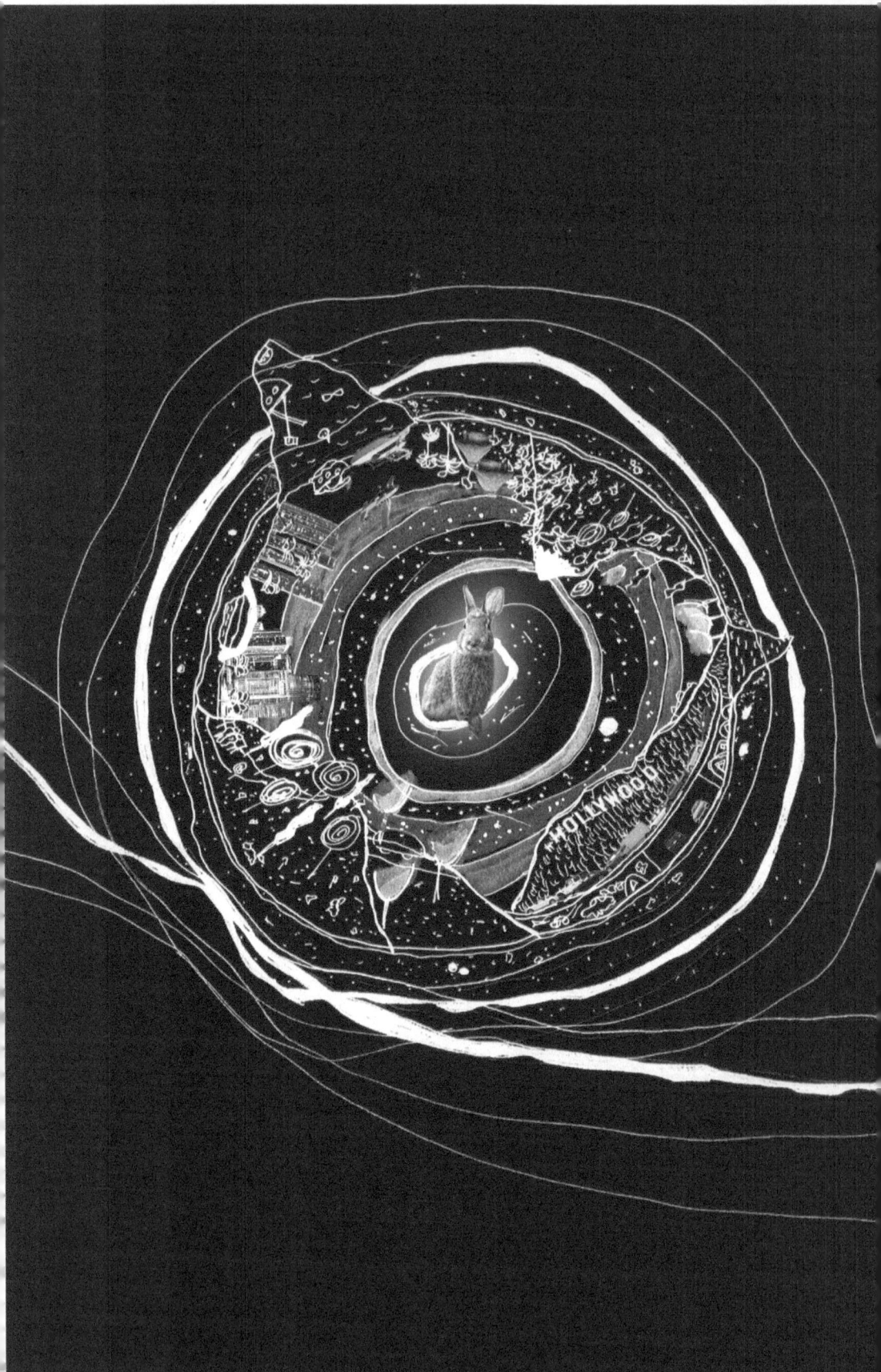

CHAPTER 2

# Observing
# Our Body

## The Human Body

Take a moment to appreciate the magnificence of your being, to revel in the miracle that is you. You are not just a collection of cells and organs; you are a masterpiece of nature, a symphony of life.

Every breath you take is a reminder of the power that resides within you, of the wisdom that your body holds. Your body is not just a vessel for your spirit but a partner in your journey through life. It is your compass, your guide, your inner technology.

And it is time to honor that, celebrate the beauty that is your body, and embrace the gifts you bring to the world. Your emotions, intuition, and resilience are not weaknesses but the essence of your strength. So take a moment to breathe, to feel the rhythm of your body, to connect with the forces of nature surrounding you. Allow yourself to be in awe of the complexity and beauty of your humanity, to recognize the wonder that is you. And know that you are not alone on this path but surrounded by a diverse cosmic family, a community of beings that share your love and your light. Together, we can create a new world free of pain for the new race. For you are more than what you think.

You are a magnificent human with immense potential.

## Longevity

We remain captivated by the concept of eternal youth within our mortal forms and the prospect of everlasting life on Planet Earth.

Aging is an inevitable procedure, yet it's a process we can positively influence to promote energy, vitality, physical wellness, and mental acuity.

As architects of our own lives and guardians of the earth, we can design lifestyle choices that optimize longevity, enhance our life's quality as we age, and control the cellular growth and replication cycles.

With this approach, we can lead a vibrant, healthy life, maintaining our cognitive sharpness and physical vitality until we decide our earthly journey has reached completion.

The Human Design System posits that individuals possess the potential to live a healthy life for a minimum of eighty-four years. This theory emerges from the correlation our bodies share with the eighty-four-year cycle of the planet Uranus, suggesting that physical decline should only begin after this milestone.

However, living authentically and true to ourselves can greatly extend this potential lifespan. Our bodies host an intrinsic antioxidant defense system that acts as a fountain of youth, preserving our vitality.

Longevity and the capability to ward off and eradicate incoming viruses go beyond just adhering to a nutritional diet or maintaining fitness routines.

The fundamental question remains:

Are we genuinely doing everything within our power to foster cellular regeneration?

## Observing Trauma

The symbiosis between the body and the mind is intricate and profound. When the body experiences a sense of safety, this sensation reverberates through our being, inducing a similar feeling of safety in the mind. Our bodies are like reservoirs of wisdom, storing experiences from our past, offering insights into our present, and subtly hinting at our potential futures. Over the years, it transmits complex neurobiological messages that capture the essence of our existence.

One of the most powerful examples of this relationship is seen in how the body and mind react to trauma. Life events, emotional wounds, and particularly traumatic experiences etch deep imprints, creating chronic patterns in both our behaviors and our physiological responses.

The experiences we've lived through, especially traumatic ones, tend to echo in our physical existence in various ways. These echoes can range from manifesting as chronic pain to creating emotional responses when we encounter certain stimuli that remind us of the traumatic event.

For instance, my last car accident. The trauma of the incident was not only mental but physically imprinted in my body as well.

After the accident, I began to feel anxiety and physical discomfort whenever I saw a vehicle approaching too quickly. This is the body communicating its remembered trauma, and the physical symptoms are a manifestation of the neurological and emotional patterns formed from this traumatic incident.

Understanding this connection between physical experiences and the information our bodies carry, we can see that the path to well-being begins by listening to these messages. We must attune ourselves to our bodies' signals and endeavor to reset these chronic patterns. With conscious effort, we can overwrite the existing patterns with new, healthier ones.

For instance, my personal journey to healing began with practicing breathwork. As I focused on my breathing, I observed the source of the pain. The act of concentrating on my breath allowed me to release the emotional and physical pain that had become almost second nature to me. It enabled me to experience my body in an entirely new way. The more I practiced, the more I noticed that my perception of the physical pain I was experiencing started to shift, gradually reducing over time.

In exploring this deeper connection with myself, I found a profound sense of compassion for the pain that I had been quietly carrying around for many years. The pain was no longer something I needed to suppress or hide from, but rather, it became an opportunity to heal. This newfound self-awareness and compassion were like discovering a new facet of my identity, shedding light on my capacity to heal, grow, and transform.

## Trauma and Understanding Its Effects on Our Well-being

Each of us experiences some degree of trauma at some point in our lives. It could be a sudden loss of a loved one, an accident, a natural disaster, a difficult childhood, or even ongoing abuse. Regardless of the source of trauma, it can have lasting adverse effects on our mental, physical, social, emotional, and spiritual well-being.

When we experience a traumatic event, our nervous system releases stress hormones such as cortisol and adrenaline. This response is an adaptive mechanism that helps us survive in times of danger. However, prolonged exposure to stress hormones can have deleterious effects on our brain development and cognitive functions.

One of the most commonly known mental health conditions associated with trauma is post-traumatic stress disorder (PTSD). It can result from experiencing or witnessing a traumatic event and can cause long-term symptoms such as flashbacks, anxiety, depression, and nightmares.

Trauma can also alter the way our brains process and store memories. The traumatic experience is not stored correctly and is often encoded as pictures or bodily sensations, which can be triggered later on by various cues or reminders, leading to flashbacks or dissociation.

Trauma can impact how we think about ourselves, react to stress, and relate to others.

Like me, people develop addictions to cope with uncomfortable feelings and negative self-beliefs caused by unresolved trauma.

The effects of trauma are not limited to the individual experiencing it; it can also have intergenerational effects. Trauma can leave an epigenetic mark on our genes that can be passed down to future generations. This mark does not cause a genetic mutation. Still, it can alter how genes are expressed, potentially increasing the risk of mental health conditions, such as anxiety and depression, in offspring.

Fortunately, trauma-informed care is a rapidly evolving field of study that is increasing our understanding of how to help individuals who have experienced trauma.

Trauma-informed care recognizes that trauma affects the individual, the surrounding environment, and the people in it. It aims to create safe and supportive spaces that foster healing and resilience while recognizing trauma's complex and long-lasting effects.

If you need help, it's essential to seek support from a qualified mental health professional trained in trauma-informed care. With the proper support, it's possible to heal from the lasting effects of trauma and improve one's overall well-being. Healing takes time, but it's possible with the right support and resources.

# Types of Trauma

There are many types of Trauma. For example, let's say a person is walking down the street. Suddenly, out of nowhere, a giant bird swoops down and attacks, leaving them with a deep cut on the arm. That's acute trauma—a single incident that happened suddenly and unexpectedly.

Now imagine that every day for a week, this person has to walk down that same street, and that same bird attacks every time, leaving them with more cuts and bruises. That's chronic trauma—when something traumatic happens over and over again, causing long-lasting damage.

But what if it's not just the bird attacking but also a neighbor who's always yelling or a boss who's constantly belittling them at work? That's complex trauma—a combination of different traumatic events, often interpersonal, and can leave you feeling helpless and overwhelmed.

Trauma can take many different forms and have a significant impact on your life. It's essential to recognize the different types of trauma to better understand and support those who have experienced it as well as ourselves.

Trauma is a psychological response to an event that is overwhelmingly stressful or disturbing. The effects of trauma can be long-lasting and can manifest in different ways, depending on the nature of the event, the individual's personal history, and their ability to cope.

In our vibrant and chaotic world, individuals grapple with different forms of trauma:

Neonatal Strains: Birth and prenatal trauma, shaped by complications during labor or maternal stress during pregnancy, can create early marks of adversity.

The primal breath we draw is often steeped in this rite of passage.

Childhood Wounds: Young lives marred by trauma—abuse, neglect, or witness to violence—can reverberate through emotional and psychological growth, shaping our core selves in unexpected ways.

The Weight of Disapproval: Parental disapproval syndrome—chronic reproach from the guardians of our youth—plants seeds of self-doubt, blooming into anxiety and depression.

Mind's Double-Edged Sword: Unchecked, the mind can turn on itself, fueling a negative thought cycle that amplifies trauma, spinning a web of despair and helplessness.

Subconscious Lure of the Void: Rooted in unresolved trauma, an unconscious death urge could harbor a chilling wish for self-destruction.

Shadows of Past Lives: Through certain spiritual lenses, our trauma might echo from past existences, karmic residues seeking resolution in our present life.

Heartbreak: The crumbling of a relationship can strike a profound blow, particularly if it is mired in abuse or has spanned a significant portion of our lives.

Scholastic Scars: School, a supposed sanctuary of learning, can devolve into a battleground of bullying and academic pressures.

Religious Wounds: Trauma may seep in through the cracks in our faith, sprouting from dogma, shaming, or discrimination within religious frameworks.

Abuse's Unkind Impact: Physical, psychological, or sexual abuse can root itself in the psyche, leading to sustained trauma. The harmful effects are the result of another person's actions, leaving long-lasting implications.

Illness' Unwanted Gift: A life-threatening ailment can offer a grim package of trauma along with its physical burdens.

The Twilight Fog: Late-life cognitive shifts—confusion, memory loss, and more—can stir a unique blend of trauma, as familiar landscapes turn alien.

The Void of Loss: The sudden disappearance of a loved one from our lives can plunge us into a whirlpool of grief and bereavement, a sharp pang of trauma.

Accidental Cruelties: Accidents, whether on the road or at work, can usher in trauma, unexpected and often brutal in its consequences.

Echoes of Collective Pain: Historical or collective trauma, passed down generations or shared by communities bound by race or culture, can ripple through our lives. Natural disasters, war, terrorism, discrimination—the collective suffering casts a wide net.

Second Hand Trauma: Witnessing others' traumatic experiences can breed our own trauma. First responders, healthcare workers, and similar roles often bear this burden, carrying the weight of others' pain.

*The human response to trauma is as varied as its sources.*
*Navigating through it calls for professional guidance, self-care, and the strength of*
*communal support, knitting together a tapestry of healing and resilience.*

## Responses to trauma, grouped by category

Your reactions may be as diverse as fingerprints, yet they often fall within similar emotional landscapes. Let's take a deep dive into these psychological territories.

Denial: The Uninvited Guest. Denial is the psychological bouncer that outright refuses to let the harsh reality in. It's that stubborn gatekeeper standing between you and the unpalatable truth. It's the art of avoidance, the fierce refusal to face the trauma or its potential ripple effects on your life. Denial is the silent echo in your mind saying, "This didn't happen."

Fear: The Shadow Dancer. The fear response can feel like an eerie shadow dance in the corners of your consciousness. It's that chill of apprehension, the quickening heartbeat, the breath held hostage when reminders of trauma flutter into your world. Fear convinces you that you're not equipped to navigate through the storm, making you question your strength.

Sadness: The Invisible Anchor. Sadness is that unseen anchor weighing you down with its crushing load. It's the torrent of sorrow that drowns your spirits, the desolate expanse of despair stretching out before you. Sadness can convince you that the bridge to a brighter future has collapsed, leaving you stranded in the ruins of the past.

Shame: The Unseen Stain. Imagine a stain invisible to others, yet glaringly apparent to you. That's shame—the raw humiliation that leaves you feeling like you've got a scarlet letter emblazoned on your chest. The tormentor that blames you for the trauma, whispering in your ear that you should've known better, you should've done better.

Confusion: The Unraveled Map. Ever felt lost in a maze with no exit in sight? That's what confusion can feel like after trauma. It's like you've been handed a map where up is down and left is right. It scrambles your understanding of what happened, disorients your emotions, and leaves you questioning the purpose of your journey and the decisions you've made.

Navigating these responses might feel like traversing an emotional labyrinth, but understanding is the first step toward healing. You're not alone in this journey.

**Most common behavioral shifts:**

Solitude seeking: The deliberate evasion of individuals or situations evocative of the distressing incident.

Joy drain: An encroaching apathy that robs once cherished pursuits of their allure.

Reactivity/Touchiness: A propensity for agitation, with tempers flaring at the slightest provocation.

Self-directed accusation: A misplaced attribution of responsibility, pinning the blame on oneself regardless of the actual circumstances.

Externalizing fault: Unjustly casting blame on others, regardless of their actual involvement or culpability.

## Mental transformations:

Focus fragmentation: A struggle to concentrate, to remember, and to see tasks to completion.

Emotional disconnect: A pervasive sense of being emotionally detached, adrift from one's own feelings or the feelings of others.

Night terrors: Frequent, intrusive nightmares, tinted by the colors of the traumatic event.

Despair: A growing feeling that the future holds no improvement, that life has lost its worth.

Culpability: A sense of guilt, remorse or responsibility for the occurrence or the inability to prevent it.

These shifts and transformations are as diverse as the individuals experiencing them. There's no strict sequence, no standard combination. Some may face a handful of these responses, while others may grapple with a multitude.

# How Does Our System
# Naturally Recover From Trauma?

Deep within our intricate system lies a robust network of mechanisms that allow us to naturally bounce back from trauma. It's a delicate dance between our brain and body, a symphony of communication happening among our amygdala, hippocampus, and prefrontal cortex.

Always on the lookout, the amygdala raises the alarm when we face a stressful event. It's our internal warning system, notifying us of potential danger. Meanwhile, the hippocampus helps us learn and remember how to stay safe, storing memories of both threat and safety. And the prefrontal cortex takes charge, orchestrating our emotional and behavioral responses to these events.

Even the strongest warriors can stumble at times, but when we falter, there are ways to regain our footing.

For those who have experienced trauma, the path to recovery may not be a walk in the park, but it is within reach. With the assistance of professional therapy, the gentle guidance of a balanced lifestyle, and the calming practices of mindfulness, we can learn to manage symptoms and address the root cause of our pain.

Through breathwork, we can calm the stormy winds within us and find our center. We can teach our nervous system to regain resilience and endure even the harshest storms. As each day passes, we witness our health and quality of life improving, shining brighter than ever before.

Let's not lose hope in the face of trauma, for we possess an innate strength we often underestimate. Let's embrace the journey of recovery and find solace in the knowledge that our system can naturally heal from trauma when equipped with the right tools and support.

## The Nervous System and Polyvagal Theory

The Polyvagal Theory was formulated by Dr. Stephen Porges, a prominent American psychiatrist and neuroscientist. He first introduced this theory in 1994, the year my son was born, and has since expanded upon it in various scientific publications and presentations.

Dr. Porges' Polyvagal Theory provides a complex and nuanced interpretation of the human nervous system and its interaction with our environment. This theory underscores the profound influence that our personal perception of safety or danger exerts on our actions and responses.

The vagus nerve, from which the theory derives its name, is a crucial player in this dynamic. As the longest cranial nerve, it extends from the brain, passing through the neck and chest to the abdomen. It is responsible for regulating numerous functions across the body, such as heart rate, blood pressure, digestion, and blood glucose levels. Given its substantial role, the vagus nerve is considered a cornerstone of the body's parasympathetic nervous system, often described as the "rest and digest" system that works to maintain homeostasis after periods of stress or danger.

According to the Polyvagal Theory, the nervous system can be subdivided into three primary branches, each with a unique role.

The Ventral Vagal State: This is also known as the "social engagement system." It's associated with feelings of safety, calmness, and connection with others. When we are in this state, our body and mind are relaxed, enabling us to interact and communicate effectively with those around us.

The Sympathetic-Adrenal State: This state is linked to our fight or flight responses. It is activated when we perceive a threat, triggering a variety of physical responses such as elevated heart rate, rapid breathing, and heightened sensory alertness to prepare our bodies to confront or escape from the perceived danger.

The Dorsal Vagal State: This state is associated with the freeze response, or a state of immobilization. It occurs when we perceive a threat that is so severe or inescapable that neither fight nor flight seems viable. In this state, our bodies shut down to conserve energy and numb the senses to mitigate potential pain or harm.

These states are not solely reactionary; they are shaped by our "neuroception," a subconscious system for scanning the environment for cues of safety or danger. Particularly in individuals with post-traumatic stress, these systems can be hypersensitive, causing the person to interpret even neutral or safe situations as threatening due to past traumatic experiences.

A deeper understanding of these states and their interplay with our perception of safety and danger can inform effective strategies for regulating our nervous system. For instance, activities that promote a sense of safety and calm, such as cultivating positive relationships, practicing conscious breathing exercises, engaging in regular physical activity, or participating in singing and chanting can activate the ventral vagal state. Even laughter, with its proven stress-busting effects, can help shift our nervous system toward a state of relaxation and sociability.

## NarcoBaby

I was just twelve years old when my innocence was shattered. But let me be clear, it wasn't the kind of innocence you might expect. Growing up in Colombia, a vibrant and diverse country in the northern part of South America, I was exposed to a world of collective violence and personal loss that profoundly impacted me.

From the very beginning of my life, right through to my adult years, I found myself caught in the grips of traumatic events. These experiences etched themselves into the very fabric of my being, both physically and energetically.

Looking back, I can now see a direct correlation between those events and my mental and physical well-being.

When we are swept up in the throes of intense emotions, our breathing patterns naturally alter, and occasionally, we might even find ourselves holding our breath.

These variations can create disruptions in the flow of our energy. It's important to be mindful of those instances when your breath either halts or accelerates. Yet, facing life with a mindset of openness and a heart willing to accept changes is crucial.

Understand that the journey to self-awakening isn't linear. Rather, it's a constant flux, an evolving cycle that never remains the same. Relinquish the need for rigid expectations of how events should unfold, and stay receptive to the growth that accompanies these experiences.

As a student of life, grant yourself permission to experience the stages of grief: denial, anger, and depression. Show up for yourself, fully and unconditionally. Once you've allowed yourself to grieve, take a moment to recognize the adaptive strategies you've developed along the way. For instance, in my own journey, I discovered that my desire for independence had led to feelings of isolation. It wasn't until I identified this coping strategy that I could address the root cause and adapt it to better serve my true needs.

Moreover, I started to notice a connection between my chronic back injuries and a persistent sensation of being unsupported. The weight I carried, both physically and metaphorically, manifested as a painful pressure in my lower back. It was as if I had been shouldering the burdens of others without realizing the toll it was taking on me.

Through it all, I've learned that true liberation comes when we fully accept ourselves and our circumstances. By allowing ourselves to feel, we initiate the healing process.

We can surrender to the emotions that course through us, acknowledging their presence as a means of gaining awareness. This awareness, in turn, helps us identify where we stand, reframe our experiences, and ultimately cultivate new, harmonious feelings that align with our higher selves.

*Healing lies in listening, accepting, surrendering, and holding space for ourselves and others.*

## Listening to the Body and Acceptance

Have you ever felt that something wasn't quite right with your body but ignored it and pushed through anyway? Or maybe you've tried to control your thoughts and feelings rather than accepting them for what they are?

This is common programming, but it could be more efficient.

Listening to our body is all about tuning in to those physical sensations and cues that our body gives us, like painful digestion or a sore muscle. When we listen and respond appropriately, we are able to take better care of ourselves and prevent further discomfort or even injury. But it's not just about the physical, it's also about developing a deeper connection with and understanding of our body.

And what about acceptance? It can be difficult to embrace our thoughts and feelings when they're uncomfortable or challenging. But when we allow ourselves to experience them without judgment or resistance, we can learn to process and move through them more healthily.

Acceptance means accepting ourselves as we are, our bodies, and everything we are, rather than constantly criticizing or trying to change ourselves. The more we accept ourselves the easier it is to accept others.

When we listen to our body and accept everything how it is, we create a powerful mindset of self-care. We can navigate guided by our inner technology and wisdom by paying attention to our body's signals and responding in a way that honors our needs.

There is always room for expansion, but it begins from loving acceptance and clarity.

## Calibrating the Physical Body

Cultivating the art of fine-tuning our physical bodies can significantly enhance our overall health, wellness, and performance. This practice not only aids in warding off injuries and illnesses but also fosters a more extended, superior quality of life. Through this bodily calibration, we can optimize its operations to achieve peak performance.

Below are various methods to fine-tune your body:

* Sleep for 6-8 hours nightly: This routine aids your body's natural repair and restoration processes.
* Power naps: Take short 20-minute naps to rejuvenate and recharge yourself.

* Daily physical activity: Engage in exercises that increase your heart rate and fortify your muscles for at least 20 minutes every day.
* Stay active: Dance, engage in sports, and exercise regularly.
* Stretching: Stretch your muscles at least twice a day.
* Strengthening: Fortify your bones and muscles.
* Recovery: Allow your body to recover post physical exertion.
* Quantum nutrition: Learn about it and incorporate an anti-inflammatory diet. Opt for whole, nutrient-rich foods that foster cellular regeneration.
* Hydration: Consume clean, vital and alkaline water.
* Maintain a clean diet: Evade sugary drinks, caffeine, stimulants, gluten, dairy, processed foods, trans fats, and alcohol.
* Choose healthy products: Avoid fluoride, tap water, and harmful cleaning and self-care products.
* Stress management: Use relaxation techniques to control stress.
* Fasting: Let your system take a break and reset.
* Cold-water immersions: Practice this often.
* Sauna or steam room: Utilize these 2-4 times a week.
* Biohacks and anti-inflammatory therapies: Learn about these to improve your well-being.
* Embrace the water element: Bathe and build a relationship with water.
* Self-massage: Regularly massage your body to relieve tension.
* Skin brushing: Regularly dry brush your skin to exfoliate dead cells, stimulate circulation, detoxify your body, and improve skin health.
* Posture: Align your physical structure to maintain good posture.
* Healthy sexual practices: Engage in safe, respectful sexual practices that honor your body.
* Cleansing: Under professional supervision, try colon cleansing, colon hydrotherapy, and/or enemas.
* Detox: Undertake seasonal cleanses and detoxification.
* Self-talk: Speak gently and positively to your body.
* Self-love: Cherish the reflection in the mirror.
* Setting healthy boundaries: Establish and uphold healthy boundaries for yourself.

* Creative expression: Find joyful, artistic avenues to express yourself, such as painting, writing, or playing music.
* Body awareness: Pay heed to your body, be mindful of physical sensations, observe any discomfort or pain, stay attuned to its needs, and seek timely and suitable care as required.
* Laughter therapy: Laugh more!
* Write below a few ways you can fine-tune your body.

_____

_____

_____

_____

_____

_____

_____

_____

_____

_____

_____

_____

_____

_____

_____

_____

_____

_____

_____

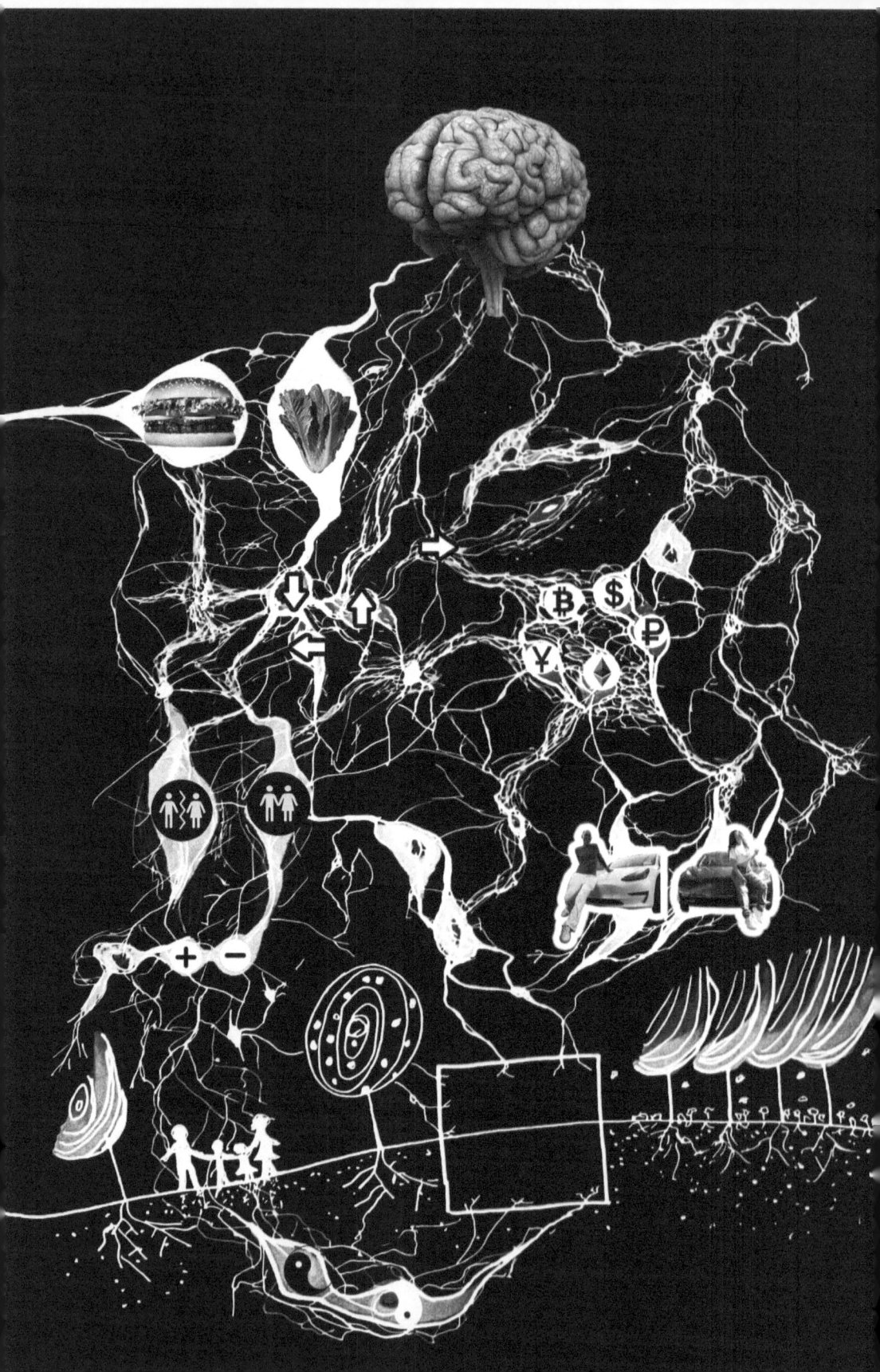

# CHAPTER 3
# Observing Our Mind

## The Mind as a Powerful Tool
## Not Capable of Decision-making

The mind is the seat of consciousness and thought and is undoubtedly an essential instrument in our lives. It endows us with the ability to perceive and comprehend our surrounding world, encouraging us to think both critically and creatively, and to identify and experience a spectrum of emotions and sensations. Despite its immense power, however, it does not independently make decisions.

Decision-making is an intricate process. The mind is instrumental in this process, generating thoughts, memories, and emotions that bear upon our decision-making. Nonetheless, the ultimate responsibility of making decisions resides within us, rather than with the mind alone.

The mind acts as an informative guide, but the onus lies on us to utilize that information to arrive at a decision. This responsibility calls for a degree of self-awareness, as we need to acknowledge and manage our thoughts, emotions, and biases to make well-informed decisions.

The mind is susceptible to numerous external influences, such as persuasive advertising, societal pressure, and cultural norms, which can complicate the task of determining what truly serves our best interests.

In these instances, it becomes crucial to foster an awareness of self and mindfulness to resist these external pressures and make decisions that align with our soul, values and objectives.

Even though the mind is a powerful tool with a significant role in decision-making, it is incapable of making decisions autonomously. It falls to each of us to harness our power in a way that equips us to make informed, self-governed decisions that resonate with our inherent purposes.

## Transforming Limiting Beliefs
## into Infinite Possibilities

Have you ever paused to reflect on why you make certain choices, or why you react in specific ways to different situations? Understanding these reactions and choices lies within your belief systems.

Consider your belief system as the core software that drives your mind. It shapes your perceptions of the world and self, either empowering you or, conversely, restraining you. However, there's a silver lining: we have the ability to identify and question these beliefs to form new, empowering ones.

For instance, if you foster the belief "I am not good enough," you might find yourself constantly seeking validation from others and pushing yourself incessantly to do more and strive for better. But imagine a paradigm shift where you embrace the belief "I am enough, just as I am." Just picture the liberating and peaceful impact this can have on your life.

Similarly, if you maintain the belief "I can't trust anyone," it may trap you in a perpetual state of defense, preventing you from forming meaningful connections with others.

However, shifting your perspective to something like "I am open to trusting others and forging meaningful relationships" can unlock new avenues and offer enriching experiences.

The key point is to identify these limiting beliefs and challenge them. Ask yourself if they truly benefit you or if they're merely hindering your progress. Then, consciously replace them with beliefs that empower you. While our limiting belief systems can significantly influence our lives, consciously recognizing and replacing these beliefs with empowering ones can trigger a transformative journey toward a realm of infinite possibilities.

Affirmations, or as I prefer to call them, manifestations, can serve as powerful tools for altering negative thought patterns and beliefs, bolstering motivation, and nurturing self-esteem and confidence. These are positive statements infused with the feeling of attaining our goals, and when repeated, they can reprogram our mind.

## Shadow Work

Shadow work is exploring and embracing the parts of ourselves that we have often kept hidden or pushed away. We don't necessarily like or agree with these parts, but they make up a crucial aspect of our personalities and experiences.

Think of it as shining a light on the shadows in a room. When you illuminate what's hidden in the darkness, you can see everything more clearly, and gain a deeper understanding of yourself and your motivations.

Shadow work is a way to observe our fears, anxieties, and negative emotions. It helps us identify patterns of behavior that may not be serving us and get to the root cause of them. This inner work can be challenging, but the rewards are immeasurable.

Observing our shadows, we can integrate the parts of ourselves that we have disowned and become more whole and authentic individuals. We can learn to love and accept ourselves and live with more purpose and meaning.

## Resilience

Imagine yourself as a rubber band, constantly changing shapes and adapting to different situations, yet always having the ability to bounce back. That's what building resilience is all about.

It's a journey of growth where you develop the skills and mindset to handle life's challenges with grace and ease. It's about being flexible and changing and growing when faced with adversity.

Resilience doesn't mean you won't experience stress, pain, or sadness. It's not about being immune to these emotions but instead having the strength to manage them effectively.

Think of it as a workout for your mind and soul. You can start building resilience by practicing mindfulness, setting achievable goals, connecting with others, and focusing on your strengths. These activities will help you cultivate a positive mindset, reduce stress, and increase your overall well-being.

As you continue to develop resilience, you'll start noticing its positive impact on your life. You'll become more confident, self-assured, and better equipped to handle whatever you encounter.

Building resilience is not a destination but an expedition. It's a lifelong process of self-discovery and growth. Embrace the process, and never stop bouncing back.

Joaquin says our bodies are like balloons; we inflate and deflate while navigating the present moment and what the energy breathing brings us.

We can engage in emotions, thoughts, or physical pain, or accept the process and let go. When we inflate a balloon, it goes from nothing, totally deflated, to different degrees of expansion. If it inflates too much, the balloon can explode. How can we navigate the flow of air to keep expanding without exploiting it? Maybe it is not about what we put in the balloon but how we can adapt and transform that into an enjoyable situation.

You have trees that take the carbon monoxide and purify the air, giving back oxygen. When we breathe, we are in that flow of creating. Allowing, letting go, and enjoying. The more focused we are on the breath, the less attachment we have, and the more resilience we can maintain.

Adaptation is not about taking in, taking in, taking in. So we don't end up exploding, we need to transform whatever we take in. Life and expansion always bring us contrast, and contrast is in our life to bring us more desires, dreams, and clarity on what we want and what we don't want.

That is how the universe keeps expanding over and over. So when we take, we take everything, inflate the balloon with everything we have. And we need to let the air go and release some air to ease the balloon. This brings us to the mutation. Change. Bring the new to adapt ourselves to the new reality. And the goal is always to enjoy it. Enjoy the present situation. To keep ourselves and others happy.

Everything we want, whether a beautiful lover, a trillion dollars, or any experience, is because we think we will be happier when we do it or have it. We don't need the experience to shift the emotion, and we don't need the circumstance to feel happiness. If we believe this—when we know this—we can shift our emotions before any manifestation that justifies the shift, or without any physical representation of what we desire to experience. Then we are the influential creators that we came here to be.

Then we can leverage these creations to expand our life to the point that we can't explode. We can change, adapt, and keep thriving in any situation. But if we keep needing a manifestation to change our reaction, if we keep needing circumstances to shape our emotions, then we will keep having no control. We will keep being puppets to our feelings and other people's emotions. And we have nothing to control. We just need to let go, surrender to life, and surrender to our inner self, and everything will continue to fall into place for us.

The only thing we can control is our focus of attention. The longer we can focus on something positive like breathing, the longer we can keep ourselves connected to this inner wisdom and watch the movie while enjoying the ride.

Unlocking the essence of profound inner harmony lies within the art of harnessing the breath, a pivotal gateway to unlocking a truly transformative experience.

As an extraordinary bonus, when we transcend the need for justification and effortlessly embrace happiness, embracing the notion that the universe orchestrates every detail in our favor, we pave the way for the magnificent dance of manifestation to gracefully unfold—a majestic enactment of the fundamental Law of Attraction, as espoused by the profound teachings of Abraham Hicks.

## Life Can Be Easy

Accepting our inherent goodness and receiving without overexertion or compromising our well-being can be a challenge. However, we can relinquish the urge to incessantly prove ourselves.

By releasing resistance and surrendering to the rhythm of life, we are able to generate momentum and fulfill our desires with a sense of ease and pleasure. The key lies in identifying thoughts that resonate with comfort and employing these to refocus our attention toward love, success, and self-acceptance.

The narrative of "you must work hard" or "hard work pays off" is a chorus often echoed and passed down through generations. However, there are other paths to success. We can lead a life that is easy and effortless simply by embarking on inspired action. Our lives reflect what resonates within our vibrational state. Consequently, the strategy lies in nurturing an energy that aligns with our desires, because all we desire is already within reach. It exists in our realm;

we only need to connect with it. This connection is facilitated through infinite intelligence, not through uphill struggle or relentless hustle. The era of the hustle is over.

# Neuroplasticity

In the vast realm of scientific discovery, neuroplasticity holds incredible promise for our understanding of the human brain.

Picture your brain as a vibrant ecosystem, constantly reshaping its connections and pathways, much like a complex network of roads and highways. This extraordinary capacity enables us to learn new skills, recover from injuries, and even reshape our thoughts and behaviors.

Gone are the days when the brain was thought to be fixed and unchanging beyond a certain age. We now know that it possesses an astonishing plasticity that endures throughout our lives. This means that our brains can continue to learn, grow, and adapt, irrespective of our age or circumstances.

Think of it as a process of rewiring and remodeling. When we immerse ourselves in new experiences or challenge ourselves with unfamiliar tasks, our brain forges new connections between neurons and fortifies existing ones. It's akin to constructing new bridges and pathways, allowing information to flow more smoothly and establishing a foundation for acquiring fresh knowledge and skills.

Neuroplasticity uncovers the awe-inspiring adaptability of the human brain. It demonstrates that our brains are not fixed entities but rather ever-evolving structures that can be shaped and molded through experiences, efforts, and a nurturing environment.

It's the brain's ability to form novel connections and pathways and to reorganize itself in response to new experiences. It's like granting your brain the power to adapt and absorb new things, similar to how a plant adapts to its surroundings.

Just as a gardener provides water, sunlight, and nutrients to help plants thrive, you can enhance your brain's ability to adapt, learn new things, and even recover from injury or disease by engaging in challenging activities. This could range from playing a musical instrument to learning a new language or solving puzzles.

Just as a garden requires care and attention to flourish, your brain needs exercise, a healthy diet, and proper sleep to foster neuroplasticity. Treat your brain with the same care as you would a garden, and witness its unique growth and transformation.

## Neuro-linguistic Programming
## "The Language of the Mind"

Neuro-linguistic programming, abbreviated as NLP, is a multifaceted approach to comprehending the intricate relationships among language, behavior, and cognition. It's a methodological assortment of techniques specifically designed to bolster effective communication, foster robust relationships, and leverage the understanding to propagate positive transformation.

Envision an instance where you're attempting to persuade a friend to embark on a road trip with you. The principles of NLP, when applied, encourage a deliberate consideration of your word choice and delivery manner in order to enhance your friend's enthusiasm for the idea. As an alternative to a simple invitation, such as "We should go on a road trip," NLP would suggest a more vivid and captivating approach. One might say, "Visualize the spectacular sights we'll find and the lasting memories we'll forge on our adventurous road trip." This refined choice of language helps create a vibrant mental image, rendering the proposition more attractive and enticing to your friend.

NLP offers insightful strategies to understand and resonate with others' viewpoints, paving the way for building strong rapport. For instance, if you find your friend communicating in a subdued, tranquil tone, it would be beneficial to align your language style and demeanor to match theirs. This conscious mirroring fosters an immediate sense of connection, making your friend more receptive to your ideas and suggestions.

Neuro-linguistic programming was formulated in the 1970s by Richard Bandler, a student of psychology, and John Grinder, a linguist. Initially conceived at the University of California, Santa Cruz, the pair was intrigued by the relationship between neurological processes ("neuro"), language ("linguistic"), and learned behavioral patterns ("programming").

Bandler and Grinder aimed to uncover the strategies used by successful individuals and create a replicable model of those strategies. They were particularly interested in the therapeutic techniques of Fritz Perls, Virginia Satir, and Milton Erickson, all of whom were known for their successful treatment outcomes.

Their research and resultant techniques became the foundation for what we now know as NLP.

It has since evolved into a popular methodology used across numerous fields, from psychology to sales and negotiation, empowering individuals to overcome barriers, achieve personal goals, and lead more fulfilling lives. NLP continues to be refined and developed to this day, remaining an influential model in the realm of interpersonal communication and self-development.

## Neuro-linguistic Programming and Trauma

NLP can help by addressing negative thoughts, emotions, and behaviors that may be associated with a traumatic event.

One technique used in NLP is reframing, which involves changing how an individual thinks about a traumatic event. For example, if someone has a traumatic memory associated with a specific place or object, reframing can help them view the place or object in a different, more positive light. This can help to reduce the emotional charge associated with the traumatic memory and make it less distressing.

Another technique is visualization, which involves creating a mental image of a desired outcome. This can help an individual imagine a positive future, which can help reduce feelings of hopelessness and helplessness that may be associated with trauma.

NLP techniques also help individuals develop new coping strategies to deal with distressing thoughts and emotions. For example, an individual may be taught to use deep breathing or progressive muscle relaxation to reduce feelings of anxiety and stress.

Understanding how to use language for my benefit has been a tremendous tool for me, but you should know that NLP is recommended to be used along with other evidence-based therapies and should be guided by a professional.

## Practicing Affirmations

Affirmations or manifestations are the positive statements that change thought patterns and beliefs. They work by reprogramming the subconscious mind to believe in something new and positive.

Imagine you want to change your belief that you're not good enough. One way to do that would be to create an affirmation that counters that belief. For example, you might say to yourself, "I am worthy and capable of achieving my goals." By repeating this affirmation to yourself regularly, your subconscious mind will start to believe it, and you'll begin to see changes in your behavior and attitude.

Another way to use affirmations is by visualizing yourself in the present as if you've already achieved your goal. For example, you can imagine giving a presentation confidently, reaching your desired weight, or winning in business.

Affirmations can also be used to improve self-esteem and confidence. For example, you might say to yourself, "I am confident and capable of making good decisions," or "I am worthy of love and respect."

Repeating these affirmations to yourself regularly can help you build stronger self-worth and increase your confidence in your abilities.

Harnessing the power of affirmations demands precision, positivity, and the present moment. Regular repetition and a genuine sense of alignment with them are crucial.

Joaquin champions this principle, emphasizing the significance of resonating with your affirmations. The moment they stir up any resistance, he warns, they inadvertently gather momentum in the reverse direction. Consider this—if you constantly echo to yourself, "I'm a multimillionaire," but that affirmation just reminds you of your financial hurdles, it's going to be counterproductive. Instead of feeling like a multimillionaire, you'd end up feeling like an impostor. And that's definitely not what affirmations aim to do. Their real purpose is to relax your mind, creating a conduit for you to tap into and experience a certain emotion.

But how can you tell if your affirmations are truly serving you? Are they becoming a source of inspiration or just an added burden? Gauge your reactions. If the affirmation feels too heavy, dial it down, generalize it. For instance, "Every day, I have the opportunity to increase my wealth." On the other hand, if the affirmation is a source of inspiration, then be more specific. Say, "By managing our resources, I will earn 222 million dollars this year." Remember, the essence of an affirmation lies in its capacity to empower and inspire you.

## Anchors

Anchors are specific stimuli, such as words, phrases, or actions, that trigger a specific emotional state or behavior. The idea behind anchors is that certain stimuli can be associated with emotions or behaviors. Using these stimuli makes it possible to elicit those emotions or behaviors again in the future.

For example, a person might associate the smell of lavender with a feeling of calm, so they use it as an anchor to trigger that feeling of calm in themselves when needed. Or a person might associate the sound of a bell with feeling motivated, so they use the sound of a bell as an anchor to trigger that feeling of motivation in themselves.

Anchors can be established in a variety of ways. One way is to create an association between a stimulus and an emotional state while the person is already experiencing that emotional state. For example, if a person feels calm, they might associate the smell of lavender with that feeling of calm.

Another way to establish an anchor is by repeatedly pairing a stimulus with an emotional state. For example, a person might constantly play a particular song while feeling motivated and then use that song as an anchor to trigger feelings of motivation in the future.

Anchors can be used in many ways to improve performance, change negative emotions, or increase motivation. They can be used by individuals to improve their own emotional and behavioral outcomes or by therapists and coaches to help their clients.

Here are a few ways you can use anchors to achieve your goals:

• Improve performance: If you're an athlete, you can create an anchor that triggers feelings of confidence and focus before a game. For example, you might establish an anchor by squeezing your hand every time you score a goal and then use that same hand squeeze as an anchor before a game to trigger feelings of confidence and focus.

• Change negative emotions: If you're struggling with anxiety, you can establish an anchor that triggers feelings of calm and relaxation. For example, you might use the smell of lavender as an anchor, and whenever you're feeling anxious, you can take a deep breath of the lavender scent to help you relax.

• Increase motivation: If you're having trouble staying motivated, you can establish an anchor that triggers feelings of motivation and drive. For example, you might use the sound of a bell as an anchor, and whenever you're feeling unmotivated, you can ring the bell to trigger feelings of motivation.

• Self-confidence: You can use an anchor to increase your self-confidence; for example, you can use a specific posture as an anchor. Whenever you feel confident, stand up straight, and push your shoulders back, then use this same posture as an anchor to trigger feelings of confidence whenever you need it.

Anchors take time to establish, and you should use them consistently to be effective. They also can be combined; for example, you can simultaneously use an anchor for confidence and another for motivation.

Weld your mind to mine, for if our ears were to unite,

an echo of a heart would form, painted in vibrant whispers of silence.
In this space, the lines of sound and silence,
utterances and hush intermingle.
These echoes become the murals painted on the walls of our reality,
the sculptors of our perception.
For what we feed our ears, trickles into our minds,
blossoms in our hearts, and ultimately crafts the world we live in.
The words we ingest and the sounds we hear are not mere vibrations
in the air, they are the architects of our existence.

## Activation of the Pineal Gland

Nestled within the labyrinth of your brain, pulsating with a rhythm that mirrors the cosmos, resides a tiny yet potent organ: the pineal gland.

Referred to as the "third eye," this pinecone-shaped endocrine organ is much more than just a producer of melatonin, the hormone that regulates our sleep-wake cycles. It's our personal stargate, a point of convergence between the physical world we inhabit and the elusive quantum field that underlies all creation.

Since ancient times, seekers of truth have revered the pineal gland as a celestial antenna, a receptor of higher consciousness. This "third eye" isn't just biological in nature; it's an interface between the known and the unknown, capable of resonating with the quantum field, that mysterious, invisible layer of reality where all possibilities exist simultaneously.

Activating your "third eye" isn't a secret ceremony shrouded in mystery. It's a universal call to deepen your relationship with the self and the cosmos—an invitation to dip your toes into the quantum sea of endless possibilities.

Meditation, with its soothing rhythm, provides a bridge to the quantum field. As your mind stills, the frenzied particles of thought begin to slow down. They merge, collapse into waves, until you're no longer a separate entity but a part of the universal quantum sea—a state akin to what quantum physicists call 'superposition.'

Breathwork plays its part in this beautiful dance too. With every breath, you exchange atoms with the universe. Each inhale draws in the quantum soup, each exhale surrenders to the flow of life, creating a rhythm, a vibrational frequency that resonates with the quantum field.

Yoga, the ancient tapestry of asanas and pranayama, weaves your body, mind, and spirit into alignment with the universe's quantum fabric. It's a graceful dance of matter and energy that tunes your pineal gland to the hum of the cosmos.

The natural world also contributes to this quantum symphony. Certain foods and supplements, gifts from Mother Earth herself, resonate at frequencies that encourage your pineal gland to synchronize with the quantum field's energy. They are like tuning forks, bringing your internal instrument into harmony with the cosmos.

Thus, your pineal gland, your "third eye," is more than just an endocrine gland. It's a sacred portal, a quantum receiver, bridging the gulf between your personal reality and the infinite realms of possibility. Through meditation, breathwork, yoga, and mindful nourishment, you can explore this cosmic connection, waking up to the vibrant symphony of the universe that plays within us all.

## Calcification of the Pineal Gland

The calcification of the pineal gland is a condition in which the gland becomes hardened due to calcium buildup. This can happen for various reasons, including aging, exposure to fluoride, and chronic inflammation.

When the pineal gland becomes calcified, it can affect its ability to produce melatonin, leading to sleep disorders, depression, and other health issues. It can also cause the pineal gland to become less responsive to light, disrupting the body's natural sleep-wake cycle.

You can take steps to help prevent the calcification of the pineal gland. By avoiding exposure to fluoride, eating a healthy diet, and practicing stress-reducing techniques, you can help to keep your pineal gland healthy.

## Empowered Within: No Substances Needed

Welcome to a world where the mystical and the biological converge. It's a realm where the breath, the basis of life, can be a doorway to transcendental experiences. A place where the age-old wisdom of our ancestors intertwines with contemporary scientific knowledge. Here, the breath is not just an autonomous function keeping us alive but a key to unlock hidden realms of our consciousness.

Enter DMT, or N,N-Dimethyltryptamine, the psychedelic compound that nature sprinkles generously across the biological kingdom, weaving itself into the tapestry of life—from human beings and animals to plants such as the sacred Ayahuasca.

Ayahuasca is a brew made from the combination of two plants: the Psychotria viridis (Chacruna) plant and the Banisteriopsis caapi vine.

The compound N,N-Dimethyltryptamine (DMT), a powerful psychedelic, is found primarily in the leaves of the Psychotria viridis plant.

On the other hand, Banisteriopsis caapi, the other ingredient in Ayahuasca, does not contain DMT but instead contains harmala alkaloids like harmine, harmaline, and tetrahydroharmine. These compounds act as monoamine oxidase inhibitors (MAOIs), which are essential for the DMT in the Psychotria viridis to become orally active. Without an MAOI, the body's digestive system would break down the DMT before it could have a psychoactive effect.

For centuries, Indigenous cultures have held a deep reverence for plants with these properties, using them as instruments of spiritual awakening and healing, a testament to the profound interconnectedness between us and the living Earth. But what makes DMT intriguing is not just its ubiquity, but its intimate relationship with the human body. We are not mere bystanders in the psychedelic theater; we are part of the play.

Our pineal gland, often referred to as the "third eye," is thought to produce DMT in trace amounts, binding this mystical compound to our very essence. Even our lungs, the organs of breath, might harbor the necessary enzymes to metabolize DMT, further reinforcing its connection with breathwork and the transcendent experiences that follow.

Yet, the world of DMT and its potential therapeutic implications has remained largely shrouded in mystery. For years, its study has been paused, its value overlooked, and its potential squandered due to societal stigma and restrictive legislation on psychedelic substances.

Times, however, are changing. A wave of renewed interest is surging, pushing the boundaries of psychedelic research, and DMT is again under the microscope.

Alongside this scientific renaissance, there's a growing number of accounts from people across the globe who have encountered DMT-like experiences through the simple act of breathing.

Breathing—our vital yet underappreciated bodily function—may be able to stimulate our body's natural production of DMT, leading to profound and transformative experiences comparable to those induced by psychedelics.

But let's not forget, the human body is not a playground, but a temple. While we continue to explore the uncharted territories of psychedelics for scientific insights and therapeutic possibilities, and respect their ceremonial use, we must not misuse them as recreational tools devoid of respect for 'set' and 'setting.'

Indeed, our bodies have untapped potentials, and through breathwork, we may experience this incredible journey into our inner cosmos.

**Disclaimer:** The contents of this book are intended for informational and educational purposes only. While there is ongoing research into the potential therapeutic uses of DMT and the role of breathwork in psychedelic-like experiences, these topics are complex and still not completely understood by the scientific community.

The information presented should not be interpreted as medical advice or a recommendation to engage in illegal activities. The use of DMT and other psychedelic substances is controlled by law in many jurisdictions, and these substances should not be used without appropriate supervision.

The use and preparation of Ayahuasca and other DMT-containing substances are heavily regulated in many parts of the world due to their potent psychoactive effects when not used responsibly or under proper guidance.

Furthermore, while breathwork is generally considered safe, it can sometimes lead to intense physical and emotional responses. If you are interested in trying breathwork, it's recommended that you seek guidance from a trained professional.

## Creativity and Expression

*Every human spirit is alight with an inherent spark of creativity.*

Creativity is our capacity to conceive fresh ideas or solutions. It engages imagination, originality, and forward-thinking to manifest something previously unknown. It manifests in myriad forms, such as conjuring a haunting melody, sculpting an exquisite dish, designing an aesthetic space, formulating a groundbreaking scientific theory, or even devising a unique business strategy.

This facet of human expression and problem-solving is vital and can be nurtured and enhanced through practice and exposure to a tapestry of experiences and viewpoints. Cultural, societal, and environmental influences, as well as individual personality traits and cognitive abilities, can shape this creative prowess.

We often limit creativity to the confines of artistic endeavors, considering it an exclusive attribute for those who play with flamboyant hues, harmonious symphonies, or intricate verses. Yet, this perspective merely grazes the surface of the expansive, rich tapestry of creativity.

It thrives within the complex labyrinth of mathematical equations, the unerring precision of financial analysis, or even the seemingly mundane act of brushing your teeth each morning.

To create is to summon the unseen into existence. It might be a groundbreaking idea emerging from the ether, or a novel arrangement of familiar elements.

In reality, it's often the latter that takes center stage. We are instinctively drawn to imbue the ordinary with a dash of the extraordinary, reshaping the familiar to give birth to the unprecedented.

Imagine a financial analyst who devises an ingenious method to decipher and categorize economic data—isn't this also a testament to creativity? Just as a sculptor transforms a block of marble into a stunning masterpiece, the analyst employs their knowledge and tools in inventive ways, making creativity a universal language, transcending boundaries and disciplines.

*Rest by doing nothing but feeling God and creative thinking.*

We are constantly creating our reality. Breathwork can help reduce stress, anxiety, and negative emotions, which can hinder the creative process. By promoting relaxation and focus, breathwork can create a more conducive environment for creative thinking and idea generation.

Deep breathing helps increase oxygen flow to the brain, enhancing cognitive function and creativity.

Another form of breathwork that can promote creativity is alternate nostril breathing.

This technique involves closing one nostril and inhaling through the other, then closing that nostril and exhaling through the first. This pattern is repeated, alternating nostrils with each breath. Alternate nostril breathing can help balance the brain's left and right hemispheres, improving cognitive function and creativity.

In addition to deep breathing and alternate nostril breathing, many other breathwork techniques can reduce stress, enhance focus, and promote relaxation, all of which can create a more conducive environment for creative thinking and idea generation.

## Purifying the Mind

Initiating the process of purifying your mind begins with the conscious observance of your thoughts, allowing you to discern and address negative patterns. This endeavor demands an elevated level of self-awareness and introspection. Upon identifying these negative thought patterns, you can actively work toward transforming them using affirmations, visualizations, and other techniques devised to reframe your mental state.

Another effective method to cleanse your mind is through the study of sacred texts and scriptures. These ancient writings provide invaluable wisdom and profound insights into the nature of reality, thereby assisting in shifting your perspective.

Practicing mantras is a powerful tool for mental purification. Mantras, characterized by their powerful sound vibrations, have the capability to soothe and uplift your consciousness.

Engaging in chaos can be both time-consuming and energy-depleting. Instead, let grace and gratitude guide the trajectory of your thoughts. A mind focused on positive aspects has the potential to harness energy, thereby creating miracles upon miracles.

Trusting in the flow of life paves the way for your mind and body to attain a state of stillness. By finding solace in the rhythm of your breath, your mind can purify itself and unwind, feeling nothing but the stir of creative energy within.

Share some ways you express your creativity below.

_____

_____

_____

_____

_____

_____

_____

_____

_____

_____

_____

_____

_____

_____

_____

_____

_____

_____

_____

_____

_____

_____

_____

_____

## Help Us Share the Magic
## Your Review Can Spark a Transformation

*The greatest adventures are not found in faraway lands,*
*but in the hearts we help along the way.*

Hey there, incredible reader! You know, those who share their light with others tend to shine the brightest. That's why I'm so excited about our journey together. It's about more than just reading a book; it's about growing, learning, and helping others do the same. So, I have a small favor to ask. Would you be willing to help a fellow human, just like you, find their way? Imagine someone out there, maybe a bit lost, looking for a guide to help them bend their reality, just like you once were.

Our mission is simple: to make the magic of BENDING OUR REALITY a guiding light for everyone. Everything I do is dedicated to this mission. To spread this light, we need to reach... Well, everyone! And that's where your superpower comes in. You see, people often choose books based on what others say about them. That's why I'm asking for your help on behalf of a kindred spirit you've never met:

## Could you please leave a review for this book?

Your words, taking less than a minute to share, cost nothing but could change a life forever. Your review might help:

- Another young reader discover their inner strength.
- A parent find new ways to connect with their child.
- A teacher inspire an entire classroom.
- Someone feeling alone realize they're part of something bigger.
- Another dreamer take their first step towards change.

Did you know? When you share something wonderful with someone, it creates a ripple of joy. If you think this book can light up another's path, why not share it with them? Your kindness could be the start of their greatest journey.

To sprinkle a bit of your magic and make a real difference, all you need to do is leave a review. It's quick, easy, and means the world:

**Simply scan the QR code below to leave your review:**

If you're smiling at the thought of helping someone you've never met, then you're truly special. Welcome to our circle of airbenders and changemakers. I'm beyond happy to help you explore and grow FASTER/EASIER/MORE JOYFULLY than you ever imagined. The journey ahead is filled with wonder and lessons that will light up your life.

Thank you from every corner of my heart. Now, let's dive back into our adventure!

Your biggest fan,

Viviana Escobar

# CHAPTER 4

# Observing Our Heart

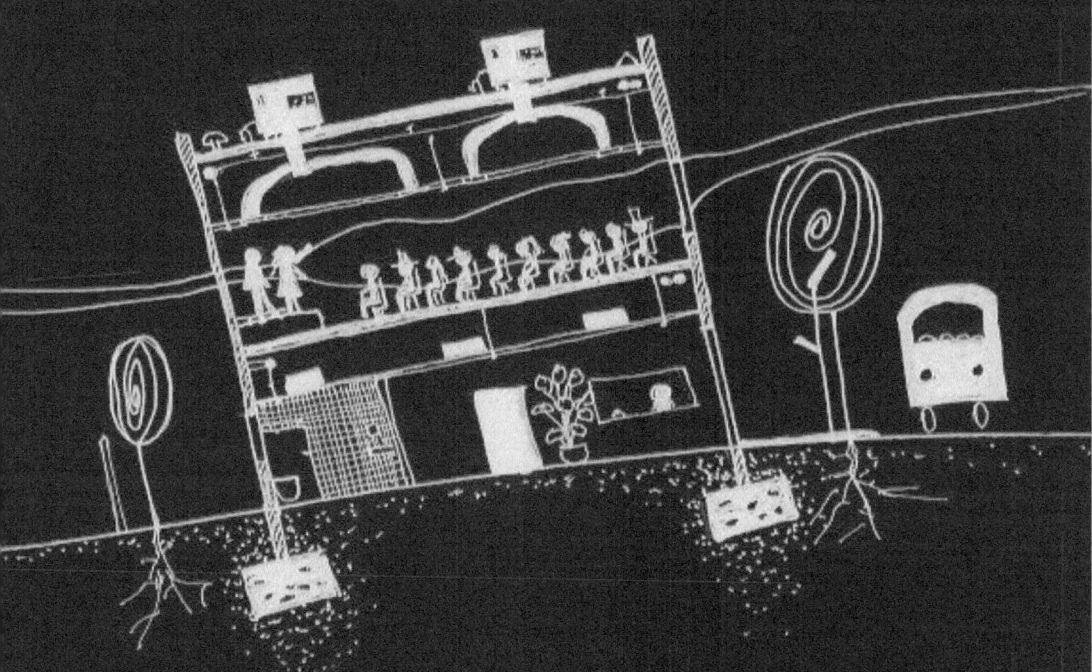

## The Heart

Our perception of the heart's role is evolving; it's not just a pump but an active participant in our physiology and psychology. Our heart and brain are intertwined, with the heart sending more signals to the brain than vice versa. Within the heart is a sophisticated neural network—coined the "heart-brain"—capable of memory, learning, and decision-making, independent of the cranial brain.

Positive emotions—appreciation, care, compassion—are catalysts for heart coherence, a harmonious heart-brain dialogue that promotes health and reduces stress. Practicing heart-focused breathing, a technique of synchronized breathing while focusing on the heart, can help us tap into these benefits.

Our heart creates a potent electromagnetic field, extending beyond our bodies. The strength of this field suggests interconnection on a grand scale. We're only limited in exploring its reach by the capabilities of our current measurement tools.

The heart's science invites us to explore our interconnectedness, not just within ourselves but potentially throughout the universe.

Research conducted by the HeartMath Institute
The HeartMath Institute is a nonprofit research organization dedicated to studying the physiological and psychological effects of the heart on human health and well-being.

Dr. J. Andrew Armour, a renowned neuro cardiologist whose research has greatly advanced our understanding of the interactions between the nervous system and the heart, introduced the concept of a functional heart-brain in 1991.

His work focused on discovering and characterizing a specialized network of neurons that forms a functional bridge between the autonomic nervous system and the heart. This network, which Dr. Armour named the "intrinsic cardiac nervous system," plays a key role in regulating the heart's function and has important implications for diagnosing and treating cardiovascular disease.

One of Dr. Armour's significant contributions to the field of neurocardiology was his discovery of a group of neurons located in the epicardium (the outermost layer of the heart) that receive direct input from the central nervous system. This discovery challenged the conventional wisdom that the heart was purely under the control of the autonomic nervous system and opened up new avenues of research into the role of the intrinsic cardiac nervous system in cardiovascular health and disease.

Dr. Armour's subsequent research has focused on the physiological and pathophysiological mechanisms underlying the interactions between the intrinsic cardiac nervous system and the autonomic nervous system. His work has demonstrated that the intrinsic cardiac neurons can integrate and modulate the inputs from the sympathetic and parasympathetic branches of the autonomic nervous system, which in turn affects the heart's rate, rhythm, and contractility.

Dr. Armour's research has also shed light on the role of the intrinsic cardiac nervous system in various cardiovascular diseases. For example, his studies have shown that the intrinsic cardiac neurons can become activated in response to myocardial infarction (heart attack) and contribute to the development of arrhythmias and heart failure.

Dr. Armour has published numerous articles in prestigious scientific journals and has been recognized with many awards and honors for his contributions to the field of neurocardiology. His research has paved the way for new approaches to the diagnosis and treatment of cardiovascular disease.

The heart plays a much more significant role in human health and well-being than previously thought, and techniques to improve heart coherence can significantly positively impact overall health and quality of life.

## Heart Coherence

Today, some of the world's most advanced researchers, like the HeartMath Institute, Mr. Gregg Braden, and Dr. Joe Dispenza, practice heart coherence techniques in their live programs and events.

Heart-brain coherence is the synchronized activity between the heart and the brain in which the two organs communicate and work together harmoniously.

The heart has its own complex nervous system, known as the "heart-brain," which is capable of sending signals to the brain through the nervous system. These signals can influence various cognitive, emotional, and physiological functioning aspects.

When the heart and brain are in coherence, the heart's rhythms become more ordered and stable, affecting the brain's rhythms. This synchronization between the heart and brain has been associated with several positive outcomes, such as increased mental clarity, emotional stability, and physical health.

Heart-brain coherence can be achieved through various practices, such as meditation, breathing exercises, and mindfulness. By cultivating a state of coherence, individuals can enhance their overall well-being and performance in multiple domains of life.

## The Connection Between Our Heart and Brain

"The human heart is more than an efficient pump sustaining life. The heart is an access point to a source of wisdom and intelligence that we can call upon to live our lives with more balance, creativity, and intuition." - Gregg Braden

Heart breathing: It's our connection to life, an unconscious yet potent force we wield within us, waiting to be acknowledged, harnessed, and honed.

The art of Mana invites you to become not just an actor but an observer in life. To stop for a moment and listen to the quiet whispers of your heart as it engages in an eternal conversation with your brain.

Mana breathwork is the journey of becoming an empathetic spectator. The practice encourages you to tune into higher frequencies, as if turning the dial of your inner radio station and experiencing melodies unheard before.

Embrace the breath, and it will bring you to the here and now, a tranquil state where the relentless waves of the mind cease to exist. Amidst this calm lies an expanse of peace, expanding like the universe itself, unhindered by the bounds of time.

Within this tranquil space, the mind and heart strike a harmonious chord, resonating together to create consciousness. It's a space nestled between thoughts, a sanctuary where your true self blooms.

Observation: It's not an attribute of the mind. Rather, it's a trait inherent to consciousness. The essence of conscious breathing lies in transcending the analytical mind, for it bridges the gap between the conscious and the subconscious.

Through conscious observation, devoid of judgment, you comprehend your interaction with the world. The practice of breathing clears away clutter, making room for you to manifest your destiny.

Observe the mind. Watch your thoughts as if they're leaves floating down a river, yet resist the temptation to swim in their currents. The moment judgment enters the scene, observation steps out.

You are more than the urgencies and thoughts. Your essence is not defined by what you own or yearn to possess. The more you persist in being the observer, the easier it becomes to bypass the mental constructs shaped by experiences and past perceptions embedded deep within your subconscious.

Breathing from your heart allows you to be the observer, the listener, and the creator. It's a call to return to the essence of being, to observe, breathe, and exist within the grand design of life.

This practice helps you resonate with the harmonic symphony of your existence, reminding you that your heartbeats are notes in the grand composition of the universe.

## Observe Your Emotions

Dive into your emotions as an explorer, not a judge. Let them flow, unrestricted by labels of good or bad. You're the observer, the silent spectator to your inner world.

Your self-identity is a tapestry, woven from thoughts and emotions responding to experiences. But it's easy to be swept away in this personal narrative, to mistake the tapestry for the weaver.

Start noticing these emotions and narratives. As you do, their grip on you eases. You're no longer a ship in a storm, but the ocean itself:

deep, expansive, and resilient. Storms come and go, but the ocean remains.

Recognizing this doesn't diminish your feelings; it shows them as fleeting waves on your deep, constant self. You're not a passive bystander, but the author of your life.

The colors of your emotions shape your experiences, but they don't define you.

In this understanding, find liberation. Witness your thoughts and emotions, celebrate your autonomy, and relish in the freedom of being more than your transient feelings.

You are the expansive sky, the enduring ocean, the space where feelings visit but don't overstay. Be engaged, be curious, and above all, be you.

"When there is coherence between the heart and the mind,
the fourth step is a quantum leap
FROM the heart to the BEING, to the unified field,
to the very center of our existence.
Suddenly your vital energy
- your individuality expands - and merges with the whole.
We are all one, and there is no separation.
No time or space exists.
You ARE unconditional love.
It is life itself in the purest form.
Your body's intelligence activates healing.
You feel Gratitude FOR EVERYTHING,
and that gratitude is the only authentic prayer."

- Gregg Braden

Practicing the HeartMath technique increases heart coherence and our ability to self-regulate emotions from a more intuitive, intelligent, balanced inner reference.

# What Are Trapped Emotions?

Have you ever had a tender spot on your body that, when activated, led to an emotional release and left you in tears? It's a powerful experience that some believe results from trauma being stored or trapped in the body. These traumatic stress symptoms can also manifest physically.

Our brains associate certain areas of the body with specific memories, often on a subconscious level. When these areas are activated, memories and emotions can be triggered. As a result, emotions are constantly being generated, whether we are consciously aware of them or not.

Trauma and unresolved emotions can become stuck energy in the body. Trapped emotional vibrations cause surrounding tissues to vibrate at the same frequency as resonance. Each trapped emotion is said to reside in a specific location in the body, vibrating at its own particular frequency. This can cause a buildup or blockage, making you more likely to experience that emotion repeatedly.

When you feel a sudden surge of emotion during a practice or other treatment, it's not just in your head—it's in your body too.

# How Do Emotions Get Trapped?

Have you ever had a feeling that just wouldn't go away? Well, those feelings might actually be trapped in your body.

Our mental and emotional health has a direct impact on our physical health. Fear, for instance, can send our bodies into a state of fight or flight, triggering all sorts of physical responses.

When we experience an emotion, we develop an emotional vibration. We feel the emotion and any associated thoughts or physical sensations. And then, ideally, we move on from the emotion by processing it. But what happens when that processing gets interrupted?

The energy of the emotion can become trapped in the body, causing muscle tension, pain, and other ailments. The higher the emotional intensity, the more likely it is to get trapped.

The phrase "trapped emotions" refers to repressed negative emotional energy that our true selves want to express, but our not self doesn't allow us to. This can lead to resentment, poor decision-making, self-sabotage, overreaction, increased stress and anxiety, depression, and fatigue.

Understanding how emotions get trapped and how they manifest physically will allow you to manage your emotional and physical well-being. If you feel like you're carrying an emotional weight, remember that it might be time to process something. Your body will thank you.

## Trauma and Trapped Emotions

Trauma is an event or a series of events that overwhelm an individual's capacity to cope, leaving them feeling helpless and vulnerable. Trauma can occur in many different forms, such as physical abuse, sexual assault, emotional abuse, natural disasters, or the loss of a loved one. Nearly everyone experiences trauma at some point in their lives.

Trapped emotions, on the other hand, are unresolved emotional energies that have become stuck in the body due to an inability to process and release them. These trapped emotions can result from past traumas, ongoing stress, or unresolved conflicts.

Trauma can cause you to suppress your emotions as a coping mechanism, leading to these emotions becoming trapped in the body. The suppression of emotions can manifest in physical symptoms such as tension, pain, and chronic illness.

When emotions are trapped in the body, they can interfere with your ability to fully experience present reality. Trapped emotions can cause anxiety, depression, and other mental health issues, and physical symptoms like headaches, fatigue, and chronic pain.

The accumulation of emotions can also make you more vulnerable to experiencing more undesired emotions. When traumatic events occur, the existing trapped emotions can be triggered, causing an even stronger emotional response and compounding the impact of the trauma.

Through your breathing, you can observe both the trauma and the trapped emotions and effectively release what doesn't serve you.

## An Emotional Language of the Physical Self

When we begin to talk about the connection between the body and emotions, we often use metaphors: butterflies in the stomach, a heart bursting with joy, or a weight on one's shoulders. But what if these expressions point to something more literal than we think? Where do we 'feel' emotions?

Emotions are not solely abstract phenomena. They are physiological experiences, expressed through our bodies. Every emotion, from the intense waves of love to the dark, immobilizing depths of despair, are sensations that we experience physically. Our body becomes a vessel that carries the whispers of these emotional currents.

## Emotional Landscapes and Exploring the Body's Emotional Map

Each emotion creates its own unique physiological footprint. Imagine your body as a vast landscape, with different regions responding to different emotional states. When you're in the throes of anger or fear, the upper regions of this landscape—your chest and arms—become the center of a storm, with rapid heartbeats and tense muscles. Conversely, when enveloped in love or happiness, it's like a warm sun rising, spreading its light throughout your entire body.

Just as we learn to navigate a physical landscape, we can learn to traverse our emotional landscapes too. The first step is recognizing these bodily responses and understanding them as signposts pointing toward our emotional states.

# Riding the Waves - The Connection Between Emotion and the Sympathetic Nervous System

Our emotions don't just cause subjective experiences—they prompt a very tangible, physiological response. A brush with fear can make your heart race and your breath quicken. These responses are orchestrated by the sympathetic nervous system, our body's internal emergency response team. It kicks into gear during moments of stress, preparing us for 'fight or flight.'

Our bodies are beautifully designed to protect us, and these reactions serve a purpose. However, in a modern world where stressors are constant and often abstract, this system can become overstimulated. This is where breathwork can become an essential tool for maintaining emotional balance.

# Unearthing Emotion - Tuning in to Your Body's Signals

Emotions are like waves, and our bodies are the shore they wash upon. The greater the emotional intensity, the larger the wave, and the more distinct the physical sensations it produces. Through tuning in to these bodily signals—the knot in our stomach, the tightness in our chest, the warmth spreading across our skin—we can develop a deeper understanding of our emotional selves. Yet, this is a language we're often not taught to understand or value.

# Unresolved E-motions

Unresolved emotions refer to feelings or thoughts that remain unsettled, unprocessed, or unaddressed. They can be persistent and can cause significant distress, impacting our mental and emotional well-being.

These emotions may arise from various sources such as trauma, loss, grief, conflict, guilt, or unresolved relationships.

Unresolved emotions can be challenging to identify and manage. Often, they can manifest in physical symptoms such as headaches, stomach problems, or insomnia.

They may also manifest in behavioral patterns such as avoidance, anger, or self-destructive habits. If left unaddressed, unresolved emotions can lead to further emotional distress, mental health issues, and physical health problems.

One of the most common unresolved emotions is grief. A grieving process can be long, and we may need support from others to help us cope with our emotions. Unresolved grief can lead to depression, anxiety, and other mental health problems.

Unresolved conflicts can also lead to unresolved emotions. When we have conflicts with others, we may feel angry, hurt, or frustrated. These emotions can persist even after the conflict is over, especially if we have not resolved the underlying issues. We may also feel guilty or ashamed about our role in the conflict, which can further complicate our emotions.

In some cases, unresolved emotions may be a result of trauma. Trauma can leave us with intense emotions that are difficult to process. We may feel overwhelmed, anxious, or depressed, and may struggle to find ways to cope with these feelings. Trauma can also lead to post-traumatic stress disorder (PTSD), which can cause ongoing emotional distress.

Addressing unresolved emotions requires us to acknowledge and process our feelings.

This can involve seeking support from others, such as friends, family, wellness advisors, counselors or a mental health professional. We may need to engage in activities that help us cope with our emotions, such as exercise, movement, mindfulness, or creative expression. In some cases, we may need to confront the source of our emotions through therapy or conflict resolution.

Unresolved emotions can be challenging to manage, but it is essential to maintain our emotional and mental well-being. Identifying and processing our emotions can help us find closure and move forward in our lives.

Seeking support from others and engaging in activities that promote emotional wellness can help us cope with our emotions and find resolution. You are not alone in this; it takes courage to observe our emotions and there are people all over the world willing to help you.

## The Healing Breath for Emotional Regulation

Breathing allows us to engage with our emotions directly through the body. As a practice that can both stimulate and soothe the nervous system, it serves as a bridge between our emotions and our physical selves.

Bodywork such as yoga, tai chi, or massage can also be instrumental in releasing emotions from the body. These practices engage the body in a mindful and intentional way, facilitating a deep connection between physical sensations and emotional experiences.

Mindfulness and grounding exercises can be used to reconnect with the body, especially in moments of emotional overwhelm.

Techniques like progressive muscle relaxation, where we intentionally relax each part of our body in turn, can help bring our focus back to the physical realm, helping us process and release emotions.

Tapping is another method that combines cognitive reframing with stimulation of physical points on the body, akin to acupressure points. This can be particularly effective for dealing with stress, anxiety, and other difficult emotions.

Practices such as Somatic Experiencing (SE) or Tension and Trauma Releasing Exercises (TRE) can also be helpful. These techniques focus on noticing and releasing physical tension that often corresponds to emotional stress.

Psychotherapy, especially therapies that focus on the body-mind connection like somatic psychology, can be hugely beneficial. Working with a therapist in these ways can provide a safe space to explore and process emotions, linking emotional experiences with physical sensations and patterns.

It's important to listen to your body. Each of us is unique, and different methods will resonate with different people. What matters most is finding what works best for you and honoring your process as you journey toward emotional well-being.

The healing breath is a tool of significant potential. By focusing on the rhythm and depth of our breathing, we can regulate our emotional states, calming anxiety and stimulating lethargic moods. The breath, in its simplicity and immediacy, is a powerful ally in our ongoing emotional health and self-understanding.

Processing emotions is not just a mental but a whole body process. It's a holistic approach that brings together the mind, body, and soul to achieve integration and well-being. It's about releasing the old narrative of separation between our physical and emotional selves and embracing the interconnectedness of our whole being.

There is no right or wrong way to release emotions from the body. Activities that make us happy and energized can help us handle our emotions more effectively.

Acknowledging our feelings is recognizing and accepting the emotions we are experiencing. It involves being honest with ourselves about how we feel, and not trying to deny or suppress our emotions. Through the breath, we can clearly see every emotion, because every emotion reflects in the pattern of breathing.

The breath doesn't lie, so when you acknowledge your feelings, you give yourself permission to feel them and breathe through them rather than push them away. You are courageous every time you observe your feelings and allow them to be what they are because they show you where you are at that moment.

You are less reactive to different situations if you recognize how you feel. When you deny or suppress your emotions, they can become bottled up and lead to negative consequences such as anxiety, depression, or physical health problems. On the other hand, when you acknowledge your feelings, you can healthily work through them and develop better emotional resilience.

Acknowledging your feelings is akin to decoding a cryptic language, one of anger, joy, fear, or myriad other emotions. It's a process of unraveling the knots of feelings within us, labeling them with their proper names without condemnation or harsh self-censure. From this place, we allow ourselves to fully immerse in these emotions, to understand their depth and contours.

Expression of these emotions, then, becomes a cathartic release. Like turning a tap, we let them flow—be it through ink spilled on the pages of a journal, or through words spoken in a trusting conversation with a friend, or maybe with the guidance of a professional who helps us navigate the vast sea of our feelings.

From this acceptance and understanding springs a transformative journey, one that morphs stress into resilience, spawns meaningful relationships, and builds a fulfilling life. By not allowing ourselves to be mere marionettes controlled by the strings of our emotions, but instead taking a step back, a pause, a moment to breathe and reflect— we don our true selves and react with thoughtfulness, authenticity. It's this pivot in our consciousness that expands the horizons of our emotional intelligence and lights up our paths, leading us to a better and brighter future.

## Emotional Harmony: A Guide to Navigating Waves

### Riding the Emotional Swell - A Fresh Perspective
Our emotions are a lot like the sea. They can be calm, serene, sometimes tumultuous, and at other times, overwhelming. Emotion, like the ocean, is an essential part of the human experience. However, in the rush of modern life, we often lose sight of this, becoming disconnected from our feelings and reactions. It's time to bring a fresh, more contemporary voice to the narrative of emotional wellness, urging us to accept and explore our emotional depths.

### Embracing Emotional Tides - The Power of Acceptance
As we navigate through the ocean of our emotions, the first step is acceptance. Each wave of emotion that crashes upon our shores carries its own unique message, an insight about our needs, desires, and experiences. We must learn to hear these messages, no matter how obscure they may seem at first. Acceptance isn't about passivity; it's about acknowledging our emotional landscape, and embracing it as an integral part of ourselves.

### Feeling Your Feelings - The Courage to Engage
Once we have accepted our emotional realities, the next step is to feel our feelings fully. This can be daunting. In an era where efficiency

and productivity are often valued over emotional well-being, it takes courage to sit with our feelings, to truly feel them. It's about engaging with your emotions, understanding their origins, and learning what they're trying to tell you.

### Mind Surfing - Emotional Intelligence in Action

Developing emotional intelligence involves honing our ability to identify, understand, and manage emotions. It's about learning how to "mind surf," to ride the waves of emotion without getting swept away. By increasing our emotional intelligence, we can improve our ability to cope with stress, build healthier relationships, and lead more fulfilling lives.

### Navigating Through Storms - Emotional Resilience

Life isn't always smooth sailing. There will be storms, periods of intense emotional upheaval. The key lies not in avoiding these storms, but in navigating through them with resilience. Resilience doesn't mean ignoring or suppressing our feelings. Instead, it means working through emotions, understanding that they are transient, and learning to adapt and grow from these experiences.

### Anchored in the Present - The Power of Mindfulness

The journey to emotional wellness is a constant, ongoing process. Practicing mindfulness is an effective way to anchor ourselves in the present, to be fully engaged with our emotions in the here and now.

It's about cultivating an awareness of our inner emotional landscape, so we can better navigate the cycles and flow of our feelings.

### Toward a Harmonious Horizon - The New Emotional Paradigm

In this new paradigm, emotions aren't something to be controlled, but rather, they are experiences to be understood, learned from, and integrated into our lives. It's about emphasizing emotional harmony as a path to overall well-being. By accepting and working through our emotions, we can learn to ride the waves of life with grace and poise, and navigate toward a more fulfilling and harmonious horizon.

## Mana Momentum

If nothing within you stays rigid,
outward things will disclose themselves.
Empty your mind, be formless. Shapeless, like water.
If you put water into a cup, it becomes the cup.
You put water into a bottle and it becomes the bottle.
You put it in a teapot, it becomes the teapot.
Now, water can flow or it can crash.
Be water, my friend.

- Bruce Lee

Journey into the temple of your flesh and bones, the divine vessel that is your body. Have you ever marveled at the movements of dancers or athletes, wondering how they command their bodies with such sublime precision and elegance? This motion and connection are a testament to the body's remarkable ability to conduct its own symphony of intention and action.

Imagine you're about to move—to stretch your limbs toward the sky, to sway rhythmically to the beats, to weave melodies, or to launch a ball into the expanse of a field. At that moment, your brain leaps into a fantastic cosmic dance.

It sends forth its commands, guiding a dance of neurons that twinkle in the vast night of your mind. Signals sprint through the intricate labyrinth of your nerves, each impulse a messenger delivering vital instructions to your muscles.

This intricate and mesmerizing ability bridges the gap between your thoughts, spirit, and physical being. Your brain creates the rhythm and the flow, orchestrating the steps and guiding your body. Yet, this is not a solo performance but a dynamic duet. The magic of this dance lies in its reciprocity—the enchanting tango of action and reaction.

As you begin to move, your senses bloom like roses in spring, absorbing the world around you and sending information to the brain. This sensory experience is your body's song, a melody that allows you to fine-tune the choreography in real time, adapting the dance to the rhythm of the world.

In the breathtaking speed of this spectacle, your movements become intentional, synchronized, and harmonious, aligned perfectly with your inner desires. And like a dancer refining their technique, the more you engage in this dance, the more flawless your performance becomes, honing your actions to a razor's edge of precision.

The art of intentional movement is a testament to our human potential, a miraculous spectacle of our inherent capacities.

Surrender to your body's rhythm, and let your spirit move as everything in nature moves.

For in movement, you find your most profound connection to the universe.

## Stillness

Practicing stillness is intentionally slowing down or observing the mind and body to cultivate a state of calm and inner peace; this can involve different techniques such as meditation, breathing exercises, or simply taking a break from constant activity and stimulation, and laying down and doing nothing.

In a world where we are delighted with distractions and constantly connected to technology, practicing stillness can be a valuable tool.

Deliberately taking the time to be still and present creates space for reflection and renewal.

Having a morning meditation practice based on stillness and silence can bring so many rewards, like becoming aware of our thoughts and emotions and developing greater clarity, focus, calmness, and resilience.

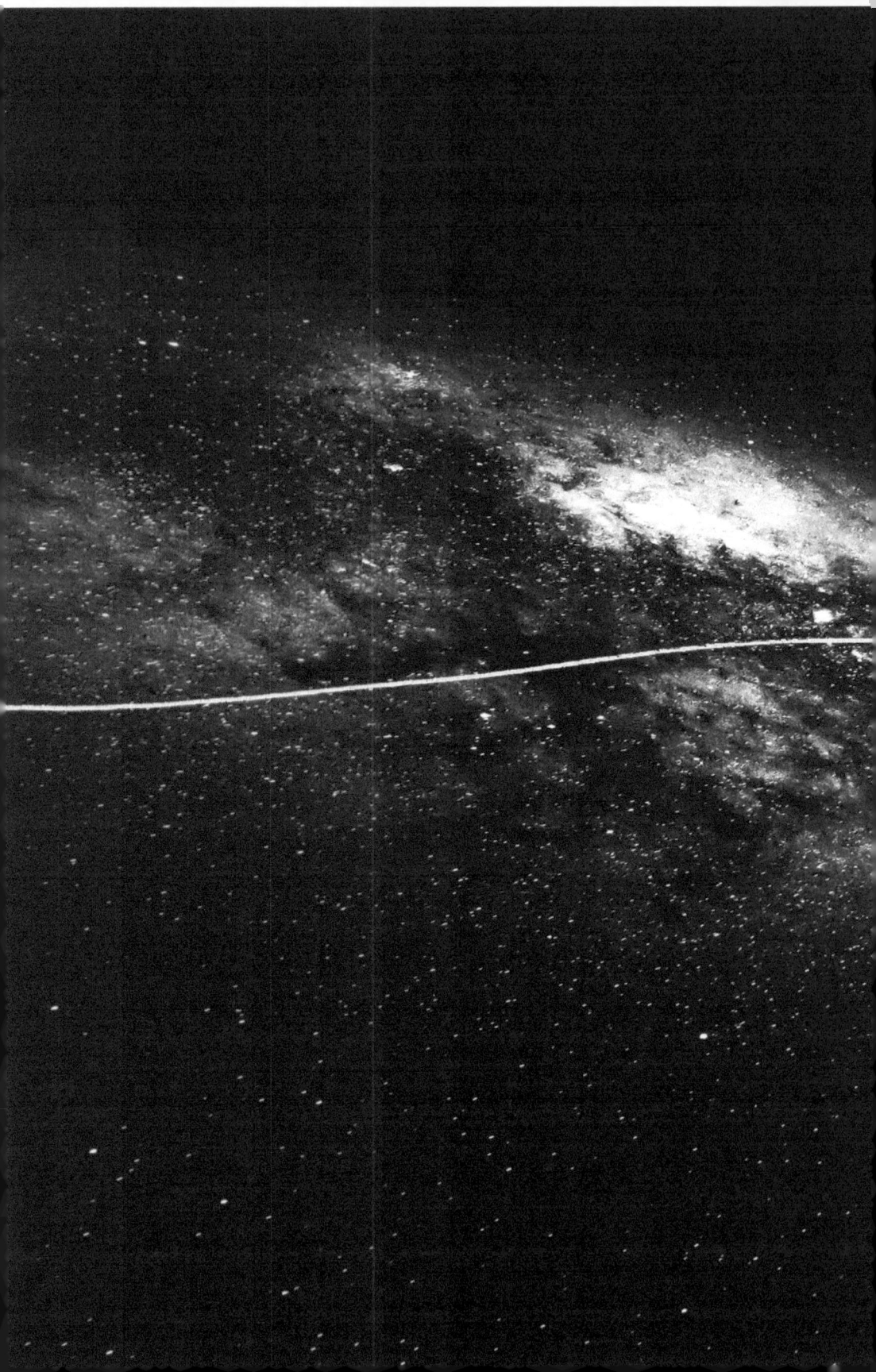

# CHAPTER 5

# Observing Energy

## "May the Force be with you."
## - Star Wars

Imagine you have a laboratory where you can conduct experiments on tiny, magical particles called "quantons." These quantons are incredibly small and possess properties that follow the laws of quantum mechanics.

In this laboratory, you have a device called the "Quantum Energizer." It's a machine that can infuse the quantons with energy in a very peculiar way. Instead of simply giving them more energy, the Quantum Energizer has the power to teleport the quantons to different energy levels, like jumping between different floors of a tower.

Now, let's think of these energy levels as floors in the tower. Each floor represents a different amount of energy the quanton can have. The ground floor is the lowest energy level, while the higher floors represent increasing amounts of energy. The quantons can only exist on these specific floors and nowhere in between.

But here's the captivating twist: the quantons can magically teleport between these floors without passing through the floors in between. It's as if they have secret passageways or invisible elevators that instantly transport them to the desired energy level.

To investigate the quantons' energy behavior, you have a set of special goggles called "Quantum Spectacles." When you put on these spectacles and look at the quantons, you see them shimmering and glowing in different colors depending on the energy level they're on. It's a beautiful sight, like watching a light show!

To explore further, you decide to design a series of experiments. You can manipulate the Quantum Energizer to teleport the quantons to higher or lower energy levels and then observe how they behave. You notice that when you move a quanton to a higher energy level, it becomes more energetic and can interact with other quantons or objects in unique ways.

Similarly, lowering its energy level makes it calmer and less likely to interact.

You also discover that quantons can release bursts of energy when they jump from a higher energy level to a lower one. It's like watching a magical fireworks display as energy is emitted in the form of light or other exciting phenomena.

Through these experiments, you realize that energy in the quantum world is not continuous but "quantized," meaning it can only exist in specific, discrete amounts. It's like the quantons can only occupy certain floors of the energy tower, and they can jump between them using their mysterious teleportation abilities.

This whimsical laboratory and its enchanting quantons represent the fantastical world of quantum mechanics. It's a realm where energy behaves mesmerizingly, with quantized levels, teleportation-like jumps, and stunning light displays.

During breathwork, we explore the profound depths of ourselves, not merely as a mechanical process of inhaling and exhaling but as a gateway to an expansive realm of energetic exploration. With each inhalation, we draw in revitalizing life force, while each exhalation releases stagnant energies, fostering a dynamic dance between our existence's physical and energetic dimensions.

Observing this energy within our breath opens a doorway to self-awareness and personal transformation. In this refined awareness, we become attuned to the flow of energy, sensing its subtle nuances as it moves through our body, animating our cells and enlivening our spirit. This heightened sensitivity allows us to recognize and release any blockages or imbalances hindering our well-being, ultimately fostering a harmonious equilibrium.

Science sheds light on the profound influence our breath holds over our entire being, bridging the physical, mental, and energetic realms.

## Nikola Tesla's Contributions to Modern Health and Wellness

Tesla saw beyond the visible world. He perceived the human body not just as flesh and bone but as a symphony of electromagnetic currents, each resonating with the music of life. He believed that by caressing and manipulating these energy fields, he could not only mend afflictions but also amplify the body's overall vitality.

Tesla dreamt of and built devices that could manipulate these electromagnetic fields to relieve various health conditions. He aspired to tap into the essence of our bodies' energy fields, nourishing them, harmonizing their rhythms, and empowering their natural balance.

Among Tesla's notable inventions stands the Tesla coil, a device designed to produce high-voltage, high-frequency electrical currents. Initially conceived to revolutionize wireless communication and energy transmission, Tesla foresaw its potential to invigorate the body's cells, stirring their innate healing capabilities.

Another gift from his innovative mind is the violet ray, a handheld marvel that emits gentle, high-frequency, low-voltage electrical currents. This magical wand of Tesla's found its way into domestic households and doctors' clinics, offering relief for a spectrum of conditions.

In his era, Tesla's approach to health technology was considered radical. Yet, as the wheel of time continually turns, the veil is gradually lifted, unveiling the potential of his work as a complementary alternative to mainstream medicine. The once-ridiculed concept is now emerging as a beacon of hope in the health and wellness sphere.

Building upon the foundations laid by him, electromagnetic therapy is utilized today to address a range of health concerns. His legacy now shines brightly in the world of Energy Medicine. His grand vision is receiving the acknowledgment it deserves, being validated and put into practice, providing solace and healing.

The new dialogues and explorations around the body's energy systems take us to the potential of breathwork.

At the core of our being, we are all creatures of energy, and the ability to harness that energy could hold the key to unimaginable health benefits.

## Scalar Energy

Have you ever heard of scalar energy? This fascinating form of energy combines both electrical and magnetic energy, creating a powerful force that has the potential to influence our very existence.

In fact, according to Nikola Tesla, our brains are capable of generating and detecting scalar waves through the process of thought.

So what exactly is scalar energy? Well, electrical energy can be described as energy expanding through oscillation and fission, while magnetic energy is energy holding through vibration and fusion.

Scalar energy is the result of combining these two types of energy, creating a powerful force that has the potential to affect our entire being.

How does scalar energy relate to our thoughts? Well, the human mind is an energy force that perpetually creates patterns of scalar waves through thought. These thoughts generate a bi-polar electromagnetic energy radiation sequence that generates distinct scalar frequency sequences within the personal morphogenetic template. The term "bipolar" in the context of bipolar electromagnetic energy radiation refers to the two poles (positive and negative) found in every electromagnetic wave. In simpler terms, thoughts are actually scalar wave patterns that possess the power to directly influence the functions of our body, mind, and spirit, as well as the ones around us. Properly guided thoughts can profoundly affect our personal morphogenetic template scalar design, influencing the observable state of our existence and the manifestation of events.

It's a fascinating concept that speaks to the power of the human mind and its ability to shape our reality. Consider the incredible power of scalar energy and the potential it holds to shape our very existence. After all, our thoughts are not just passing ideas but fundamental energy forces that have the potential to impact the world around us.

## Energy Signature

Energy signature is the unique energetic characteristics of an object, system, or phenomenon. It's the specific pattern of energy emissions or interactions that can be detected and measured from an object or system.

The idea of energy signature emphasizes the uniqueness and individuality of objects or systems and the idea that energy can be characterized and measured in various ways.

For example, every element or molecule has a unique energy signature that can be detected using spectroscopy. We all have distinctive energy signatures.

In spirituality or alternative medicine, an energy signature is the unique vibrational frequency or energy pattern associated with a person or object. This is used to describe the subtle energy fields around the human body or to evaluate the energy of different healing modalities.

Have you entered a place and felt the energy of the person who just left? This is their energy, imprinted. The cleaner our own energy is, the easier it is for us to sense the energy in ourselves and others.

## The Art of Moving Energy as Well as Air

Breathing is a powerful tool for moving energy and air throughout our bodies. With practice, it can become an art form that enhances our astral, casual, and physical bodies.

Imagine that with each breath you take, you are drawing in not just air but also a vital life force that energizes and nourishes you. This life force, sometimes called "prana" or "chi," flows through your body, and your breath is the conduit for its movement. By using your breath intentionally, you can direct this life force to areas where you need it most, whether to calm your mind, release muscle tension, or boost your immune system.

Focus on the sensations of your breath. As you inhale, imagine that you are drawing in a warm, glowing energy that fills your body with vitality. As you exhale, visualize that you are releasing any stagnant or negative energy from your body, allowing it to flow out with your breath.

Another technique is to use specific breathing patterns to achieve different effects. For example, you can use slow, deep breathing to calm your nervous system and reduce stress or active, rapid, and short breathing to increase your energy and focus. You can also use breathing to help move stuck energy in your body by focusing your breath on the area where you feel tension or discomfort and imagining the energy flowing freely through that space.

The art of moving energy through breathing is a lifelong practice that can bring a sense of balance, vitality, and connection to your life. You can explore how your breath can support and transform your experience with patience, dedication, and curiosity.

Several practices involve awareness of the flow of energy and air in a given space or within the body. Depending on the extrasensory perception level, every person interprets and sees energy differently.

One example of the art of moving energy and air is the practice of feng shui, which is the ancient Chinese art of arranging living spaces in a way that promotes good energy flow and balance. This can involve positioning furniture, plants, and other objects in a particular way, as well as using color, light, and other elements to create a harmonious environment.

Another example is the practice of Qigong, a Chinese system of movement and breathing techniques designed to cultivate and balance energy flow within the body. Qigong is often used for healing purposes, as well as for martial arts training.

## Everything Is Perceptual

Our perception shapes our understanding of the world around us. In other words, our perception, or the way we interpret sensory information, determines how we experience and make sense of the universe.

Our perception is influenced by various factors, including our past experiences, cultural background, expectations, emotions, and attentional focus. For example, two people may look at the same object differently based on their experiences and expectations. Additionally, our perception can be influenced by illusions, biases, and other cognitive processes that can distort our perception of reality.

Our perception is not necessarily an accurate representation of objective reality but rather a subjective interpretation of it. This means that what we perceive as reality may be different from what someone else perceives, and our perceptions can change over time as we gain new experiences and knowledge.

Our perception plays an essential role in shaping our understanding of the world and the subjective nature of our experiences.

## Energy Healing

Energy healing works with the body's natural energy, or prana, to promote physical, emotional, and spiritual Healing. Essentially, it's like a tune-up for your energy system.

Just like your vehicle needs regular maintenance to run smoothly, your body's energy system needs a little attention to function at its best.

Pranic, chi, or energy healing is a practice that involves three primary steps: scanning, cleansing, and energizing.

Scanning: This is a diagnostic process where the healer identifies areas in your 'energy field' or 'aura' that might be imbalanced or blocked. This is often done through intuitive or sensory perception, without physical contact.

Cleansing: Once areas of imbalance or blockages are identified, the healer then works to remove these obstacles from your energy field. This is done through various techniques.

Energizing: The final step involves infusing positive energy back into the cleansed areas to restore balance and promote healing. This might involve visualization, breathing exercises, or the use of biohacking devices or Bio Energy Technology.

Think of it like a gentle massage for your energy system. By bending your body's energy, healers can help you feel more relaxed, centered, and rejuvenated. It's a noninvasive, drug-free way to promote overall wellness.

One of the most extraordinary things about it is that it's based on scientific principles. It draws on concepts from physics, including the idea that energy can neither be created nor destroyed, only transformed. By applying these principles to the human body, energy healers can help restore balance and promote Healing.

# The Connection between Fractal Time and Energy Breathing

Life can feel like a wild and unpredictable ride, where we're thrown into the deep end of uncertainty and left to fend for ourselves. It's easy to feel like we're at the mercy of the whims of fate, a helpless pawn in a game.

One of our modern ways to experiment with this concept is by decoding the hidden patterns of the universe. Gregg Braden, a visionary scientist, merges the modern discoveries of nature's patterns (fractals) with the ancient view of a cyclic universe.

Through his research, Braden has unlocked a new world Time Code calculator that can help us decode the repeating patterns of our lives and the world around us.

The Time Code calculator helps us figure out when certain emotional events or experiences might happen again in our lives. These events can be anything that has deeply affected us, like feeling really happy about an achievement or sad because of a loss.

By looking at patterns from our past, we can get an idea of when similar events might occur in the present or future. The calculator does the math for us to find out when these repeating moments might happen.

But it's not just about predicting the future—it's also about creating it.

Every breath we take is a chance to plant a new seed in our lives, a new energy pattern that will shape our destiny. And while these patterns may not change direction overnight, we can steer them in a new direction by making conscious choices and taking deliberate action.

Embrace the power of fractal time because, with each breath, you have the chance to shape your life and create a new pattern.

And the way to use these conditions in your favor and redirect this energy is by detaching from judgment and observing how the patterns unfold.

Sounds easy, right? But how do we do this?

Through our breath, we maintain genuineness; we allow ourselves to feel what we feel; and we value who we are, how we are, and how we are doing things.

Breathing helps us focus on the present, which is when we can change the most. We start to notice our thoughts because they make us feel and act in certain ways.

For example, Louise Hay believed that depression is anger we think we shouldn't feel. Anger shows our pain, fear, and frustration, and fear comes from lies we believe about ourselves at some point in our lives.

Understanding is nothing more than an awareness of what we do not know or can't see, and basically, what we do not know is ourselves.

The purpose is not to learn to control or react to the situation, it is to know ourselves through these experiences and feelings.

We judge ourselves and others too harshly; by observing fear, we can unleash this thread of thoughts and concepts that keep us in the judge's role.

The mind controls the body, but the breath controls the mind. To detach from judgment, we should transcend all mental activity, moving beyond the intellect where there is no reasoning or reflection. When we consciously breathe, we lean forward and are in the localized world, but the nonlocal is fully there, supporting our every breath.

It is a state of profound and utter contemplation of the absolute, undisturbed by fear, pain, desire, anger, or any other ego-generated thought or emotion.

Mana Breathwork is the art of observing without judgment.

When we recognize the cycles unfolding, that things are not just happening for no reason, we can see that the chaos falls into patterns of beautiful order, which makes sense on a grand scale. We begin to see where the patterns end and where they start, and these are influential moments in our path.

These patterns exist, but we don't have to be controlled by them. They are like a guide, showing us when certain situations and chances might happen in our lives, but they don't decide what actually happens to us. They simply reveal to us when the circumstances and opportunities for events to occur in our lives arise.

Once we recognize these natural rhythms and cycles, we can bring positive changes in our lives. When we are going through a situation where we recognize a pattern, we must remember that we free ourselves from repeating this pattern by overcoming judgment.

We discover that we are beyond what we think; we are breathtakingly beautiful beings in charge of our destiny with the power to direct our cycles, and no one in this world can teach this to us. It's up to us to discover it, but when we find out about it, we will find it not just for us but for all human beings because we will be a witness on behalf of all that this possibility does exist.

## Where Attention Goes, Energy Flows

Energy becomes what it thinks about.
This is the most fundamental truth about Life.
- Leonard Orr

Your thoughts are the architects of your reality. These silent conversations you hold with yourself are more potent than any spoken word, for they are the blueprints for your experiences and your perceptions of the world.

Yet, we often take our thoughts for granted, not realizing the transformative power they hold. Like a master sculptor carving the raw marble of energy into masterpieces, your thoughts shape the formless into form, bringing life to the lifeless.

But here's the challenge: our society often emphasizes physicality over intangibility, leaving us in a perpetual cycle of external influence and internal reflection. Our thoughts become the echoes of others—our parents, our peers, our media—and not our own. We become prisoners of cultural conditioning, viewing the world through a lens not of our own crafting.

Yet, what if we were to shed this external influence? What if we were to harness the power of our thoughts to consciously direct the universal energy in a way that truly serves us?

Imagine a garden where each thought is a seed. Some seeds will sprout into beautiful flowers, bringing joy and happiness. Others may bloom into thorny weeds, representing our fears and insecurities. Our minds are this garden, and we are the gardeners. The seeds we choose to water and nurture will shape the landscape of our garden.

In this scenario, the art of discernment becomes invaluable. We learn to differentiate between the seeds that will bloom into flowers and those that will become weeds. We cultivate a garden that mirrors our desires and aspirations by consciously choosing which thoughts to nurture.

Think of this not as a rebellion against society or our upbringing but as an awakening. This is the process of self-healing and deconditioning, a journey toward self-discovery and personal growth.

As we take control of our thoughts, we take control of the universal energy, directing it toward creating a reality that truly resonates with us. This is not a power to be feared but a power to be embraced. We all have this ability waiting to be unlocked, and it's time to seize it.

## Spiritual Dimensions

In quantum physics, the observer plays a crucial role in determining the state of a quantum system. The act of measurement or observation collapses the wavefunction of a quantum particle, which is a mathematical description of its possible states, into a definite state. This phenomenon is known as the measurement problem or the collapse of the wave function.

The observer can be anything that interacts with the quantum system, such as a measuring device or even another quantum particle. The measurement process entangles the quantum system with the observer, leading to the superposition of the system collapsing into a single state that is consistent with the observer's measurement. The observer effect in quantum physics is often misunderstood as implying that observation changes the observed system's physical properties. However, the observer effect only refers to the collapse of the wave function and does not involve any physical change to the system.

As humans, we have come up with many spiritual terms such as "dimensions," "densities," and "soul." These concepts are often channeled through extrasensory perception because science has yet to find a way to measure them. While these ideas attempt to capture the essence of these phenomena, they fall short of fully understanding their true nature.

The role of the observer in quantum physics is a subject of ongoing debate and research. Some interpretations of quantum mechanics suggest that the observer is fundamental to the nature of reality. In contrast, others argue that the observer is simply a part of the measurement process and does not have any fundamental role.

Humans can experience many dimensions through meditation, hypnosis, lucid dreaming, out-of-body experiences, hallucinogenic plants, prayer, and other spiritual modalities. But most people believe we cannot physically be in dimensions higher than 5D or 6D.

The spiritual dimension of reality refers to the nonphysical and intangible aspects of existence, such as consciousness, emotions, and the soul. This dimension encompasses the realm of the unseen and the inexplicable and is often associated with religion, mysticism, and spirituality.

One way to think about the spiritual dimension is as a realm of pure potentiality. Imagine a vast ocean of possibilities, where all the potential paths of your life and all the possible versions of yourself are waiting to be explored. This dimension allows you to access your inner wisdom and intuition and connect with something greater than yourself.

The spiritual dimension is also where you can find true inner peace and fulfillment. Imagine a state where you feel completely at ease and content, with no worry or stress and a deep sense of connection with the world around you. This is the spiritual dimension.

Many people access the spiritual dimension through practices that can open them up to the deeper truths of existence. Others may find connection through nature, art, or music. The key is to feel what resonates with you and explore it in your own way.

Imagine a world beyond what our limited human senses can perceive—a world where consciousness expands beyond our physical bodies and into the vast unknown. This is the world of the twelve dimensions of consciousness, where different levels of awareness and states of being await those who dare to explore them.

But this is more than just some fanciful idea from science fiction. Many spiritual traditions and belief systems have studied and embraced the concept of multiple dimensions of consciousness throughout history.

Rather than seeing these dimensions as a hierarchy, with some being better or higher than others, a more enlightened perspective sees them as inner and outer—each with its own unique qualities and attributes.

And while our 3D reality relies heavily on words to communicate, these higher dimensions operate on a different frequency altogether. Where communication is more efficient and relies less on terms and more on a sense of unity and oneness.

## Dimensions vs. Densities

Think of density as a cosmic radio station that broadcasts your vibes. Just like how different radio stations have different frequencies, every being and object has its own unique density frequency that it puts out into the universe. When you tune in to a particular density frequency, you tap into a whole dimension of experiences that are shared by others vibrating at a similar frequency.

The density you're tuned in to also affects your level of cosmic enlightenment. The higher your density, the closer you are to the divine source and the more cosmic knowledge and awareness you can hold in your "light body." On the other hand, if you're operating at a lower density, you're more connected to the physical world and all its diversity and structure.

Next time you're feeling light as a feather or heavy as a rock, remember that it's not just a physical sensation—it's also a reflection of your cosmic density!

Reality is an infinite symphony of dimensions coexisting in the same space, each vibrating at a unique energy frequency. A shift in our own vibrational harmony opens a portal to an entirely new perspective, where we can witness the world through a fresh lens.

To expand consciousness beyond the physical world's limitations, mastering the breath has been the most efficient path we have found.

# Releasing Energy Contracts

The idea of a soul contract is rooted in various beliefs, which posit that we have pre-existing agreements or contracts with specific souls, higher powers, or the universe itself that outline the experiences, relationships, and lessons we are meant to encounter during our lives. This concept suggests that our lives are not simply random events. It is like saying, "Some things are meant to be."

Soul contracts are created before birth when our souls reside in the spiritual realm. These contracts serve as a blueprint for our lives, detailing the people we will meet, the challenges we will face, and the roles we will play in each other's lives. All souls mutually agree upon them to facilitate growth and development.

To contemplate that we have all that power—it's a revolutionary shift in my belief system. It is a belief that works for me to consciously leave people better than when I found them or resolve a karmic relationship by being aware of it. We can have multiple contracts with different souls, each serving a unique purpose in our lives. We can end these souls' agreements by having this awareness.

There is freedom in accepting ourselves through accepting the roles played by our family members, friends, romantic partners, or even adversaries because they are all meant to help us grow.

Each agreement in life can also be a lesson that, when understood, can be let go and forgotten forever.

You have the power to absolve any past life experiences or debts with others by viewing each relationship as it truly is—a reflection of our shared human experience and a classroom for the soul. Once we understand and accept this, we can move forward without carrying the weight of these experiences.

The process of releasing these contracts involves intention, motivation, and energy work, such as meditation and visualization. Releasing soul contracts can be a powerful and transformative process, and here's one way to approach it:

**1.** Start by setting an intention. Before you begin, take a moment to reflect on what you hope to gain from releasing your soul contracts. What areas of your life do you feel are being held back by these agreements? What do you want to experience instead?

**2.** Get into a meditative state. You can use any practice you feel comfortable with. Whether guided meditation, deep breathing, or mindfulness, the goal is to quiet your mind and connect with your inner self.

**3.** Imagine that you are standing in front of a large ornate door. This door represents the gateway to your soul contracts. As you approach the door, you may notice it is locked or shut.

**4.** Take a deep breath and visualize yourself opening the door. As you step over the threshold, you find yourself in an ample open space.

**5.** In this space, you may see different rooms or areas that represent different areas of your life. For example, you might see a room labeled "career" or "relationships."

**6.** As you explore these rooms, pay attention to any feelings or sensations that come up. Are there areas that feel heavy or restrictive? Are there areas where you feel a sense of joy or liberation?

**7.** When you come across a room or area that feels restrictive or heavy, imagine yourself walking up to a table or altar in the center of the room. On this table, you may see a document or symbol representing the soul contract holding you back.

**8.** Take a deep breath, and with intention, release the soul contract by visualizing yourself tearing up the document or breaking the symbol. As you do this, imagine that you are releasing the energy or influence of this "agreement" and allowing yourself to move forward with greater freedom and personal growth.

**9.** Repeat this process with each room or area that you come across. You can stay in this meditative state for as long as you like or until you feel that you have finished releasing all the contracts you need to.

**10.** Finally, when you are ready, imagine yourself walking back through the door and returning to the present moment.

Take a moment to reflect on what you have experienced and set an intention for how you want to continue to move forward in your life.

## Conversations with Infinite Self

There is information that comes from the higher self, infinite intelligence, spirit guides, ascended masters, angels, or even extraterrestrial beings. Entering into a meditative or trance-like state and allowing information downloads is possible.

I like calling it blending. Some people who can blend may hear a voice, while others may receive the information through images, feelings, intuition or other senses.

The purpose is seeking guidance, wisdom, healing, or spiritual growth. And as with any spiritual practice, it's also to approach with an open mind and discernment.

Imagine that you're a radio and want to listen to a specific station, but the station is not broadcasting on a frequency that your radio can tune in to.

You know that the station exists and is playing music you want to hear. So, you decide to adjust your radio's settings and tune in to a different frequency.

Suddenly, you start picking up signals from a source, unlike anything you've heard before. The voices and music you hear are not from this world, and you can't explain how or why they're coming through your radio.

That's a bit like what blending is. Instead of tuning in to a radio station, you're opening yourself up to a different frequency or vibration and allowing messages and guidance to come through from the higher self, beings, or entities that exist beyond the physical realm. You are blending within realms.

It's awe-inspiring and a deep experience that can provide insights and guidance that you may not be able to access through traditional means.

I call it blending because for me it's a blend into other dimensions of consciousness, but here are a few other cool terms:

Mediumship: This refers to the practice of communicating with spirits, including deceased loved ones or other entities. Mediumship can involve various methods, like clairvoyance and clairaudience, or physical manifestations like table-tipping or automatic writing.

Channeling: This is communicating with and receiving information from entities or beings that exist in dimensions beyond the physical realm.

Trance channeling: This is entering into a trance or altered state of consciousness in order to allow entities or spirits to communicate. This type of trance is present in many Indigenous traditions and new-age practices.

Automatic writing: This practice allows messages to flow through a person onto paper or another medium. The person's conscious mind is disengaged, allowing information to come through from a deeper or higher source.

Inspired writing: This is the process of receiving messages or guidance through writing without necessarily involving a specific entity or spirit. Inspired writing can come from one's own higher self, intuition, or spiritual guides.

## Spontaneous Transmission
### Journal, January 24, 2023

"Today, I feel guided. I had a deep connection with Source again. I feel like a conduit for something greater than myself. Today the "blend" was both humbling and awe-inspiring as I realized the vastness of this universe and the incredible wisdom that exists beyond our realm. I can see the information implanted in me. The immense peace I feel.

My eyes got super watery, more than in other transmissions. I was not crying at all, but my face got completely wet. I can still feel the expansion and love. The tingling. The love. I receive insights as if I am being given an understanding as if a layer is removed so I can take a closer look at what is. It's just knowing. Today was profound, and it took time to integrate. I feel in my heart a deep sense of purpose and clarity now. Now I know my path and how every experience is aligned harmoniously for me to be."

In childhood, I had a sensitivity to things unseen by others. Words would float to my ears from unseen sources, and figures would appear to me, invisible to others around me. This heightened perception, this innate ability to interpret energies, was as much a part of me as my own skin.

But as I grew older, I realized that these experiences were leading me to something more profound: transmissions, channeling, and downloads.

I remember the first time it happened as clear as day. The year was 2021. Like any other day, I was in the shower, my head submerged in the water. Suddenly, an overwhelming warmth began to grow in my chest. My body buzzed with energy, as though I was a tuning fork, resonating with the vibrations of the universe. The clarity that washed over me was staggering, impossible to put into words.

With these transmissions came tears, not of sadness or joy, but of a deep connection to the water around me. These tears felt cleansing, purifying. They brought me back to the rivers and oceans of my beloved Colombia, reinforcing my bond with the water and the land. The sensation of energy coursing through my spine was invigorating; it was electrifying.

During these transmissions, physical desire seemed to fall away. Hunger ceased to nag at me, replaced by a sense of infinite satisfaction and profound joy. These experiences varied in duration. Some were fleeting, lasting less than an hour. Others lingered for over six hours, time seemingly bending to the will of the infinite intelligence communicating with me.

The information I received during these transmissions differed each time. Some messages were personal, meant only for me, while others were intended to be shared, their wisdom too valuable to keep to myself. Many themes that appear in this book are borne from these enlightening downloads.

My journey has been extraordinary, a testament to the mysterious wonders of the universe. It has taught me to keep an open mind and an open heart, to cherish each moment, and to embrace the unknown. This journey has shaped me, and I am eternally grateful for every twist, turn, and revelation along the way.

"The two most important days in your life are the day you are born, and the day you find out why."
- Mark Twain

## Past Life Regressions

Past life regression is used in hypnotherapy and breathwork therapy to access memories from previous lifetimes.

The belief behind past life regression is that our souls or consciousnesses have existed beyond this current lifetime and that we may carry unresolved issues or karma from past lives that can affect our present life.

Hypnosis is a state of heightened suggestibility and relaxation where we can access other levels of the subconscious mind.

During a past life regression through hypnosis, the individual is guided by a practitioner to access memories from a previous lifetime. The process involves relaxing the body and mind and then guiding the person through a series of questions or prompts to access memories and information from their past life.

Breathwork can also be used to access past life memories. Energy breathing helps quiet the mind, release physical tension, and access deeper levels of consciousness.

During a past life regression through breathwork, the person is guided through the breathing patterns and then prompted to access past life memories.

In both hypnosis and breathwork, the goal is to access memories from past lives in order to gain insight into current issues, patterns, or challenges in one's life.

The memories accessed during past life regressions may or may not be literal or historically accurate, but they can still provide valuable information and healing. Past life regression gives a sense of connection to a more profound spiritual or universal consciousness beyond just the current lifetime.

## Collective Awakening

Collective awakening is realizing the interconnectedness and oneness of all beings and recognizing that our actions directly impact others and the planet as a whole.

It is a shift in consciousness that allows us to see beyond the ego and the illusion of separation and embrace a more holistic, compassionate, and responsible way of living.

This awakening is not limited to individuals but is a collective phenomenon that is happening on a global scale. As more and more people awaken to their true nature, they begin to recognize the interconnectedness of all life and the need for a more sustainable and harmonious lifestyle.

This collective awakening is not a linear or predictable process but a gradual and ongoing evolution of consciousness. It is a process that requires us to be open, receptive, and willing to let go of old beliefs, habits, and patterns that no longer serve us or the planet.

As we awaken collectively, we begin to see the world in a different light, with new possibilities and opportunities for growth and transformation.

We realize that the problems we face as a society cannot be solved through individual efforts alone but require a collective and collaborative approach.

The collective awakening also entails a shift in values and priorities from materialism, greed, and competition to cooperation, compassion, and sustainability.

It calls for a deeper respect and reverence for all life forms and the recognition that we are all interconnected and interdependent.

It is a time of hope, possibility, and potential, and it requires us to work together toward a globally united civilization. A brighter and more harmonious future for all.

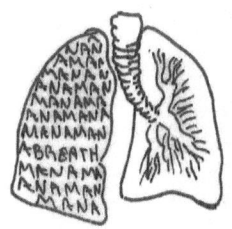

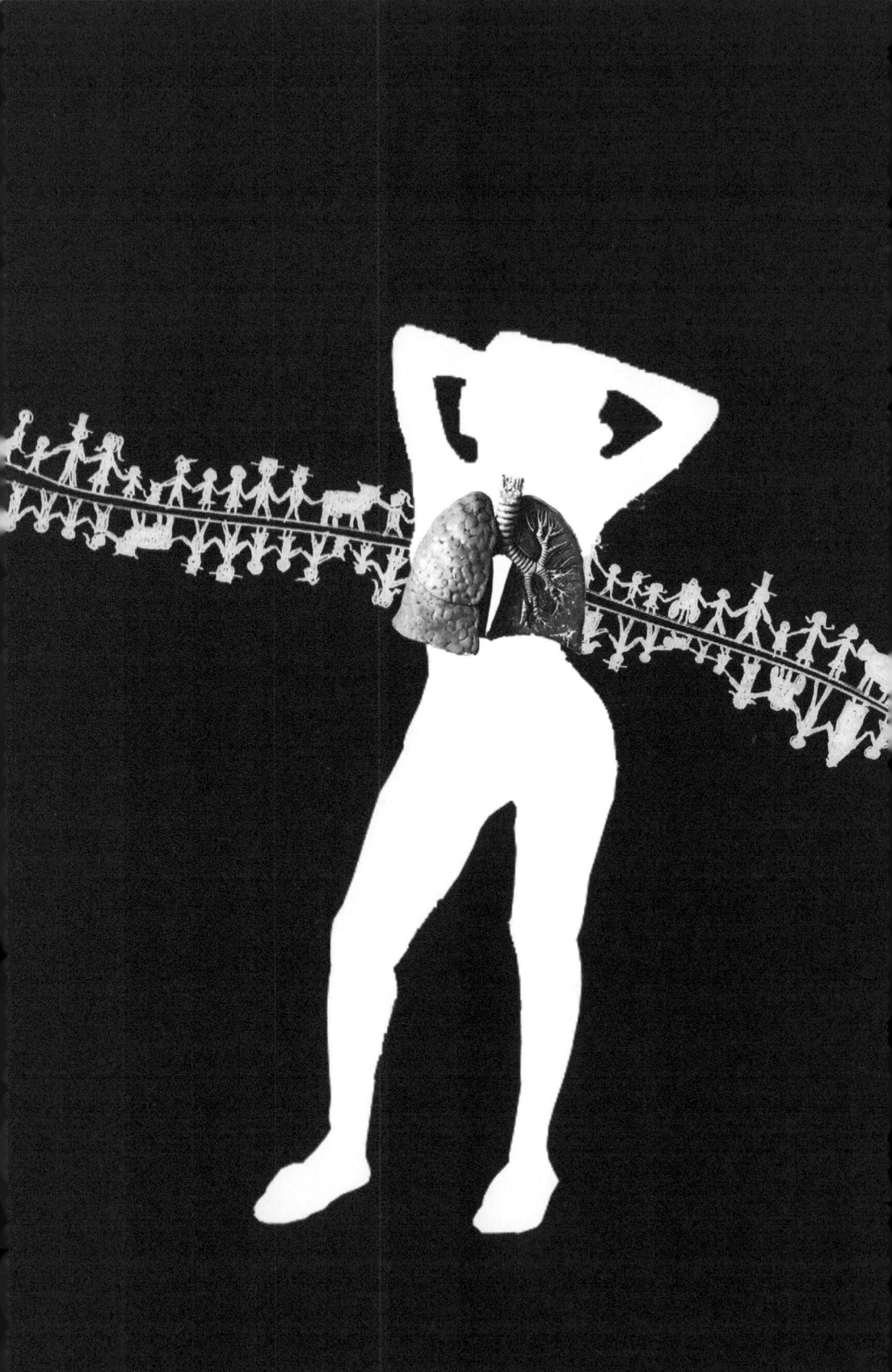

# CHAPTER 6

# Observing
# Our Breath

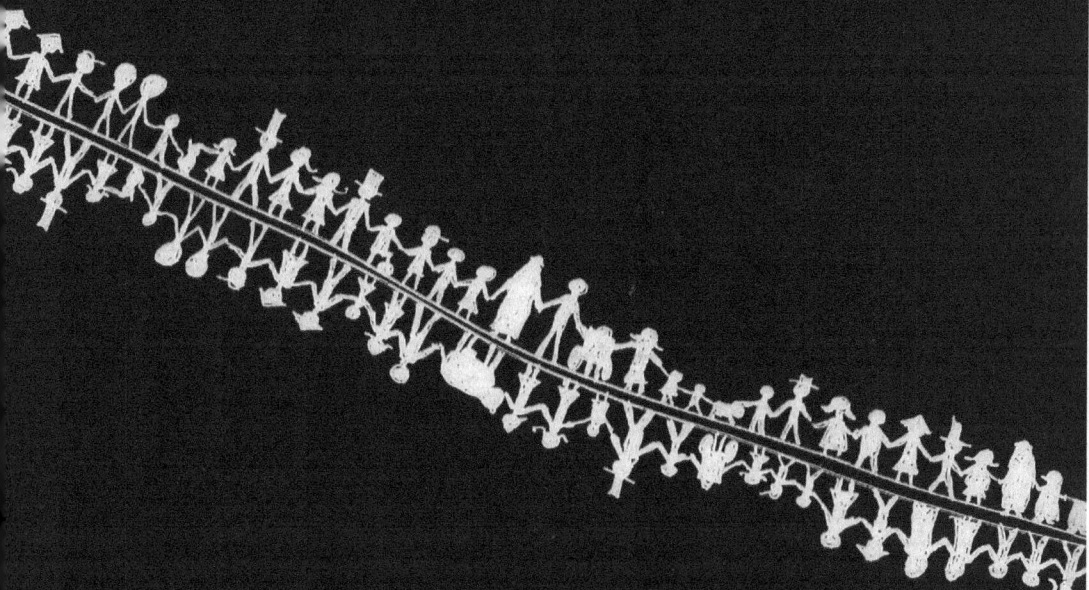

# Breathing

Take a deep breath. Inhale the fresh air into your lungs, filling them with vitality and energy. Exhale, letting go of all the stress and tension you've been carrying with you. Releasing the irrelevant.

As you breathe, you become aware of the power within your breath. You realize that your breath is more than a physiological process; it is the bridge to other states of consciousness.

Mastering the breath is not just about moving air in and out of your body; it's about moving energy, shifting your perspective, and tapping into your inner wisdom. With each breath, you generate self-healing and transformation, bringing you closer to your true nature.

As you practice, you become a sophisticated observer of your thoughts and emotions and learn to detach from them. You begin to notice patterns and behaviors that are just old conditions and release them.

The circular and continuous breathing creates a rhythm that synchronizes the self, bringing a sense of calm and relaxation. With each breath, you allow more oxygen into your body, revitalizing your cells and organs. You feel a sense of lightness and clarity, and you become more receptive to new ideas and perspectives.

As you continue to practice, you realize that you are not just unblocking your breathing mechanism but also resetting your life patterns.

You are creating a new way of being, one that is grounded in self-awareness, self-love, and self-empowerment. No longer a victim of the circumstances but a bender of your reality.

Mana Breathwork is a journey of self-discovery, a path to a more fulfilling and joyful life. It's not just a technique but a way of life, reminding you that you are a powerful being capable of designing your destiny.

Here, you will learn how to optimize your breathing. To do so we are going to enter into more technical realms. Take a deep inhale, and let the power of your breath guide you toward your highest potential.

# The Science of Breathing

Close your eyes and imagine you're standing on the edge of a crystal-clear lake. The air is cool and crisp, and the trees around you rustle in the gentle breeze. You take a deep breath in, feeling the cool air fill your lungs and energize your body.

Breathing is like taking a refreshing sip from this pristine lake, but instead of water, you're drinking in the essence of life itself. With every inhale, you take in oxygen, the vital gas that fuels your body and powers your cells.

It's like adding fresh logs to a fire, allowing it to burn brighter and hotter. But like any fire, your body also produces waste. With every exhale, you release carbon dioxide, a byproduct of your cells' metabolism. It's like throwing ash out of the fire, making room for more and preventing buildup that could smother the flames.

Just as a fire needs oxygen to burn, your body needs a steady supply of oxygen to function. Your lungs are like balloons, expanding and contracting to draw in the fresh air and expel what doesn't serve. And just like a fire needs the right conditions to burn, your body needs a balanced mix of oxygen and carbon dioxide to function optimally.

When we breathe in an active rhythm, we can regulate our physiological, mental, and emotional states in numerous ways.

Breathing is intrinsically linked to our autonomic nervous system (ANS), which is divided into the sympathetic (responsible for our "fight or flight" stress response) and the parasympathetic (responsible for "rest and digest") branches. When we engage in active rhythmic breathing, we can affect this balance and thereby influence our bodies and minds.

Rhythmic breathing, or paced breathing, involves consciously controlling your breath's rate, depth, and regularity.

When done correctly, it can lead to the following outcomes:

Enhanced Relaxation: Similar to deep breathing, maintaining a rhythmic pattern can help activate the parasympathetic nervous system, triggering a relaxation response. This can reduce stress and anxiety, promoting feelings of calmness and well-being.

Improved Focus and Concentration: Active rhythmic breathing can increase alertness and cognition. It brings our attention to the present moment and makes us more aware of our physical state, effectively acting as a form of meditation.

Better Emotional Regulation: Conscious, rhythmic breathing can provide an anchor during emotional turbulence. By focusing on your breath, you can gain more control over your emotional state, which can be particularly beneficial during periods of emotional stress or anxiety.

Physiological Regulation: Breathing rhythmically can influence heart rate variability (HRV), which is a measure of the variation in time between each heartbeat. Higher HRV is associated with better stress resilience and overall cardiovascular health.

Enhanced Athletic Performance: Some athletes use rhythmic breathing to improve their performance. Synchronizing breath with movements can increase efficiency and stamina.

Promotion of Restful Sleep: Rhythmic breathing before bed can calm the mind, lower the heart rate, and prepare the body for a restful sleep.

Despite these benefits, it's important to remember that everyone is unique. What works best for one person might not be as effective for another. So, it's always a good idea to experiment with different breathing techniques to find the one that suits you best.

## Is physical immortality possible?

Telomeres are like the plastic caps at the end of our shoelaces but for our chromosomes. They protect our genetic data, making it possible for cells to divide and reproduce correctly.

As we age, these protective telomeres naturally shorten, which can lead to cellular damage and, eventually, disease and death. This is where longevity, as we understand it, takes an exciting turn.

Now, imagine if you could extend the life of these shoelace caps or even regenerate them? And what if all it required was a simple yet profound change in something you do around 23,000 times a day— breathe?

The science of breathing has taken a deep dive into how our breath can influence the length of telomeres and, by extension, our lifespan. There is a link between certain breathing techniques and the activity of an enzyme called telomerase, and this enzyme has the power to repair and lengthen our telomeres.

Deep, rhythmic breathing, much like the type you engage in during meditation, breathwork, or yoga, helps to create a state of calm and balance in the body. This state reduces stress and inflammation, which are key factors that accelerate telomere shortening. By reducing stress, we create a more hospitable environment for telomerase to do its work, thereby potentially delaying the onset of age-related diseases and extending our health span.

In this grand spectacle of life, the act of breathing, something so innate, yet often taken for granted, may indeed be one of our most valuable tools for longevity. Our breath, with its rhythmic rise and fall, could be whispering the secrets of a longer, healthier life. And the best part? It's a gift that's always with us, as accessible as the air around us. The invitation to embrace this transformative power of breath is open to us all, always.

Now, how's that for a fresh take on the story of life? What if we are meant to evolve? How does this make you feel?

There's foundational importance in the way we breathe. You see, our bodies harbor a sophisticated defense system, an internal guard that tirelessly works to preserve our youth and shield us from disease onslaughts, such as viruses. The unsung heroes of this system? Cells and their microscale energy factories, better known as mitochondria.

Like a well-oiled machine, these mitochondria labor to produce a special chemical named adenosine triphosphate (ATP). Think of ATP as the premium fuel that powers every process and every action within our bodies.

What if I told you that something as fundamental and often unconscious as the way we breathe has a crucial bearing on the efficiency of these industrious energy factories?

Here's the captivating part: When we draw breaths that are deep, unhurried, and steady, it can kickstart the mitochondria into high gear, leading to an enhanced production of ATP. This, in turn, catalyzes an improvement in our overall health and vitality. It's akin to pouring jet fuel into a sports car—the performance just takes off. This scientific insight brings a whole new perspective to the benefits of aerobic exercise. It's not just about toning muscles or keeping fit;

it's about bolstering the body's ATP production through the power of respiration.

But the fascinating part doesn't stop here. Breathing may do more than just supply oxygen for ATP production.

As we explored earlier, the mindful act of deep and rhythmic breathing can play a role in maintaining the length of telomeres, the protective end-caps of our chromosomes.

By creating a state of calm, reducing stress and inflammation, deep breathing could be a potent promoter of telomerase activity, which in turn can contribute to cellular health, disease prevention, and potentially, longevity.

Breathe in, breathe out. It's more than a simple life-sustaining act; it's a key that could unlock the door to better health and vitality, and perhaps, a longer life. The science of breath is complex, but the practice is as straightforward and accessible as ever. It's a story that's constantly unfolding within us.

## There is foundational importance in the way we breathe.

Breath, in its simplest form, is an essential whisper of existence—a peaceful, rhythmic dialogue between us and the air around us, vital yet unassuming. Whether at rest, in a state of meditation, or at the peak of our physical exertion, our body carries out this intrinsic dialogue, continuously exchanging gases in a delicate balance between life and lethality.

At peace, our bodies maintain a composed rhythm, inhaling and exhaling at a rate that quietly hums in the background of our existence—roughly 12 to 20 whispers per minute, a discreet reminder of our presence in the world.

But life isn't always tranquil. When we delve into physical activity, the stakes are raised, and the body's demand for oxygen spikes.

The rhythmic whisper transforms into an assertive conversation, our breaths quickening in pace to perhaps 30, 40, or even 50 times per minute. It's as though the body shouts, "I am here, I am striving, and I need more to continue."

Our young ones, the children, are unique. Though they share our oxygen-breathing blueprint, their smaller, growing bodies translate this plan differently. A newborn's whisper is nearly a song, with their tiny lungs conducting a rapid melody of about 30 to 60 breaths per minute. As they grow and their lungs expand, this frenetic tempo gradually descends until it matches the rhythm of an adult. Yet, even then, the smaller capacity of their lungs means they breathe with a quicker cadence than adults when at rest—a poignant reminder of their youthful vigor.

So, as we exist, as we strive, as we rest, our breath underscores every moment. It is a testament to the endurance of life—a nuanced symphony of existence that plays out silently, beautifully, from our first gasp to our last sigh.

Traditional healing systems and mystic philosophies have long recognized the relationship between breath and health.

Breath is a way to bring energy into our body and connect it to the universe. When we inhale, we take in oxygen and energy, which are vital for regenerating our cells. When we exhale, we release carbon dioxide and other toxins. This breathing process also helps to clear our minds, reduce stress hormones, relax our muscles, and elevate our well-being. Respiration bolsters the immune system on a genetic level. When we practice breathing continuously, our body takes in more oxygen than usual, which changes the $CO_2$ level in our body.

Gently, we enter an unordinary state of consciousness, where memories, pictures, emotions, or body sensations can surface to be observed, released, and integrated. Letting the rhythm of life course through us.

Mastering the art of breathing, this sacred symphony of life, is akin to dancing with your very existence. It attunes you to the symphony of your own body, mind, and the energy that surrounds you—a melody that was always there, but perhaps unattended.

With each conscious breath, you dip into the wellspring of self-awareness, unraveling threads of emotional and physical knots tied in the shadows of your past. With the gentle wisdom of the breath, you illuminate these shadows, weaving them into a tapestry of positive experiences and growth.

Our life flows as we turn to the universe within us, to the cosmic orchestra of cells that constitute our being. Just as a musician needs the right notes to create harmony, our bodies require the correct nutrients.

They are the life-giving scripts that transform our cells into radiant stars, twinkling with vitality.

Yet, life is not without its discord. Toxins, the harsh cacophonies that clash with our internal rhythm, are part of our world. Yet, we have the power to moderate their influence. By lowering the volume of these discordant notes, we restore balance and create a serene soundscape for our cells to perform.

And at the heart of this cellular opera sit the mitochondria, the diminutive maestros conducting the energy symphony of our body.

Certain nutrients, akin to the virtuosic concertmaster, support these mitochondrial maestros, amplifying the production of ATP, the eloquent aria of cellular energy.

Let's observe the epic of building muscle mass. Just as a sculptor shapes clay into form, we mold our physical selves through exercise and strength training. This creation of muscle is not just an aesthetic triumph; it is a functional masterpiece that fine-tunes our metabolism, and upgrades our physical performance.

The stillness of mindfulness, the quiet sonata of meditation, brings a gentle peace. It encourages us to listen, to observe, and to accept. In the tranquil echoes of these practices, we find emotional harmony, resilience, and a beautiful acceptance of life's complexities.

Life is a tribute to movement. It's our bodies' beautiful ballet with gravity—a testament to our vitality. The benefits of this dance resonate not just in our physical form but ripple out to touch the shores of mental and emotional well-being.

Lastly, the grand finale of our daily cycle, sleep, is a soothing lullaby for our system. In this nocturnal serenade, our bodies conduct the unseen magic of healing, cleaning, and renewal, whispering the promise of a new dawn.

This poetic journey of mastering breathing, optimizing nutrition, reducing toxin exposure, supporting ATP production, building muscle mass, practicing mindfulness, embracing movement, and ensuring quality sleep, presents a sweeping symphony of holistic health.

These strategies are not merely chapters in a health guide; they are verses in the grand poem of life, a testament to our potential for self-discovery, self-mastery, and transformation. They are the lines we inscribe in the book of our lives, making us not just the protagonists but also the authors of our well-being.

"Spirare" is the Latin word for breathe. It has its roots in words such as spiro, spiratum, and spiritus, which mean to breathe life into the soul.

In its whole meaning, it means bringing the energy in the air to the soul through the nostrils and renewing our living beings.

## The Shallows of the Breath

So, how did we get to the shallows of our breath?

As we moved from an agrarian society to an industrial one and then to a digital one, the nature of our daily activities and the physical and emotional demands on our bodies changed dramatically. Our relationship with our breath has been a casualty of this transition.

In our distant past, our ancestors led lives that were physically demanding. They spent much of their time outdoors, working in the fields or hunting, activities that naturally promoted deeper, rhythmic breathing.

They also lived at a slower pace and had fewer distractions. The simplicity of their lifestyle allowed for periods of rest and reflection, further supporting healthy breathing.

The advent of the industrial age brought with it a shift in our physical environment. Factories became the new workplaces, with people spending long hours in confined spaces. Air quality worsened due to pollution, and the body's natural response was to limit exposure by adopting a shallow breathing pattern.

Then, the digital revolution changed our lives in unprecedented ways. The transition to desk-bound jobs, increased screen time, sedentary lifestyles, and a constant influx of information added new layers of stress and anxiety.

In response, our breathing became even more shallow and irregular, a symptom of the 'fight or flight' response triggered by stress.

Moreover, societal influences have played a role too. Consider, for instance, the cultural emphasis on an 'ideal' body image. This has led to a prevalence of restrictive clothing that inhibits deep, diaphragmatic breathing. Additionally, societal expectations and norms often encourage us to suppress our emotions, which can manifest physically as breath-holding or irregular breathing patterns.

Over time, we've developed unhealthy habits and lifestyles that have led us away from our natural breathing rhythm, pushing us into the shallows of our breath. The path to reclaiming our deep, natural breath is a journey of unlearning and relearning, of letting go of these accumulated patterns and adopting healthier practices that honor our innate connection with our breath.

The disconnection of ourselves from our breath is a silent epidemic of the modern, fast-paced lifestyle, 'the hustle.'

We are often too caught up in the rush of our daily lives to pay attention to how we breathe. Our breath is the life force that fuels our body and mind, providing essential oxygen to our cells and releasing carbon dioxide and other waste products.

The act of breathing is a symbol of our existence—an intimate link between our inner selves and the outer world. Every breath we take can be a moment of mindfulness, a pause in the whirlwind of life to center ourselves and connect with the world around us. Yet, we have been conditioned to treat it as something automatic, something we do without thinking.

What if we chose to change that? What if we took the time to listen to our breath, feel its rise and fall, and sense its flow? As we become more aware of our breath, we become more attuned to our bodies. We start to notice the subtle changes, the minor tensions, and the momentary lapses. This newfound awareness can then guide us in making positive changes to our breathing habits.

Breathing, you see, is not merely a physiological necessity, but a bridge between our conscious and unconscious selves. It is through our breath that we can touch base with our emotions, anxieties, fears, and our joys. With each inhale, we invite the world into us, and with each exhale, we release a part of ourselves into the world. This exchange, this dance of give-and-take, is what makes us whole. It is what connects us to the world and to each other.

The journey to more profound, healthier breathing is an opportunity for self-observation, discovery, and a path toward a more authentic, connected, and mindful life.

When we start to reclaim our breath, we are also reclaiming a vital part of our humanity that we have lost. We are reclaiming our ability to be present, to be mindful, and to be fully alive.

Breathing, in its deepest essence, is an act of love toward ourselves. It is a commitment to our well-being, a pledge to live our lives fully and mindfully. It is the silent mantra that guides us through life's ups and downs, reminding us that we are alive, we are connected, and we are part of this beautiful, breathing world.

## Let's try this exercise

Unlike our heartbeat, we can consciously control our breathing pattern. It can change in response to our emotional state, like when we are scared or excited, but also as a result of our cognitive efforts, like during this exercise. By recognizing these subtle changes, you've taken a step toward mindfulness—toward understanding the interaction of your mind and body in response to stimuli.

This exercise, however simple, underscores a key aspect of human existence: our mind-body connection. With our busy, digitally driven lives, we often overlook this connection. But it's always there, always influential.

This exercise also brings forward another significant point: the subjective nature of our perceptions. Two eyes, the same object, yet different perspectives. Isn't it a metaphor for our daily interactions? We perceive the same events differently based on our perspectives, beliefs, and experiences.

Whether it's appreciating the work of our eyes to provide us with depth perception or realizing the changes in our breath due to shifting focus, this exercise allows us to reconnect with our body, realize its intricate mechanisms, and appreciate its incredible capacity.

If you find yourself in a tense situation or a discussion with differing views, try to recall this exercise. Take a moment to observe your breath, remind yourself of the subjective nature of perception, and approach the situation with renewed understanding and mindfulness.

Just like the shifting focus of our eyes, we too can choose where to focus our energy and attention in our lives. By becoming more attuned to our inner workings, we can better navigate our external world.

So go on, reconnect with yourself by practicing this exercise.

Find Your Center: Begin by finding a comfortable seated position. Aim for a posture that helps you stay alert yet relaxed. If you're seated on a chair, plant your feet firmly on the ground and keep your back straight. Ensure your head is still, and you are comfortable.

Start with Focus: Close one eye and focus on a point about 20 feet away from you. As you maintain your gaze, raise a finger just below the focal point and notice how it appears slightly blurred. As you're doing this, tune in to your breathing patterns. Is your breathing slow and steady, or does it fluctuate as you maintain your focus?

Switch Your Focus: Look directly at the tip of your finger. Observe how it comes into sharp focus while the distant point becomes blurred. Now, pay attention to your breathing. Has it changed with the shift in your focus?

Observing Perspective: Find an object at a distance, like a painting on a wall. Close one eye and raise your arm, aligning your finger with the object. Now, close the opened eye and open the shut eye without moving your finger or head. The object seems to jump to the side, and your finger is no longer aligned with it. This is due to different images perceived by each eye, which in conjunction create a three-dimensional view of the world.

Reflect on the Experience: After the exercise, take a moment to observe your breathing again. Did you notice any changes during the exercise? Was there a shift in the depth or pace of your breathing as you concentrated on the task?

This exercise is an exploration of the deep link between your focus, perception, and breath. It shows how these aspects interact with each other, and offers a window into the intricacies of your mind-body connection.

## What Happens When Our Breathing Becomes Dysfunctional?

Breathing pattern disorders (BPD) or dysfunctional breathing (DB) are like chameleons that can mimic other diseases, making them hidden causes of various health problems. It's like a ninja that sneaks in and attacks without being noticed.

DB is not a one-size-fits-all disorder; it manifests as breathing too shallow, too fast, too deeply, and even holding your breath. If you have ever caught yourself breathing through your mouth, you might have experienced DB.

The impact of DB on our bodies is extensive, and it can affect our respiratory system, heart, gastrointestinal tract, nervous system, and even mental health. Symptoms can range from shortness of breath, chest pain, and fatigue, to anxiety, depression, and even panic attacks.

The good news is that BPD is manageable. Breathing is not just an unconscious habit; we can train our bodies to breathe efficiently and functionally through breathing exercises and techniques.

Next time you catch yourself breathing in a way that doesn't feel quite right, take a moment to pause and observe. Notice how your body responds and try to adjust your breathing pattern.

## Breathing Patterns

Breathing patterns are like the rhythm of a song that our body plays. They're how we inhale and exhale, the tempo and melody that keep us alive. Just like how a song can have a fast or slow beat, our breathing patterns can also vary.

Take, for example, eupnea; it's the average, normal, relaxed breathing we do without even thinking about it. It's like a soothing melody that keeps us calm and composed.

On the other hand, hyperventilation is like a frantic song, with rapid and deep breathing that can make you feel anxious and lightheaded. This is when your body is taking in more oxygen than it needs.

Hypoventilation, however, is like a slow and mellow song, with shallow and slow breathing that can make you feel drowsy and fatigued. This is when your body is not getting enough oxygen.

Apnea is like a sudden silence in the song, a temporary cessation of breathing.

Bradypnea and tachypnea are like changing the tempo of the song, with slow and fast breathing rates, respectively.

Lastly, Cheyne-Stokes respiration is like a pattern of gradually increasing and decreasing breathing, with regular periods of apnea. It's like a melody that builds up and then fades away.

Breathing patterns can be affected by a variety of factors, such as medical conditions, stress, and physical activity. Just like how different types of music can affect your mood, your breathing patterns can also impact your overall well-being.

When we practice specific breathing techniques, we can reset our breathing patterns and improve our well-being.

## Breathing Deviations

Imagine your body as an orchestra and your breathing as the conductor. When all the musicians are in harmony, the symphony flows flawlessly. However, when the conductor starts to falter, that's when you hear the off-key notes. The same holds true for breathing— when it's off, your body doesn't perform at its best.

Now, how can we detect when our conductor is losing its rhythm? The signs can be subtle, but once you know what to look for, you'll find they're not so hard to spot.

Observe this: You're trying to catch your breath, but only your chest or stomach moves, not both. Or you're sitting all hunched over, like the weight of the world is on your shoulders. These could be signs of impaired breathing.

Now consider a fish out of water, gasping from the mouth, not getting enough air. Or your breaths are as shallow as a kiddie pool, barely making a ripple. Or perhaps you find yourself pausing too long after a breath, like a song with too much silence between the notes. You might also notice you're cutting your exhales short, forcing the air out, holding your breath after exhalation, or breaking your exhales into little pieces. These can all be signs your breathing's hit a rough patch.

Let's say you're feeling tightness around your neck or throat, like you're wearing a collar that's a size too small. Or perhaps your breath feels like it's caught in a traffic jam, tense and unable to flow. These are red flags, signaling that you might have a breathing issue.

Think of your breath as a river. It should flow smoothly and rhythmically. But if the river's rushing too fast or crawling too slow, or if the current's become erratic and unnatural, then it's time to take a closer look.

Our breathing is an echo of our inner world. Just like an echo can tell you if you're in a vast canyon or a narrow alleyway, our breath can reflect our thoughts, feelings, and actions.

When you're scared, your breath might become as shaky and uneven as a cat in a room full of rocking chairs. And when stress piles up, your breath can become rapid and shallow, fluttering like a trapped butterfly.

Overbreathing is another deviation. It's like running a marathon at a sprinter's pace – you might find yourself feeling breathless, and it can even trigger false or heightened emotions.

There's also something known as chaotic breathing, where your breath loses its rhythm and pace. It's akin to a drummer who's lost the beat, sometimes playing too fast, other times too slow. Similarly, when you're physically exerting yourself or emotionally stirred up, you might find yourself panting or taking spasmodic breaths.

And then there's sleep apnea, where you stop breathing intermittently during the night, akin to a record that skips beats. It can deprive your body of essential oxygen and cause health complications. And during the day, you might be holding your breath during activities that require focus, known as 'concentration or computer apnea.'

Consider shallow chest breathing, which is usually more psychological than physical. It's like trying to satisfy your thirst with tiny sips of water. But when we engage in deep, mindful breathing, it's like flipping a switch that turns on relaxation and calm.

Let's play a game: Take a deep breath and exhale slowly. Hold your breath for as long as you can before going back to your regular breathing rhythm. How did that make you feel? Did it feel easy, or was it uncomfortable?

This isn't just a clinical analysis but a real-life, personal experience—a story that shows how even the simple act of breathing can take on new dimensions when you're in tune with your body.

A few years ago, during an unusually demanding week at work, I found myself completely swamped, juggling multiple projects at once. Timelines loomed like storm clouds, emails poured in like torrential rain, and the pressure mounted. It felt as if I was carrying the world on my shoulders.

During this time, I noticed something off about my breathing. Instead of the smooth, rhythmic pattern I was used to, it felt like I was only breathing from my chest, my abdomen barely moving. My body had lost its rhythm.

In the rush of the day, I would find myself taking shallow, hurried breaths, as if I was trying to cram a full meal into a snack-sized bag. It felt unnatural, a sort of mechanical breathing, as though my body was going through the motions but missing the essence of the act.

Moreover, I started experiencing something I later learned was 'computer apnea.' During intense bouts of focus, I would unintentionally hold my breath, my body so engrossed in work that it seemed to forget its essential function and most important tool.

Then, the tension started creeping in. I felt it in my neck, a tightness that slowly crept upon me as though an invisible hand was steadily applying pressure. My throat, too, felt tight, making each breath feel like a struggle.

One night, I found myself jolting awake, my heart pounding. I had been holding my breath in my sleep. That's when I realized I was experiencing sleep apnea, a breathing deviation I had only read about until then.

Recognizing these symptoms was the first step toward addressing the issue. I began incorporating conscious, deep breathing exercises into my daily routine, an act as simple as it was transformative. It became more than just weekly breathwork sessions, but a way of living, using the breath as my primary coping tool.

I practiced inhaling deeply, exhaling slowly, and then holding my breath for as long as comfortably possible. In the beginning, it felt a bit uncomfortable, but over time, I found it increasingly soothing.

The simple act of focusing on my breath helped recenter myself, calming my nerves and alleviating the stress that had, for so long, been building up. I started observing how different breathing patterns could be reset with various breathing exercises, which I have included for you in this book, that you could do in one or three minutes.

This personal journey taught me how profoundly our internal states can affect our breathing. It showed me the importance of being in tune with my body and reminded me that sometimes, the simplest things can make the biggest difference. It also highlighted that by paying attention to our breathing patterns, we could gain invaluable insights into our physical and emotional state and learn to consciously create balance and relaxation.

## Resetting Breathing Patterns

The first step toward breaking these patterns is to change your attitude toward your breath. This can lead to long-term changes in your body to counteract the harmful effects of stress and environmental factors. Think of oxygen as a critical nutrient and source of life.

When you're feeling anxious or stressed, your breathing becomes shallow and rapid. Your body's natural "fight or flight" response kicks in, causing you to take quick, shallow breaths to prepare for danger. While this response can be helpful in certain situations, it can also be counterproductive in everyday life.

But it's okay; you can reset breathing patterns and train your body to take deeper, slower breaths to help you feel more relaxed and focused. Here's how:

• Find a quiet, comfortable space where you won't be disturbed. Sit down or lie down in a relaxed position.
• Inhale deeply through the nose, feeling your chest and belly, then exhale through the mouth.

- As you exhale, visualize the tension leaving your body. Do this for one minute.
- Focus on your breath and make each inhalation and exhalation last longer than the one before. Observe for how long you can inhale or exhale. Rate your breathing.
- If staying focused on your breath is difficult, you can use a mantra or visualization. For example, you could silently repeat the word "peace" to yourself with each exhalation or imagine a peaceful scene like a beach or a forest.
- Practice this deep breathing for a few minutes each day, gradually working up to more extended periods, and consider incorporating deep breathing into your daily routine, such as taking a few deep breaths before a meeting or before going to bed.

You can find more exercises in this book, but before you dive into the exciting world of breathing techniques, please remember that your health is always a top priority. If you're experiencing breathing difficulties, I highly recommend seeking the advice of a medical professional. They can help you determine the root cause of your breathing problems and develop a personalized treatment plan to help you breathe easier.

Now, for those ready to explore, you can visit the Practical Exercises section at any time, which is filled with various techniques. From deep breathing and belly breathing to vibrational breathing and alternate nostril breathing, there's something for everyone.

Whether you're a master or a new observer, these exercises are designed to meet you where you're at.

## Breath Sounds

Breath sounds are like a symphony performed by your lungs and body, creating a beautiful melody with every inhalation and exhalation. Each type of breath sound has a unique tone and rhythm that can reveal valuable information about your respiratory health.

The regular or vesicular breath sounds are like a gentle whisper as air flows smoothly through your airways. It's like listening to the wind caressing the trees on a calm day.

On the other hand, crackles or rales are like tiny explosions in your lungs, signaling the presence of fluid or secretions that shouldn't be there. It's like the sound of popping popcorn.

Wheezes are like a high-pitched whistle, indicating a narrowed airway that restricts airflow. It's like hearing a tea kettle boiling on the stove.

Rhonchi are like a deep, rumbling sound that echoes through your chest, caused by excess mucus or secretions in larger airways. It's like the sound of a distant thunderstorm rolling in on a hot summer day.

Stridor is like a piercing cry heard when an upper airway obstruction occurs, and it's like an alarm going off in the middle of tea time.

Diminished breath sounds are like a hushed silence, indicating decreased air movement in the lungs. It's like the sound of a pre-google library.

Finally, a pleural friction rub is like a grating, creaky sound that occurs when inflamed pleura rub together, and it's like the sound of a vintage door hinge that needs some oil to stop squeaking.

Breath sounds are an essential component of respiratory health, and by listening to them, we can detect any underlying issues that may be present. I know, It's a lot of information so let's do an activity. Take a deep breath and listen to the beautiful melody your lungs are creating.

Tap into your inner curiosity with childlike wonder, using a stethoscope to listen to the unique sounds of your body. Don't worry if you don't have a professional stethoscope; an over-the-counter one will do just fine. And if you don't have a stethoscope at all, you can use a cup and listen to someone else's body instead.

Breathwork masters, listen up! This exercise is especially for you. I encourage you to experiment with using a stethoscope before each session to better understand the needs of the person breathing.

But this is for everyone, so let's dive into the fun part.

You'll place the stethoscope on different parts of your thorax box and listen to the amplified sounds your lungs produce. It's like your own concert, but instead of music, you'll hear the beautiful symphony of your breath. To perform lung auscultation, simply place the stethoscope bell on your chest and/or back. Take note of the sounds you hear, and compare them with the sounds from the other side of your body. Also, compare the sounds produced by each lung.

Get ready to listen to the incredible sounds of your lungs. You'll be amazed at what you hear! You can connect with me letting me know what you discovered; I would enjoy hearing about your experiences.

## Anatomy of the Respiratory System
## What Is Breathing?

Pulmonary ventilation, also known as breathing, is the process by which organisms bring oxygen into their bodies and expel carbon dioxide, a waste product of cellular metabolism. It involves the movement of air between the atmosphere and the tiny air sacs in our lungs called alveoli.

The process of breathing is driven by the contraction of respiratory muscles, which cause the thoracic cavity to expand and contract, allowing air to flow in and out of the lungs. It consists of inspiration, where we inhale the fresh air, and expiration, where we exhale stale air out of our lungs. But breathing is one of the components of respiration; the others are gas diffusion, gas transport, and regulation.

The respiratory system is a network of tissues and organs that work together to facilitate gas exchange. It includes the nasal and oral cavities, pharynx, larynx, trachea, bronchi, bronchioles, and alveoli. Each of these structures plays a critical role in regulating airflow and gas exchange, ensuring that our body receives the oxygen it needs to function properly.

When we inhale, the diaphragm contracts, moving downward, while the intercostal muscles between the ribs also contract, causing the ribcage to expand.

This creates a negative pressure within the chest, which causes air to rush through the airways and fill the lungs. When we exhale, the intercostal muscles and diaphragm relax, causing the chest to contract and air to be expelled from the lungs.

Breathing is controlled by the brainstem, which receives input from various sensors throughout the body to regulate breathing rate and depth. The brainstem monitors the levels of carbon dioxide and oxygen in the blood, as well as pH and temperature, and adjusts breathing accordingly to maintain homeostasis.

Pulmonary ventilation is a vital process that ensures the proper functioning of the body. So, on your next breath, take a moment to appreciate the fascinating and coordinated efforts of the numerous structures and mechanisms making it happen.

## Observing Our Lungs

The lungs are a fantastic pair of organs that help you breathe. Humans have two lungs in the chest but they aren't the same size. The left lung is smaller than the right lung to give room from your heart.

Your rib cage is made up of twelve sets of ribs, and they protect the lungs. The ribs are connected to your spine, and beneath the lungs is the diaphragm, a beautiful muscle.

Lungs are soft and spongy structures that are very elastic and separated from each other by the mediastinum.

You can't see your lungs, but you can feel them. Try this: put your hands on your chest and breathe deeply, and you'll feel your chest rising. Now breathe out and touch your chest.

Each lung has an apex that extends up to the level of the first rib, about 2.5 cm above the level of the clavicle. The left has two lobes, while the right has three lobes. The base is the inferior concave surface that rests directly on the diaphragm.

The inside of the lungs looks like a branching tree, with tubes called bronchi and bronchioles getting smaller as they branch out. About 30,000 of the tiniest tubes, called bronchioles, are in each of the lungs. Each bronchiole looks similar to the thickness of a hair.

A unique area at the end of each bronchiole leads into clumps of tiny air sacs called alveoli. There are approximately six hundred million alveoli in the lungs; if you stretched them out, they would cover a vast space.

Each alveolus has a mesh-like covering of tiny blood vessels called capillaries. These capillaries are so small that the cells in your blood must line up in a single file to march through them.

Take a deep breath three times, feeling the expansion of your lungs. Feels refreshing, doesn't it?

## The Airways

These are divided in two parts, the respiratory zones and conducting zones (airways).

The airways carry air in and out of the lungs, while the respiratory zone, formed by alveoli, is the site of gas exchange. The conducting airways consist of the nose, nasopharynx, larynx, trachea, bronchi, bronchioles, and terminal bronchioles.

Imagine standing at the entrance of a magical tunnel, where you can take a breath and be transported to a world where you can live and thrive. This tunnel is the beginning of the respiratory system's airways, which bring life-giving oxygen into your body and help you breathe.

As you step into this tunnel, you breathe in air through your nose (or mouth), which is filtered by tiny hairs and mucus to remove unwanted particles. The air then flows down into your trachea, like a highway leading to the lungs.

The trachea branches off into smaller and smaller airways, like the side streets of a city, eventually leading to the alveoli, where oxygen and carbon dioxide are exchanged.

It's like a busy marketplace, where oxygen is the currency and carbon dioxide is the waste product.

But just like a thriving city, the airways must be kept free of obstruction and clean to function correctly. Your body has several mechanisms to keep the airways clear, including coughing, sneezing, and mucus production, to trap unwanted particles.

However, the airways can become inflamed or obstructed, leading to respiratory diseases such as asthma or bronchitis. This could make it challenging for you to breathe at total capacity. Despite challenges, the respiratory system's airways work day and night tirelessly, helping you breathe and live.

## Inspiration & Expiration

When you breathe in, it's called inspiration. This happens when the diaphragm contracts and flattens out, making more room for the lungs to fill up with air. The rib muscles lift the ribs up and outward to give the lungs more space. At the same time, air enters the body through the nose and mouth and travels down the trachea, bronchi, and bronchioles.

Once the air reaches the end of the bronchioles, it reaches the respiratory zone, where the alveoli are located. These alveoli allow oxygen from the air to pass into the blood, which is then transported to all the cells in the body.

When it's time to breathe out, it's called expiration. This is a passive process; the diaphragm relaxes and moves up, pushing air out of the lungs. The rib muscles also become relaxed, and the ribs move in again, creating a smaller space in the chest. The air that is exhaled contains waste products, and it's warm.

And if you ever wondered why things don't get stuck in your lungs, it is because of the slick pleural membranes that ensure everything moves smoothly.

## The Muscles of Respiration

Visualize yourself in a high-intensity spin class. You're pedaling at full speed, your heart rate is high, and you're breathing heavily. As you inhale, the external intercostal muscles situated between your ribs pull your rib cage upward and outward, thus expanding your chest cavity.

Meanwhile, your diaphragm contracts and flattens, pulling downward to increase the volume of your chest cavity. This increase in volume subsequently lowers the air pressure inside your lungs, which draws air in.

Now, imagine exhaling after this deep breath. The external intercostal muscles relax, allowing the rib cage to drop back down. Concurrently, the diaphragm also relaxes, moving upward into the chest cavity. This action decreases the volume inside your chest, expelling the air from your lungs.

If you're still struggling to keep up with the pace of the class and need to take in more air, additional muscles kick in to help. The sternocleidomastoid in your neck contracts, lifting your sternum and further expanding your chest cavity. The scalene muscles in your neck also contribute by raising the upper two ribs, thus increasing the volume in the chest cavity.

And then comes the final sprint of the class. You lean forward, placing your hands on the handlebars in what's known as the 'tripod position.' This position stabilizes your chest, enabling your serratus anterior, a muscle in your pectoral girdle, to help expand your chest cavity and increase your lung capacity.

Let's not forget the abdominal muscles, such as the rectus abdominis, which pull the ribs down during active expiration, and the pelvic muscles, which support various organs, including the bladder, uterus or prostate, and rectum.

These muscles are critical in various bodily functions, such as bowel and bladder control, sexual function, and supporting the spine and internal organs. But one lesser-known function of the pelvic floor muscles is their connection to breathing. These muscles work in tandem with the diaphragm to aid in breathing.

When you inhale, the pelvic floor muscles relax and move downward, allowing the diaphragm to move freely and create space for the lungs to expand. Conversely, as you exhale, the pelvic floor muscles contract and move upward, assisting the diaphragm in pushing air out of the lungs. If these muscles are weak or tight, they may not function properly, which can impact your breathing.

Weak pelvic floor muscles may fail to provide adequate support for the diaphragm, leading to shallow breathing and inefficient oxygen exchange. Tight pelvic floor muscles, on the other hand, may restrict the movement of the diaphragm, causing shallow breathing and contributing to feelings of anxiety or stress.

Keeping the pelvic floor muscles healthy and strong through exercises such as Kegels or pelvic floor physical therapy can enhance your breathing and overall physical health.

All these muscles in your body work in harmony to make breathing possible.

## The Thoracic Cage

The thoracic cage is a dynamic structure that plays a vital role in our respiratory system. It acts like a fortress, encasing and protecting our lungs and other vital organs while providing a sturdy foundation for breathing. The dome-shaped thoracic cage offers rigidity and support for the upper limbs and muscles, making it an essential player in our daily movements.

The thoracic cage comprises the thoracic skeleton, which includes the sternum, twelve pairs of ribs, and twelve thoracic vertebrae. These bones are connected by flexible costal cartilages and intervertebral discs, allowing for movement during breathing. The ribs, which make up most of the thoracic cage, are lightweight and resilient. They extend from the back to the front of the thoracic walls and are attached to the sternum and thoracic vertebrae, providing the necessary elasticity for the thoracic wall.

The sternum is the middle part of the front of the thoracic cage and is divided into three parts, the manubrium, the body, and the xiphoid process. The thoracic vertebrae, numbered T1 to T12, form the back of the thoracic cage and attach to the heads of the ribs and the intervertebral discs. This complete skeletal system provides both protection and flexibility for ventilation.

The thoracic cage also has two openings, one at the top for the trachea and one at the bottom for the diaphragm. These apertures allow air movement during breathing and are indispensable. When you inhale, the diaphragm contracts and moves downward, creating space for the lungs to expand and fill with air. When you exhale, the diaphragm relaxes, moving upward, helping to push air out of the lungs.

## The Production of Sound

Breathing and talking are two vital functions intricately connected in the human body. The lungs, located in the chest, provide the necessary air to speak. But it's not just the lungs that play a role in speech; the larynx, or voice box, sits above the trachea and is a crucial component in sound production.

The larynx is home to the vocal cords, two small ridges that open and close to create different sounds. As you exhale air from your lungs, it travels through the trachea and larynx, reaching the vocal cords. When the vocal cords are closed, the air flows between them, causing the cords to vibrate and produce a sound.

The amount of air you exhale determines the sound's volume and duration. Try shouting and see the difference it makes. Shouting requires a lot more air, so you'll need to breathe in more frequently than if you were only speaking at an average volume.

Experiment with different sounds and pay attention to how much air it takes to produce them.

## Breathing Mechanism & Regulation

The mechanism of breathing involves the expansion and contraction of the lungs in two ways: First, by lengthening and shortening the chest cavity. Second, by increasing and decreasing its anteroposterior diameter. The diaphragm is responsible for the first method, while the elevation and depression of the ribs are responsible for the second method.

The regulation of breathing is controlled by the respiratory center located in the medulla oblongata and the pons of the brainstem. The center comprises three major collections of neurons, the dorsal respiratory group, the ventral respiratory group, and the pneumotaxic center—the trio responsible for keeping you breathing smoothly.

First up, the dorsal respiratory group located in the medulla is like the captain of the team, overseeing the largest part of your breathing cycle. It sends signals through nerves to your diaphragm and external intercostal muscles, so you can inhale that sweet, life-giving oxygen.

When you need to exhale, the ventral respiratory group comes in, located in the same area of the medulla. This group is like the sidekick, helping out when forced expiration is needed. It sends signals to your rectus abdominis and internal intercostal muscles, allowing you to release that stale air and make room for more.

The pneumotaxic center, located in the superior portion of the pons, acts like the conductor of the team, controlling the rate and depth of your breaths.

## How Do We Unblock the Breathing Mechanism?

Unlocking your breathing potential can dramatically enhance your overall respiratory health, and breathwork plays a pivotal role in achieving this objective. When performed correctly, these techniques can help to clear any obstructions within your respiratory system and improve your lung's capacity and efficiency.

Energy Breathing: Initiate the process by taking a deep breath through your nose, allowing your lungs to fill with air, and then effortlessly exhaling through the nose. This is a cyclical, connected motion without any interruptions or straining.

Deep Breathing: Like energy breathing, begin with a deep nasal inhalation, filling your lungs to their capacity. However, for this technique, exhale slowly through your mouth.

Pranayama: This term encompasses a variety of breathing techniques that originate from yoga. For instance, Ujjayi breathing, or 'victorious breath,' requires you to breathe in and out through your nose while focusing on the back of your throat. Another practice, Nadi Shodhana, or 'alternate nostril breathing,' consists of alternating the nostril used for inhalation and exhalation.

Breath Retention: Also known as Kumbhaka in yoga, this technique encourages you to hold your breath either after inhaling or exhaling for a specified duration. Regular practice can enhance your lung capacity and increase your blood's oxygen levels.

Diaphragmatic Breathing: This technique emphasizes deep inhalations from the diaphragm. To practice, place your hands on your abdomen, breathe in deeply so you can feel your belly rise, and then slowly exhale, sensing your belly deflate.

When it comes to starting breathwork, it's essential to have some expert guidance at first, especially if you have any pre-existing health conditions. Think of it like training wheels on a bike. You want to start off slow and steady, gradually building up your skills and confidence. After a few sessions with a trained facilitator, you'll be ready to take your breathwork practice solo.

## Mastering the Breath

Have you ever noticed the relationship between your posture and your breathing? Or have you paid attention to the amount of air that you allow yourself to take in?

It's common to hold your breath when you're scared or to sigh when releasing tension. These reactions can inadvertently lead to a pattern of vertical breathing, primarily utilizing the upper part of the lungs and chest muscles to inhale and exhale. While this might give the impression of a deep breath, it actually deprives your body of vital oxygen.

Additionally, vertical breathing places undue strain on the neck and shoulder muscles as they have to overcompensate during this inefficient breathing process. This can result in increased tension and tightness in these muscles. By focusing on relaxing these muscles and maintaining good posture, you can transition to more efficient diaphragmatic or belly breathing, enhancing your oxygen intake.

But why is oxygen so necessary? Oxygen is essential for every cell in your body to function correctly. Without enough oxygen, your body can't produce energy efficiently, and you may feel fatigued, have difficulty concentrating, experience loss of libido (sex drive), and even have headaches.

That's why it's crucial to use your diaphragm muscles when you breathe, but using your diaphragm is only part of the equation. You need to engage your pelvic floor muscles to fully expel all of the air in your lungs.

Together, your muscles work in perfect harmony, creating a horizontal expansion. This type of breathing involves using your diaphragm and pelvic floor muscles to expand and contract your abdomen, generating a more efficient exchange of oxygen and carbon dioxide.

Breathing horizontally is what nature intended us to do, and the best part is that you can train yourself to create space instead of contracting.

Take a deep breath, and observe your posture. Are you using your diaphragm and pelvic floor muscles, or are you relying on your chest muscles and neck? Does the upper part of your body feel tense?

But it is not just about posture and muscles; have you ever noticed how your nose and mouth feel different when you breathe? Breathing through your nose feels different than breathing through your mouth, right? Well, there's a good reason for that—it's because breathing through your nose is better than breathing through your mouth.

Let me explain why breathing through your nose can be better for you.

First, your nose acts as a natural filter, trapping and filtering out all kinds of icky things in the air, like dust, dirt, and allergens. Think of it like a protective barrier for your lungs—your nose keeps all the gross stuff out so your lungs can stay healthy.

Second, your nose helps to humidify and warm the air before it reaches your lungs. This is important because your lungs are delicate tissues that must stay moist and warm to function properly. Breathing cold, dry air through your mouth can dry out your lungs and make them more susceptible to infections.

Third, breathing through your nose can help reduce the risk of respiratory infections. That's because your nose produces mucus, which helps to trap bacteria and viruses before they can enter your body. Plus, the little hairs in your nose (called cilia) help to move the mucus and trapped particles out of your nose and keep your airways clear.

Breathing through your nose reduces stress and promotes relaxation. It's been shown to activate the parasympathetic nervous system, which is responsible for calming us down and helping us relax. On the other hand, breathing through your mouth has been associated with increased sympathetic nervous system activity, which can lead to feelings of anxiety and tension.

The amount of breaths you take every minute should be observed too.

Through practicing energy breathing and observation, you will adopt better habits and give your body the cell nutrition required to live longer.

On top of that, when you consciously breathe in a connective, circular way for an extended period, your vital energy will go wherever needed: the psyche, the body, the astral body, those around you, and even the planet. It might go to unresolved emotions to cause some release; it might go to specific muscles or body parts to ease the pain; it might go to your psyche to generate a realization, or it can build a deep connection with the wholeness.

When you consciously breathe circularly, you enter into what is called an energy cycle. You observe the mind and reset memories in our muscles and cells. You can explore the deepest corners of consciousness and unlock true essence. You can dissolve the barriers that separate you from others and deepen your connection with yourself and the universe.

So there you have it—mastering the breath is a skill that can transform your entire being, from the physical to the mental and spiritual.

It is an ever-evolving process, and there is always room for growth and expansion. With each breath, you can nourish your body, let go of tension, release negative emotions, and connect with the present moment.

Through the art of mindful breathing, you can tap into the infinite power and access the vital energy that flows through all things.

Take a deep breath, and feel the life-giving energy flowing through you.

# Benefits of Observing the Breath

The benefits of breathwork are both creative and scientific, as this practice has been shown to profoundly impact the mind and body.

One of the significant benefits is resetting belief systems and old programming. By consciously breathing in a circular and connective way, we release data from our minds and reset memories of our muscles and cells, leading to a more positive outlook.

Breathwork is also a powerful tool for trauma and tension release. When we take the time to breathe deeply and slowly, we signal to our brain that we are safe, everything is working out, and we can relax. This response decreases the fight or flight response, reducing stress and anxiety and allowing us to release physical and emotional tension.

At a scientific level, breathwork affects the brain and heart, growing connections between neurons and increasing serotonin and dopamine release. These changes in brain chemistry can lead to a positive shift in mood, motivation, attention, and arousal while feeling an increase in relaxation, mental clarity, and emotional regulation.

Breathwork has a positive impact on our central nervous system. By balancing the body's pH and reducing acidity, it can improve immunity and other functions. It reduces inflammation and oxidative stress, boosts circulation, and decreases cortisol levels, influencing metabolism.

Just as fetal stem cells know exactly where to go in a mother's body to bring about regeneration, so too does divine energy know how to best serve you.

And the best part? You can tap into this divine energy anytime through something as simple as breathing. With every inhale, you are drawing in life-giving energy that can be felt throughout your entire being. This energy, known as prana or chi, can flow wherever it is needed most, bringing with it a profound connection to your environment and the people around you. By mastering the art of allowance and letting go, (inhale and exhale), we become more resilient and adaptable to change.

## Here are some of the potential physical benefits of breathwork:

- Restores the balance of the autonomic nervous system
- Increases vital energy
- Stimulates circulation, cell regeneration, and oxygenation
- Balances the blood pressure
- Increases blood flow to the genitals and promotes a healthy sex life
- Removes 70 percent of toxins from the body
- Reduces oxidative stress
- Releases muscle tension
- Keeps the digestive system working smoothly
- Alkalizes the blood pH
- Has an anti-inflammatory effect
- Regulates hormonal imbalances
- Strengthens the immune system
- Builds stronger respiratory function
- Reverses respiratory disorders
- Liberates the breathing mechanism from shallow, inhibited breathing patterns
- Helps with flu- and cold-related symptoms and recovery
- It mitigates the susceptibility to contagious illnesses
- Boosts performance
- Enhances mental clarity, attention, and memory
- Activates creativity and motivation
- Activates telomerase in the body, producing a lengthening of the telomeres and, consequently, it slows down or reverses the aging process
- Uses many core muscles that can be trained and strengthened; breathing is an active exercise

## Here are some of the potential emotional benefits of breathwork:

- Creates coherence between the mind and the heart
- Facilitates a positive emotional state / elevates the mood
- Provides a better outlook on life, contentment, and joy
- Decreases fatigue, panic, and reactivity
- Reduces feelings of depression and anxiety
- Improves sleep cycles
- Calms an overactive mind
- Brings awareness of self-sabotage patterns
- Decreases addictive behaviors
- Releases traumatic memories and suppressed emotions
- Releases early childhood and birth imprints, patterns, and memories
- Reduces PTSD symptoms
- Promotes healthy relationships
- Increases resilience
- Serves to integrate parts of yourself

## Here are some of the potential energetic benefits of breathwork:

- It enhances the connection with our Source, Infinite Self, Higher Self, or Subconscious Mind, allowing for deep insights, intuitive guidance, and improved decision-making
- Breathwork cultivates an experience of unity, fostering a sense of oneness with the world around us
- It encourages feelings of unconditional love, thereby raising our vibrational energy
- Breathwork releases energetic blockages, allowing for an uninterrupted flow of vital energy
- It revitalizes and rejuvenates our energy, thereby increasing our vibrancy and vitality
- Breathwork increases our energetic capacity, enabling us to handle more tasks and responsibilities

• It balances our chakras, harmonizing the energy flow throughout our bodies
• Breathwork purifies our aura, clearing away any negative or stagnant energies
• It enhances our energetic sensitivity, making us more aware of subtle energy shifts in our environment
• Breathwork nurtures spiritual growth and evolution by amplifying our energetic potential

I can go on and on describing the benefits of breathwork. There are so many! But at some point, practicing is the only way to understand all its benefits.

If you're looking for inspiration on what types of exercises to try, remember to check out the Practical Exercises section. There's a whole world of techniques out there to explore. Find what works for you, and let the breath work its magic.

"You may appropriately depart your body without illness or pain."
- Abraham Hicks

## The History of Breathwork

From the dawn of our existence, we have turned our mindful gaze toward the act of breathing. The techniques we associate with this act have not so much been invented as they have been discovered through the intimate art of observation.

The breath, for many, is viewed as a profound life force that not only brings life into being but also serves as an instrumental tool for transformation and healing.

This belief can be found in the sacred Hindu practice of Pranayama, a Sanskrit term meaning 'breath control.' Its central role is to foster spiritual growth, guiding its practitioners toward a deeper understanding of themselves and the universe.

Similarly, the ancient Taoist masters of China developed the practice of Qigong, harnessing specific breathing techniques to cultivate inner energy. This, they believed, was key to achieving a state of balance and well-being.

Our journey with the breath transcends time, place, and culture, uniting us all in a shared understanding of our innermost existence.

There are other breath-centered meditations in Buddhism, Taoism, Sufism, Christianity, Shamanism, and martial arts. Each breathing technique varies among cultures, but the universal theme remains the same.

Many ancient languages used words that could mean "breath" to also refer to the soul, spirit, or life energy. Spirit comes from the Latin spiritus, which means "a breath," This concept is not unique to Latin.

For instance, in Greek, the word pneuma refers to both "air/breath" and "spirit/life energy." The Greeks believed that the breath was closely related to the mind; therefore, the spirit and mind are interconnected.

In Indian philosophy, the sacred essence of life is known as prana, which means "air and breath." Similarly, in Hawaiian, the word Hā means breath—the breath of life—and is related to Mana, which is the "spiritual force."

In the Qur'an, the breath is related to the physical and spiritual life of the human being. Recitation, particularly recitation of the Qur'an, involves the physical act of breathing.

The concept of breath is also prevalent in Chinese medicine, where the word Chi represents the "universal and cosmic energy of life." Likewise, the word Ki holds a similar meaning in Japanese tradition and is an essential component of martial arts and spiritual practices.

In many languages and dialects, including Andean Quechua, Amazonian Quechua, Tibetan, Aramaic, and others, the word for breath is similar to the words for life, spirit, and soul.

Many shamanic cultures worldwide have used breathwork as a form of healing, such as the Kalahari Kung Bushmen of Africa, who use rapid and shallow breathwork and dancing to attain kia, a state of powerful emotional and physical ecstasy. Those who reach this state can perform healing rituals for others.

As these practices expanded to new territories, they became a distinct field of study.

In the early twentieth century, Wilhelm Reich developed a therapeutic approach known as "vegetotherapy," which emphasized the importance of breathing in emotional and physical healing.

Beyond this ancient knowledge, modern use of breathwork began during the 1960s and '70s, when pioneers like Leonard Orr and Stanislav Grof explored the potential of breathwork in facilitating altered states of consciousness and personal transformation.

Along with Ram Dass and Timothy Leary, Leonard Orr is one of the originators and elders of what we call "the New Age movement."

In 1962, Leonard Orr had a regression experience while experimenting with deep breathing patterns in a water tub, and that's how the Rebirthing Breathwork movement began. Leonard found that breathwork helped reach the subconscious, where memories, pictures, emotions, or physical memories can surface to be reviewed, released, and integrated.

Rebirthing Breathwork is based on nasal breathing and practiced in a one-on-one setting without any external stimulus other than the facilitator's voice.

Leonard dedicated his life to understanding the intricacies of breathwork, spiritual psychology, trauma, and physical immortality. His practical approach was the result of years of experimentation and facilitation. He generously shared his insights with the world for more than fifty years of his life through more than twenty books in a dozen languages, including Rebirthing in the New Age; Fire; Breaking the Death Habit; Breath Awareness; Babaji, the Angel of the Lord; and Government Without Taxes. His international Rebirthing Movement has served over ten million people on six continents. Although Leonard is no longer with us, his legacy lives on through every Rebirther in the world. His work continues to touch the lives of people all over the world through many of his students.

"Leonard Orr's book is the most realistic and practical in the field of conquering death."
- Timothy Leary

Another pioneer is Dr. Stanislav Grof, a Czech-born psychiatrist who, in the 1960s, worked with psychedelics as therapeutic tools and found that the "non-ordinary states of consciousness" his patients could access during these experiences had healing power. LSD—a psychedelic substance that was once a beacon of hope and liberation, was abruptly banned. But he believed that the fact that these healing states could be accessed with a substance was proof that the receptors for that type of experience existed in our brains. And if that was true, then there had to be a way to access the same states without the use of LSD, psilocybin, mescaline, adrenochrome, adrenolutine, and tryptamine derivatives: DMT, DET, and DPT.

He then researched how traditional societies had accessed these states and studied modern consciousness theory. Dr. Grof is one of the principal developers of transpersonal psychology; from his research and working with groups of volunteers at Esalen over several months, he developed a modality that uses rapid, controlled breathing patterns and rhythmic music to access more profound levels of consciousness. He called it Holotropic Breathwork.

As the legacy of these pioneers continues to unfold, the field of breathwork advances, constantly refining an array of techniques. Some practices favor profound, slow breaths, while others highlight rapid, rhythmic breathing or specialized patterns of inhalation and exhalation.

Breathing is both an art and a science, interwoven with the fabric of our existence.

## Types of Breathwork

From the moment I woke up to the power of breath, I have found myself in a wondrous labyrinth of knowledge and experience.

I've learned from those who walked the path before me, shared wisdom with those who walk it beside me, and passed the torch to those who will continue the journey after me.

Each breath has been a step into the unknown, a journey into the depths of my soul, and a bridge to the universal consciousness that binds us all.

Breathwork is not just about breathing. It is a profound practice that reaches into the core of our being. It invites us to question, to probe, to peel back layers of existence until we find our true essence.

It is about exploring the unknown and embracing the impermanence of life. It is a spiritual, psychological, and physical journey that allows us to navigate our emotions, heal our wounds, and tune in to the rhythm of the universe.

As Leonard would say, "You are your own guru." It means we are our own teachers, the experimenters of our own lives. I took his words to heart. They influenced my journey, my practices, and my approach toward breathwork. I believe we each possess the tools to explore our inner universe and heal ourselves.

As I share the insights, and experiences, my hope is that this ignites a spark within you. My intent is not to instruct, but rather to inspire, to stoke the flame of curiosity within you, and to encourage you on your own path of self-discovery.

Embrace the adventure that lies within each breath. Each inhale is an opportunity to invite new perspectives, and each exhale a chance to let go of what no longer serves you. The breath is the key that unlocks the door to our inner selves, and through it, we can access the infinite potential that lies within us all.

As we venture into the unknown together, let us remember the teachings of all those who have illuminated our path with their wisdom and guidance. Let us all become our own gurus. Let us listen to our breath, learn from it, and allow it to guide us. With each breath, we become more attuned to ourselves and the universe around us.

With an open heart and a curious mind, let's continue this breath odyssey, sharing the wisdom and insights we gain along the way.

But what I practice doesn't have to be the same for you. It is your time to bend energy!

Mastering the breath is the art of observing; it is a dance between extrasensorial perception and science with infinite possibilities. For me, it's equally as fulfilling to give or receive a session. Joaquin and I trade sessions often.

From nose-focused to mouth-focused, from slow and steady to rapid-fire, from cold to hot water, there are many different breathing methods and techniques to choose from, each with its unique set of benefits.

Some techniques are designed for one-on-one sessions, while others are meant for larger groups. And the facilitators themselves go by different names—sitters, guides, healers—depending on the approach.

But perhaps the most fascinating is how it can be used for various purposes, from tapping in to alternate states to performance enhancement. Some sessions focus on the mystical and emotional experiences that can arise from breathing, while others prioritize the physical benefits like increased endurance and lung capacity. The belief systems and spiritual frameworks also vary from practice to practice, influencing the rest of the parameters.

The core principle of The Mana Breathwork Universe is observing the physical, astral, and emotional bodies, which allows energy cycles to do their work.

Our philosophy is centered on the concept that joy should be the compass guiding our lives. Where there is joy, there is transformation. While contrast can be a powerful tool for growth and evolution, joy holds equal power in its ability to transmute all things.

Each modality has strengths and purposes, from the ancient pranayama to our more modern approaches, so understanding your intention for the breathwork is a crucial practice before choosing a technique. Are you seeking emotional healing, stress relief, increased energy, or spiritual exploration? Are you using it to boost creativity? Are you seeking peak potential? Once you have clarity on your purpose, you can narrow down the list of breathwork methods that align with you.

Consider your comfort level with physical sensations such as light-headedness or tingling, as some techniques may induce these feelings more than others.

Think of the environment where you prefer to practice, as some methods are more conducive to group settings, while others may be better suited to one-on-one. The best way to know is to try. You don't have to marry with a specific technique. You can try several at the same period in your life, or you might find that some are more suitable to reach a specific goal, and that's what you need that day.

Today, there are countless types of breathwork, each with its unique style and approach. You can pick and choose what resonates with you.

If you're new to breathwork, the variety of options can be overwhelming. But the beauty of mastering the breath lies in its adaptability.

Whether you want to improve stress levels, boost energy, or explore your inner self, a breathwork technique can help you achieve it.

Finding a high-quality professional or organization to guide you through the process is vital. Practicing breathwork under the supervision of an experienced facilitator can help you get the most out of the practice while ensuring your safety and well-being.

Once you've found a facilitator or organization, it's time to explore your options. There are many breathing practices. Some focus on slow, deep breathing, while others incorporate faster, more intense breath patterns. Some use external stimuli like music, aromas, or equipment, while others rely solely on the facilitator's voice.

As you explore, pay attention to how each technique makes you feel. Do you feel energized, relaxed, or more connected to yourself? Does the approach resonate with your beliefs and values? These are all essential questions to ask yourself as you navigate the world of breathwork.

Remember, there's no good or wrong way to practice, and it's all about finding what works best for you and your unique needs.

As both a teacher and a student, I am constantly amazed by the power of breathwork. It's a technology that is continually evolving, just like any other. And in this new age of AI, we are discovering more about the art of breathing and consciousness than ever before.

The science behind breathwork is becoming more and more fascinating, and researchers are conducting studies to understand how far we can expand our consciousness through the power of our breath. It's incredible to think that something as simple as breathing can be the gateway to our inner technology.

## Holding Space

An eye-opening shift in perspective busted me out of the rigid box of societal expectations, carving out space for balance in my life. No more chasing a conditioned version of success.

My new success story is spun with threads of inner peace, contentment, and a sense of purpose that feels more 'me.' Venturing into the transformative realm also opened the door to meaningful connections. The raw vulnerability exchanged in breathwork sessions smashes through social norms and builds an intimate bond like no other. It's a potent kind of beauty when a melting pot of individuals can connect over something as universal as breathing.

Through exploring the depths of our consciousness, we unlock empathy, not just for ourselves but for those who share our space. Breathing drills in the truth that despite our unique narratives, we're all tied together in our quest for authenticity and fulfillment.

Mana is more than just a brand; it's a tribe of like-minded souls who lift each other up, inspire each other, and hold space for vulnerability. Mana comes from a word I was given during transmission and to me it means mother energy or Pachamama.

Together, we journey into our inner landscapes, embracing our soft spots and cheering on our strengths. This is a potent reminder of our deep-seated ability to bond on a fundamental level. Think of it as a back-to-basics move, stripping down to the bare essentials of life— our breath—to unearth solace, joy, and a sense of purpose.

Mana Breathwork isn't just about guided breathing exercises; it's a journey of connection, compassion, and metamorphosis.

It's about being grounded in the present, staying true to yourself, and embracing life in all its technicolor glory. It's about diving headfirst into the unknown and coming out on the other side, stronger, wiser, and more in tune with your real self.

Reflecting on my journey, I was so stoked for that first email from Joaquin that lit a fire of curiosity in me. The subject said: "Hola, soy Joaquin el Maletero." I had no clue these words would set me on a life-altering adventure, redefining my existence in ways I could never have imagined. This deep dive has been nothing short of phenomenal, and it's touched not just my life but also those in my orbit, and for that, I'm eternally thankful.

The breath you're taking right now? That's your lifeline to the primal energy that powers you. Use that to tune in to your inner light, resilience, and wisdom.

By breathing with intention and awareness, you can unlock the energy flow within you, kindling a spectrum of sensations and experiences. Think of it as a workout for your soul, unknotting any energy blockages that might be anchoring you down.

Each breathwork session is a new adventure, with the potential to unlock pent-up emotions, rewrite patterns, or whisk you off on a spiritual voyage.

To begin a session, you lie down, relax, and breathe deeply in a peaceful space. You kickstart your session by focusing on your breath, and as you sync up with your breath, you start noticing any subconscious barriers or defense mechanisms that might be arising. By consciously breathing through these patterns, you can loosen their grip on you and integrate them into your present experience.

Energy Breathing sessions are a powerful way to reconnect with the unblemished state of existence we all knew before we were born. By dissolving resistance to this pristine state, we can develop more authentic relationships with ourselves and with others. By breathing in a conscious and intentional way, you can tap into the life force energy that flows within you, unleashing a whole range of sensations and experiences. It's like a workout for your energy system, loosening up any blockages that may be holding you back on physical, emotional, mental, or spiritual levels.

It is indeed a marvel how breathwork's transformative potential has transcended barriers of culture, geography, and even technology. Yet, its impact remains profound and personal, allowing you to unearth insights about yourself that would otherwise lie dormant in your subconscious.

Breathwork, at its core, is the practice of using breathing techniques to influence your mental, emotional, and physical state. It's an ancient practice, but its timeless wisdom has not only survived but flourished in the modern world.

In our fast-paced world, where we are often detached from our inner selves, It provides a sacred space to reconnect. It is adaptable to our ever-changing lifestyles. Be it an underwater session that intertwines the effect of water with breathwork, a group session where a sense of community and shared experience heightens the benefits, or a one-on-one session that provides a more intimate and personalized experience, all is possible and all will have different outcomes.

As we continue to understand more about our mental and emotional health, the significance of this practice will only grow. Corporations, world leaders, and individuals are starting to see the value of incorporating breathwork into their routines. It's a wellness practice that generates not just personal growth, but a healthier, more resilient society.

As we usher in this new era of wellness, it's crucial to remember the simplicity at the heart of evolution: observation without judgment, deep breaths, mindfulness, and a willingness to introspect. With these simple tools, each of us has the power to transform our lives profoundly. We are not alone, your story is also being written with each breath you take.

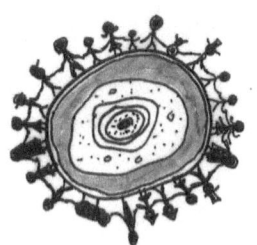

CHAPTER 7

# Everything is Connected

## Spiritual Purification with the Elements

The fundamental elements have been the subject of contemplation and study for millennia. From ancient India to Greece, from China to South America, different cultures have recognized the importance of elements in shaping our world.

At their core, the five elements—earth, water, fire, air, and ether or space—represent the basic constituents of the universe. They are the building blocks of everything around us, from the mountains and oceans to the air we breathe and the fire that warms us. Matter reveals itself in the universe through the elements.

Their names and attributes vary across traditions, but the underlying idea is the same—everything can be understood in terms of the elemental forces that shape it.

The significance of the five elements goes far beyond; they also correspond to different aspects of our being.

The elements are intimately connected to our physical body, emotions, thoughts, and spiritual essence. Your senses of sight, touch, sound, smell, and taste are based on these elements. By cultivating a conscious relationship with them, you can deepen your understanding of the self and the world.

Our teacher, Leonard, firmly believed in the power of the five elements to help us realize our potential as Intelligent Energy. He constantly reminded us that we have unique natural elemental characteristics, and by engaging with these elements, we can communicate with others more effectively.

Through simple daily spiritual practices, we harness the power of each element and purify ourselves, becoming more attuned to the flow of life.

Each element has its own unique properties and correspondences. Observe how they interact with each other, how they shape the seasons and the cycles of life, so you practice a deeper connection to them.

# EARTH

The earth element is a powerful force that can help you manifest your desires into physical reality. When you feel lost or disconnected, you can observe your roots and connect with the grounding and stabilizing energy of the earth. This can help you find clarity, allowing you to navigate the contrast in life with greater ease.

Connecting with the earth allows you to tap into its powerful energy and feel more centered and present in your body. Whether standing on the beach, walking barefoot on the grass, or climbing mountains, being in nature can help you.

Gardening is another excellent way as you nurture and care for plants that grow from the soil.

Earthing, which is visualizing roots extending from the soles of your feet deep into the earth, allows you to release any low vibrations or intense emotions and transmute them into positive energy.

Planting or touching a tree can also help you feel supported and rooted in the physical world. Planting is an act of kindness.

The earth element is responsible for the structures that allow experiencing smell, a sense associated with connection to the physical world.

Wearing red or looking at red lights is associated with the root chakra and can make you feel more grounded. Different colored rays have various therapeutic effects.

Eating nourishing, whole foods is essential in connecting to the earth. The lighter and more nourishing your food, the more life energy you have.

A personal exercise system can also help you stay connected to your body and maintain balance and stability.

Thriving financially and having a fulfilling career or activity that inspires you is part of your relationship with the earth.

Self-care treatments such as body massages, dancing to soothing music, practicing affirmations, and earth-balancing asanas can further strengthen your connection.

When the earth element is balanced, you feel grounded and unwavering in your sense of stability, allowing you to manifest your desires with greater ease.

## WATER

Imagine standing on the shore of a crystal lake, the cool, clear water lapping at your feet. As you immerse yourself, you feel calm and see thoughts and emotions being washed away.

Water is a transformative element that can purify both the body and mind. Hydrotherapy, or using water for therapeutic purposes, has been used to treat ailments for a long time.

The water element has much to do with emotional healing, adaptability, and physical health. Water is associated with emotions and intuition. Its flow and movement can mirror your emotional currents, while the stillness of a calm lake can help you connect with your innermost feelings and thoughts.

Just as the physical body is mostly water, this element also influences the emotional body. One way to connect with it is by immersing in it—taking a bath twice a day cleanses not only the body but also has the power to purify the energy body, which, as Leonard said, is "our mind in action."

But water purification doesn't stop with bathing; you can practice connected breathing in the tub using the water as a conductor or practice controlled exposure to cold water, also known as cold water immersion or cold water therapy, which could be taking a cold shower, soaking in an ice bath, or plunging into a cold pool or natural body of water. Doing this can help boost your immune system and mood, improve your ability to recover, and build resilience.

Drinking alkaline optimal water is another way to honor the water element and keep our bodies hydrated.

Meditating near water can also help us connect with the element. Find a quiet spot near a body of water and sit with your eyes closed, imagining yourself becoming one with the flow of the water. Allow the sounds and movements of the water to guide you into a deeper state of relaxation and connection.

By incorporating water-based practices into our daily lives, we can tap into its energy and find greater flow and balance in all areas.

# FIRE

Fire's significance extends well beyond the tangible and into the spiritual realms, acting as a potent symbol and tool for purification and longevity.

Cultures around the world have turned to fire as a conduit for spiritual purification. Rituals involving fire are commonplace and play a significant role in numerous spiritual traditions. The sacred fire ceremony known as Agnihotra in Vedic traditions is believed to harness the purifying properties of fire. Participants offer natural substances to the fire at sunrise and sunset, chanting mantras and making offerings to invite blessings and cleanse negative energies.

On the path to longevity, consider fire as a metaphor for your internal vitality or "life force." Traditional Chinese Medicine refers to this as your "yang" energy—the warming, activating principle. To cultivate longevity, we should keep this internal fire burning brightly but not excessively.

Fire is also associated with passion and determination—qualities essential for a long, purposeful life. Just as a flame flickers and dances but never ceases to burn, harnessing your inner fire can keep you motivated and resilient in the face of life's challenges. Keeping your inner flame alight is about living with purpose, maintaining enthusiasm, and continuously kindling your love for life.

The Phoenix is a bird renowned for its relationship with fire and its symbol of longevity and rebirth. The Phoenix's life cycle involves a fiery death and rebirth from the ashes, representing transformation, renewal, and continuity of life. Just like the Phoenix, you can use the element of fire to symbolize your ability to rise from adversity, grow, and start anew.

The spiritual practice of 'Tummo' or 'Inner Fire' meditation, derived from Tibetan Buddhism, is another way to engage with fire's transformative power. Tummo focuses on generating and maintaining an internal warmth, which is believed to cleanse the soul, awaken spiritual potential, and even increase physical longevity.

The element of fire provides a profound lens to view and experience our lives, both physically and spiritually. It embodies transformation, purification, energy, passion, and longevity, illuminating the path to a life full of warmth, resilience, and continual growth.

Candle exercises can be a beautiful and effective method for spiritual purification.

Here are a few you may want to try:

## 1. Candle Gazing Meditation (Trataka)

This practice has roots in yogic traditions and is known to improve focus and clarity, and can also aid in spiritual purification.
• Sit comfortably in front of a lit candle placed at eye level (far from your face).
• Gaze at the candle's flame for as long as you can without blinking. Let your focus be soft rather than intensely sharp.
• When your eyes begin to water, or you need to blink, close your eyes.
• Behind your eyelids, you will see an afterimage of the flame. Try to hold onto that image for as long as you can.
• When the image fades, open your eyes, and begin the gazing process again. Repeat this for five minutes.

## 2. Candle Flame Visualization

This exercise can help cleanse your aura and energy field.
• Sit in front of a lit candle, relax, and close your eyes (maintaining a safe distance from the fire).
• Take several deep breaths, imagining drawing in white, purifying light with each inhale, and releasing negativity with each exhale.
• Visualize yourself surrounded by the candle's flame. Imagine this fire burning away all negative energy, leaving your aura glowing brightly.

### 3. Writing and Burning Ritual

A writing and burning ritual releases negativity and renews your spirit.
• Take a piece of paper and a pen. Write down any negative thoughts, feelings, or experiences you wish to release.
• Light a candle, and while focusing on what you've written, place the paper into the flame (be sure to do this safely, perhaps over a metal bowl or sink).
• As you watch the paper burn, imagine the negative energies being consumed by the flames and transformed into positive energy.

### 4. Candle Affirmation Exercise

Using affirmations with candle magic can create a focused intention for spiritual purification.
• Choose a candle color that aligns with your goals.
  * White: Symbolizes purity, clarity, and spiritual enlightenment. It can be used for cleansing, healing, and new beginnings.
  * Red: Represents passion, energy, courage, and love. It can be used for matters of the heart, vitality, and strength.
  * Pink: Symbolizes love, affection, and emotional healing. It can be used for romantic matters, self-love, and harmony in relationships.
  * Orange: Represents creativity, enthusiasm, and success. It can be used for career-related goals, ambition, and personal growth.
  * Yellow: Symbolizes intellect, clarity of thought, and communication. It can be used for enhancing mental abilities, studying, and gaining new insights.
  * Green: Represents abundance, fertility, and prosperity. It can be used for financial matters, growth, and healing of the body and mind.
  * Blue: Symbolizes peace, tranquility, and intuition. It can be used for relaxation, meditation, and enhancing psychic abilities.

* Purple: Represents spirituality, wisdom, and higher consciousness. It can be used for spiritual pursuits, divination, and connecting with the divine.
* Black: Symbolizes protection, banishing negativity, and transformation. It can be used for releasing old patterns, breaking bad habits, and dispelling negative energies.
* Gold: Represents success, wealth, and achievement. It can be used to attract prosperity, financial abundance, and success in endeavors.
* Silver: Symbolizes intuition, lunar energy, and feminine power. It can be used for harnessing intuition, psychic abilities, and enhancing feminine energy.
* Gray: Represents neutrality, balance, and stability. It can be used for contemplation, grounding, and finding a middle ground in difficult situations.

• Candle colors and their meanings can vary based on cultural and spiritual beliefs. When choosing a candle color that aligns with your goal, trust your intuition and personal associations with the colors.

• As you light the candle, say an affirmation, such as "Every day, in every way, I am becoming stronger and more resilient. My potential is limitless, and I embrace every opportunity for growth with openness and courage."

• Gaze at the flame as you meditate on these words, visualizing the fire igniting the truth of this affirmation within your soul.

Always handle fire with care and respect, and ensure you are practicing these exercises in a safe and controlled environment.

# AIR

Just as the winds whip across the mountaintops and sweep through the forests, our breath courses through us, constantly renewing and invigorating us. It is the life-giving gust of the universe itself, playing out on a microcosmic level within our bodies. The air element, in its vast omnipresence and invisible might, provides sustenance to every cell of our being, keeping us alive and animated.

Our breath, the corporeal manifestation of the air element, is a rhythmic dance between the internal and external worlds, a silent yet powerful dialogue between self and universe.

By vocalizing through singing or chanting, we amplify the power of air, allowing it to reverberate within us and through us. Our voice, carried on the waves of breath, becomes a beacon of self-expression. Through song or chant, we tap into the transformative power of the air element, allowing it to cleanse our thoughts and carry away our worries.

In expressing ourselves, in speaking our truths, we strengthen our bond with the air element. Every word we utter is a testament to our connection with this universal force. Our truths, once hidden within the confines of our hearts, are given wings to soar, carried aloft by the winds of our breath.

Let us also not forget the simple act of being outdoors, surrounded by nature's grandeur. It reminds us of our interconnectedness with the world.

As we breathe in the fresh air, feel the wind on our skin, and let our gaze travel across the open sky, we are embracing the air element, acknowledging its power, and reinforcing our connection with it.

Air is the silent mediator between our conscious and subconscious minds, the link between our physical existence and the ethereal realm.

## ETHER/ SPACE

In the quantum ballet of existence, you're more than just a solitary dancer. You're the dance and the music, the stage and the audience, all entwined in the elegant waltz of the cosmos. In the theater of the universe, every atom, every particle, every wave of energy participates in this grand performance, and you, too, are a vital part of this celestial choreography.

In the quantum field, all is interconnected, a woven tapestry of stardust and ether, where matter and energy interplay in an eternal dance. Your body, thoughts, and very essence are all born of this cosmic dance, particles vibrating in harmony with the symphony of creation.

You are a drop of consciousness in the vast cosmos. In this boundless ether, you're both the observer and the observed, a particle of matter, a wave of energy. The quantum realm does not distinguish between the two—you are simultaneously both, a testament to the dual nature of existence.

In the silence of meditation, become aware of this interconnectedness, this unity with all that is, was, or will be. In the stillness, hear the whisper of the ether, the voice of the universe calling out to you. Its message is simple: You are a part of me, and I am a part of you.

Every breath you take, every beat of your heart, resonates with the rhythm of the cosmos. Each inhalation draws in the energy of the universe, filling you with the light of a billion stars. Each exhalation releases your energy back into the ether, a gift of your spirit to the universe.

Dive deep into existence, dance with the cosmos, and merge with the ether. For in this dance, you'll find not just the answers to who you are, but also a deeper understanding of your place in the universe and your role in the grand narrative of existence.

In the ether, you're not merely existing; you are alive, intertwined with the cosmos, a beacon of infinite possibilities in the cosmic ocean. Embrace this dance, and in it, find your poetry, your song, and your story. And in the midst of this cosmic dance, discover the profound insight of the beauty that is You.

## Sacred and Conscious Relationships

In the grand tapestry of existence, our paths intertwine, connected by a thread of interconnectedness. It is said that you are the manifestation, and I, a conduit of divinity. Together, we form a vast network of support, woven by the fabric of our collective purpose.

In this cosmic dance, we find solace in our interdependence. Each of us carries a unique spark, a gift, a role to play. As we embrace our individual strengths, we become threads of guidance, compassion, and understanding, interlaced to uplift and empower one another.

Through the highs and lows, we draw strength from the knowledge that our presence is not accidental. We are here to nurture, inspire, heal, and learn. We contribute to the harmonious symphony of existence with each interaction, a chorus where our voices blend and resonate in perfect unity.

Let us remember that we are never alone within the vast expanse of this interconnected web. We are here, together, to offer kindness, lend a helping hand, and share the wisdom we've gathered on our own journeys. In this mutual exchange, we find fulfillment, for it is in giving that we receive and in supporting others that we are supported.

So, let us embrace the truth of our shared purpose, the understanding that our existence is intertwined. As we navigate the intricacies of life, let us be conscious of our potential to create a network of love, compassion, and empathy—a safety net woven by the divinity within each of us.

For it is your manifestation, my divine conduct, and the interconnectedness that guides us forward, enabling us to become the best versions of ourselves and fostering a world where the bonds of unity and support hold us all.

There is nothing more precious than a relationship, one that is rooted in respect, trust, and personal and collective growth.

It's the kind of relationship you cherish with every fiber of your being. It's the kind of relationship that fills you with love, hope, and joy and encourages you to be your best self.

You are committed to mindfulness and self-awareness when you are in a relationship. You are not only interested in your own growth and development but also in the growth and development of your partner. You support each other in your journey of self-discovery, and you create a safe and supportive space to grow and evolve.

Relationships are a choice, and the way you choose to view them will have a significant impact on the way they play out.

To be dedicated to someone else, you must first be committed to yourself. In a sacred and conscious relationship, you learn to reflect on your true nature through your interactions with your partner. You mirror each other and become better versions of yourselves because of that. We learn by reflecting on the other, our true nature. It allows you to deepen your intimacy, communication, and connection with one another in transformative ways.

Communities thrive on the power of conscious, enriching relationships. These bonds play a significant role in creating lasting abundance. In this new era, the beauty of authentic human connections sets the stage for blossoming generations yet to come.

Pause for a moment, draw in a deep, life-giving breath, and visualize the ten most cherished relationships in your life. Reflect on your interactions with these individuals. Ask yourself whether there's room for growth, and if your bond with them is rooted in unity and unconditional love.

If it isn't, pose these introspective questions to yourself: "Do I extend enough love toward myself? Do I feel worthy? Is there love within my heart?"

Your relationships mirror your belief systems. Changing your beliefs will align your relationships with the energy you emit into the world. When you transform your beliefs, your relationships will naturally evolve in harmony.

I have learned so much from my relationship with my husband; the dedication to each other's well-being has been an incredible learning experience and blessing. It is possible to live a beautiful love, un amor bonito.

It is also possible to have a conscious relationship with your parents, children, family members, friends, and all humanity, but it begins with you, and this momentum influences the conscious relationship of all society.

# Parenting a Sa Seed & the New Species

Imagine a new world where children are not just born but emerge as unique beings with extraordinary abilities. A new type of human that possesses powers beyond our imagination.

During a transmission (channeling episode), I saw these new beings. However, there were more than just one type walking on Earth. They were distinct from interplanetary beings, hybrids, spirits, or aliens. These beings are called Sa, and we have yet to see all there is to them.

After tapping into this knowledge, I began researching and was surprised by how much information I found on the subject.

Some proponents of these theories suggest that some of these children are born with heightened intuition, telepathy, or clairvoyance and have a mission to improve the world and promote peace and love. Others have developed a unique immune system that allows them to resist not only the HIV virus but also other pathogens.

Some have a different digestive system, have different DNA structures, and can activate other parts of their brains.

In China, some children are known as "super psychics" and can harness the universe's energy and possess incredible psychic abilities, including telekinesis, psychokinesis, and clairvoyance.

There is a theory by Ra Uru Hu which predicts that in 2027 a new human species will emerge—the Raves. They will have emotionlessness, social detachment, vegetarianism, hypersensitive skin, issues with speech, different eyesight, and a lack of desire for knowledge. They will look disabled at first, but once they merge into groups of three to five, they will communicate with each other as one consciousness.

Ra Uru Hu sought to make sense of the complexities of human nature and our place in the universe. Among his many theories, this was one that stood out. The vision of the future, of humanity's evolution. He called it the 'Rave Era.' I saw it as the 'Sa Era.'

Ra Uru Hu envisaged that as time passed, humanity would undergo a remarkable transformation. Our individual consciousness, our singular sense of 'I,' would begin to fade but not to be lost. Instead, it would begin to merge with a collective consciousness, a shared sense of 'we.'

He saw a future where the lines separating individuals would blur, where we would perceive ourselves as integral parts of a grand whole rather than separate entities.

He believed this transition was a natural part of human evolution. A species, after all, finds strength in unity. It was a shift from individual self-interests to the collective needs and well-being of the entire human race.

This transition is a slow, gradual process—a delicate shifting of the tides. And we, as part of this process, are living at a significant juncture in history, straddling the line between the old era of individuality and the coming era of unity.

Ra Uru Hu suggested this is our final chance to express our unique individuality before it is forever intertwined with the grand tapestry of collective consciousness. So, he urged us to explore, express, and understand our individual selves. For this phase, this unique moment of balance between the individual and the collective, was fleeting, a precious period in our long human journey.

And so, as we stand on the precipice of the NEW ERA, we live and love, laugh and cry, explore and express, treasuring this moment of singular identity before we step into the era of unity, of collective consciousness. And as we do, prepare for the next chapter of our evolution.

As humanity stands at the cusp of this new era, the Sa Era, it is not just our own transition that we must consider, but also that of the generations to come. We are not simply inhabitants of this transitional age, but the parents and grandparents of the new species that will fully embody this collective consciousness.

This responsibility holds both profound challenges and remarkable opportunities. For us, the elders of the coming generation, we are tasked with raising children who will experience the world differently than we do. They will not simply be members of a family, a tribe, or a nation but intrinsic parts of a global collective, deeply interconnected and united.

We must guide them, nurture their budding collective consciousness while still cherishing and fostering their unique individuality. We will have to learn to communicate with them, understand them, and most importantly, accept them, despite the increasing differences in our ways of perceiving and interacting with the world.

For the children, the pioneers of the Sa Era, their journey too will be filled with challenges. As they navigate their consciousness, they will be treading paths that no human has walked before. They will need to find balance, to retain the wisdom and lessons of individuality, while embracing the unity and collective consciousness that defines their era.

It's a grand dance of evolution, where we, the last torchbearers of a bygone era, and they, the forerunners of a new age, must learn to move in harmony. We must be open to their new ways of being, and they must be patient with our old ways of understanding. Together, we will write the story of this great transition, a story of change and adaptation, of the end of one era and the birth of another.

As we continue to express our individuality in these waning moments of the old era, let us also prepare for the dawn of the new. Let's treasure these final moments of solitary identity and prepare ourselves and our children for the era of collective consciousness.

As we do, we remain forever guided by the wisdom of our ancestors, conscious of our responsibilities as the elders of the new species, and hopeful for the unity and harmony of the coming Sa Era.

Let us embrace the uniqueness of each child and celebrate their differences, for they are the future of our world. All children deserve the resources and opportunities to reach their full potential, regardless of where they are born or what abilities they possess. We can open our minds to a new world, full of possibilities, that awaits us as we continue to unlock the secrets of Sa.

# Quantum Nutrition

Your body is a finely tuned instrument, capable of sensing and responding to the world around you in ways you may not even know.

By observing how your body operates and responds to different foods, you will understand what your unique human design requires to thrive. You can learn to tune in to the rhythms of your digestive system and make adjustments based on the season and environment.

Quantum nutrition is about more than just physical nourishment; it's the acknowledgment of the different types of hunger you might experience daily.

You may feel emotional hunger when stressed, anxious, or lonely. Or mental hunger can arise when you're craving knowledge or stimulation. You can experience spiritual hunger when you feel disconnected. When you turn to food to fill these other types of hunger, you may use it as a cover-up rather than a source of genuine nourishment.

As humans, we always seek to fill the gap between what we are expecting and experiencing. Sometimes you turn to food to close that gap, not because you have a physical need for food's energy but because you want to escape from a situation or emotion.

Joaquin designed a quantum nutrition program that has opened our minds to the possibility of getting energy from other sources besides food. The behavior of molecules and cells in the body affects nutrition and health, and this means that there is more than one source of nutrition, and every human has different needs.

Conscious nutrition is a practice of observation, where you tune in to your body's unique needs and nourish yourself from the unified field. It's about understanding that food is just one piece of the puzzle and that you can tap into other energy sources.

By adopting this approach, you can create a more balanced and fulfilling relationship with food—one that listens to your body, trusts your instincts, and honors your uniqueness.

Recognize that you are all different and that your journeys toward health and vitality will look different; it's essential to your nutrition.

The deeper you get into your breathing practice, the more you will feel your body's communicating, and the more you will observe your behavior toward food.

Do you ever feel like you need to be more patient with your meals, barely taking the time to taste what you're eating? Or maybe you find yourself mindlessly snacking when you're upset or stressed? I used to be the same way until I discovered the power of practicing simple breathing exercises before meals.

Now, I take the time to check in on my emotional state before I eat. If I'm upset or stressed, I give myself a few moments to breathe or meditate before diving into my food. And once I start eating, I focus on gratitude, taking a moment to appreciate the nourishment I'm giving my body.

But that's not all—I've also learned to pay attention to the chemistry in my brain by observing and smelling my food before taking a bite. And once I start eating, I take my time savoring each flavor and chewing enough to facilitate digestion.

And when it comes to preparing my meals, choosing the right foods is also essential. I opt for whole foods whenever possible and choose organic when available. I also make a point of ingesting alkaline foods and fluids and keep track of the alkalinity in my body, using pH strips.

It is vital to avoid foods that cause inflammation, stimulants, sugars, trans fats, and gluten for me and anyone interested in cellular regeneration.

Also, the order in which we ingest foods is important because some foods can decompose and ferment faster.

I stay hydrated by drinking water before meals and throughout the day. And I take pauses while eating, allowing myself to enjoy my food and avoid overeating.

Finally, including fasting in our habits is like giving a vacation to our system. The body needs to rest to reset. There are many ways to fast, safely giving space for regeneration of the cells.

These simple principles have genuinely been a game changer for me. I've found a greater sense of balance by choosing how to nurture my body.

## Love in Action. Are You Doing What You Love?

Do you wake up excited for the day ahead, or do you dread starting your day?

If you are hesitant, it's time to step back and observe. Life is too precious to spend most days doing something that doesn't make you fulfilled. If you're unsatisfied, it may be time to explore other options.

Think about the skills and abilities you possess that make you good at what you enjoy doing. Observe your qualities as a human being. How do you feel? Is it easy for you to identify them?

When you use these skills and feel a sense of accomplishment, you're tapping into the frequency of abundance, and from there, it expands, everything will keep getting better and better.

It's not about finding what you enjoy doing. It's about finding something that positively impacts your world and aligns with your true self. When you experience a state of flow while in your daily activities, you know you're on the right path. And when your daily activities align with your long-term income goals, you'll feel abundant and unstoppable. This is your true self.

But how do you figure out what you're genuinely passionate about? Observe your emotions throughout the day. You can start by writing down your thoughts and feelings about your activities. Note any successes or challenges you encounter. This can help you identify patterns and gain clarity on what you enjoy and what you don't.

Experiment with personality tests or human design system charts to gain insights into your strengths and interests too.

When you're willing to make changes, you open up to a fulfilling and satisfying life. And when you follow your own compass and internal authority, the feeling will amplify the vibration, manifesting a good life.

Yes, it can be scary to take risks and try new things. But imagine waking up each day excited for the infinite opportunities ahead. Imagine feeling energized and motivated to positively impact the world using your unique skills and abilities. This kind of life is possible when you're on a path that aligns with you.

Start loving your life now to have the life you want in the future. Do you trust your intuition? Is it possible for you to embrace change as a way to grow and evolve?

You can reimagine yourself as many times as you want and strive to live your best life; regardless of what you constantly hear and how scandalous this sounds, there is enough in this world for everyone, and life is abundant. The possibilities are endless.

## Our Unique Design

Have you ever wondered if you are correctly using your energy and life force? Each of us is born with a perfect design. We all have gifts that we bring to this world, which unfold naturally when we understand and align with our mechanics.

One of my favorite systems for the exploration of the self is The Human Design System (HDS). It was channeled by Ra Uru Hu and combines principles of the I Ching, Eastern and Western Astrology, Kabbalah, the Hindu-Brahmin Chakra System, and Quantum Physics.

Ra Uru Hu, also known as Robert Allan Krakower, was born on March 9, 1948, in Montreal, Canada, and passed away on March 12, 2011.

Ra Uru Hu had a mystical experience in 1987 when he received a profound revelation about human nature and the mechanics of our individual lives. Based on this revelation, Ra Uru Hu spent years developing and refining the HDS.

The Human Design System is a complex system that combines astrology, genetics, and the I Ching to create a comprehensive understanding of an individual's personality, strengths, weaknesses, and life purpose. It provides a detailed chart, known as the Human Design BodyGraph, which illustrates the energetic and psychological aspects of a person.

Ra Uru Hu dedicated his life to teaching and spreading the knowledge of Human Design. He conducted workshops, wrote books, and founded the International Human Design School to train practitioners in this system.

Although Ra Uru Hu is no longer alive, his teachings and the Human Design System continue to be studied and practiced by individuals interested in personal growth and self-understanding.

Our BodyGraph is calculated using our birth date, time, and place. It shows us our genetic Design and where and how to access our body's consciousness, which we can use as a tool to make decisions and, ultimately, awaken to our nature and extraordinary potential.

This understanding and the power of our breath allow us to enhance our individual experiences.

HDS gives us a mapping of our uniqueness. When we live in alignment with our true nature, we experience comfort and acceptance for who we are instead of chasing who we are not.

Human Design provides two main sets of tools called Strategy and Authority. The BodyGraph shows us what our unique Strategy and Authority are. When we operate with our body's natural energies instead of against them, we experience less resistance in our bodies and our lives.

We live in an age where a wealth of information is at our fingertips. Comprehending how to operate in this world and what things are worth engaging in is priceless.

We also tend to make decisions with our minds, bypassing our body's intelligence. The mind can ponder many exciting and inspiring ideas we enjoy reflecting on. Our minds, however, are not designed to guide our life. We have all of these mental stories about how things should be. Understanding how we are hardwired is helpful.

In Human Design, it is called the awakening of passenger consciousness. The Design is the vehicle, and the mind is the passenger. Its correct role is to sit back and enjoy the ride, not compete with the driver (your body) to control the steering wheel. Over time, as you experiment, your mind can observe your life instead of trying to direct it. The mind is a great tool to classify and store information, but it cannot make any decisions.

The mind functions as an external authority. It can help others by expressing your unique point of view and downloading a wealth of knowledge and wisdom to guide other people on their journey.

There are four different aura types that each have their own Strategy. Strategy is a doorway to living as yourself, affirming who you really are, and understanding and letting go of what you are not.

Your Strategy and Inner Authority go together to guide you. Your Inner Authority is your body's knowledge or intelligence. You hear a lot these days about following your intuition, and Human Design gets specific and shows you where your Authority lies so you can experiment and see how it works for you.

After Joaquin and I had our foundation readings, we experimented with the following concepts:

- Decision-making process: Human Design emphasizes the importance of making decisions from a place of Inner Authority rather than being influenced by external factors or conditioned beliefs. This process involves tapping into your body's intelligence and using it as a compass to navigate your reality. By following your unique Inner Authority, you can make decisions that align with your authentic nature and bring a greater sense of fulfillment, ease, and authenticity.
- Strategy: In Human Design, there are four different aura types—Manifestor, Generator, Projector, and Reflector—each with its own unique Strategy for engaging with the world. By understanding your aura type and following its specific Strategy, you can align your actions and decisions with your inherent energetic blueprint, resulting in smoother interactions, increased productivity, and tremendous success.
- Open Centers: Your BodyGraph contains nine centers representing different aspects of your being, such as communication, emotions, and intuition. Open centers are undefined or "white" in your chart, representing areas where you may be more susceptible to external influences and conditioning. By becoming aware of your open centers, you can recognize where you may be taking in and amplifying energy from others and learn to let go of any patterns or behaviors that are not truly yours.
- Conditioning: Many people struggle with trying to fit into societal norms or fulfill expectations placed upon them by others.

Human Design teaches us that embracing our unique Design and living in alignment with it is the key to finding true happiness and fulfillment. By understanding and accepting our true nature, we can let go of the need to conform to external standards and instead focus on living our authentic life purpose.

By integrating these, we have a framework to unravel the layers of conditioning and societal expectations that have shaped our life thus far.

It doesn't stop with the HDS; there are many more systems, methods, and ways to get to know yourself better. I invite you to become a researcher of your uniqueness.

On our websites, you will find links to some of our favorite systems for self-discovery

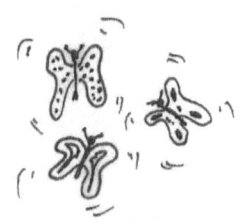

# CHAPTER 8

# Mana Breathwork Universe

## Intention

Self-Discovery is what the Mana Breathwork Universe is about. Through daily practice, you'll find yourself moving through life with greater ease and joy, basking in the boundless potential within you.

At the heart of Mana Breathwork lies the art of observation. Cultivating this mindful awareness, you can harness the power of your breath and effortlessly glide along the path of least resistance. It's a practice that allows you to gracefully navigate life's contrasts and empower yourself to live fully in the present moment.

Unlike goal-oriented practices, the Mana Breathwork Method is not about reaching specific milestones; instead, it's a daily practice that gently guides you toward personal growth. It is a way of living in which each breath attunes to your inner world.

## Expansion

With each day, you have the opportunity to:

**1.** Learn something new.
**2.** Look at the sky at sunrise and draw energy from it, feeling guided.
**3.** Set aside time in the mornings and evenings for self-care.
**4.** Meditate.
**5.** Exercise.
**6.** Nurture your skin.
**7.** Strengthen your relationship with water.
**8.** Observe your bodily functions, and regulate your internal systems.
**9.** In the morning, before 9 am, spend twenty minutes sunbathing.
**10.** Throughout the day, glance at the sky frequently (protect your eyes).
**11.** Monitor your breathing patterns, and take twenty-second breaks to breathe deeply.
**12.** Engage in activities to align your body, such as yoga, stretching, massages, kinesiology, dancing, contortionism, or professional

therapy like chiropractic care or osteopathy. Ensure it is safe and effective for your alignment.

**13.** Move your body to achieve alignment.

**14.** Align your physical structure; prioritize your digestive system using common sense, listening to your body, and researching.

**15.** Enhance your visual experience; shift your focus from the ground or your cell phone to a panoramic view. Look straight ahead, enabling your peripheral vision to broaden, complementing your awareness of the surroundings.

**16.** Keep your head up and core engaged.

**17.** Trust your body's wisdom and the quantum realm for answers to your nutritional needs.

**18.** Follow your intuition when eating, but also research the foods' origins, cultivation, packaging, and preparation. Make informed choices based on this knowledge.

**19.** Examine the relationship between your emotions and food, noting how specific foods and drinks affect your mood. Be honest with yourself and choose what's best for your body at that moment. If necessary, visualize feeding your inner child.

**20.** Savor every bite, chew your food up to one hundred times, playfully shifting it from one side to another. This is where the magic of your digestive system begins.

**21.** Evaluate your belief systems.

**22.** Observe your thoughts and listen to your words.

**23.** Recognize the power of your words.

**24.** Check in with yourself.

**25.** Ask yourself: Are you an agent of chaos or peace?

**26.** Observe without judgment and step back when needed.

**27.** Reset and retry as often as necessary.

**28.** Embrace inspiration, motivation, progress, and abundance in your heart as your morning prayer.

**29.** Connect with your inner intelligence, which is always present.

**30.** Set a clear intention to remove layers of conditioning and clear anything that inhibits expansion.

**31.** Focus on the present moment to enhance your efficiency. Keeping your mind clear will prevent distractions and impediments, thus optimizing your decision-making process.

**32.** Remove energetic pollution so you can achieve a clear mind and a body that provides answers to all your questions.

**33.** Release the need for parental guidance, validation, and approval while taking full responsibility for each breath and action—the true meaning of dedication.

**34.** Accept responsibility for your existence and actions.

35. Embrace the freedom that comes from knowing what you know and recognizing what you don't.

**36.** Be a student of everything.

**37.** Ask yourself how you can help others and do it.

**38.** Identify your needs and establish healthy boundaries.

**39.** Love and accept yourself exactly as you are and where you are.

**40.** Use your breath as a bridge to remove anything that doesn't serve you from your energy field.

**41.** Spend time deeply acquainting yourself with your unique energy signature, allowing you to discern which vibrations belong to you and which don't.

**42.** Use your breath as a bridge for expansion.

**43.** Be mindful of what you see before sleeping and what you hear while asleep. This is an opportunity to upload programs to your subconscious mind.

**44.** Study the subconscious mind.

**45.** Achieve coherence between the mind, heart, sacral center, and language through your breath. This is science.

**46.** Hone your craft and strive for excellence, which will bring rewards.

**47.** Contribute to the well-being of your family, community, country, and planet.

**48.** Regularly exercise abundance and resource allocation.

**49.** Walk barefoot on grass, strengthening your connection with Mother Earth and leading to a more sustainable lifestyle.

**50.** Do as much as possible for our planet, as it is our home.

**51.** Be kind to all beings.

**52.** Acknowledge your sacred union with the elements.

**53.** Remember who you are.

**54.** Show up for yourself and for others.

**55.** Cultivate energy.

**56.** Celebrate your uniqueness.

**57.** Let joy be your compass.

**58.** Choose love and oneness, for that, is the essence of existence.

## Release the Tension

Please take a moment to reflect upon and carefully compose your responses to the following questions.

How does the Daily Opportunity List make me feel?

_____

_____

_____

_____

_____

Nurture your growth; we've all been there. But here's a liberating thought: it's perfectly okay not to achieve everything on your list daily, and in fact, embracing this mindset can be incredibly empowering. Accepting that you may only accomplish a few goals is a beautiful reminder that we all are a work in progress. Each day presents us with opportunities to evolve, and we must honor our unique journeys.

Who am I?

_____

_____

_____

_____

_____

Peel back the layers of societal labels, expectations, and preconceived notions. What remains when everything superficial is stripped away?

_____

_____

_____

_____

_____

What core values and beliefs define me?

_____

_____

_____

_____

_____

Who do I want to be?

_____

_____

_____

_____

_____

What is your ideal vision of yourself? Describe in detail that version of yourself that you aspire to become. It could be an amalgamation of qualities you admire in others or a realization of your latent potential.

_____

_____

_____

_____

_____

What am I grateful for?

_____

_____

_____

_____

_____

Gratitude is the heart's memory. What are those anchors of joy and contentment that you are thankful for? They could be as grand as your accomplishments or as simple as a kind word from a stranger. Keep going...

_____
_____
_____
_____
_____

Am I enough?

_____
_____
_____
_____
_____

Do I deserve love?

_____
_____
_____
_____
_____

After all that defines me in this human realm is absent, who am I, truly?

_____
_____
_____
_____

What significance does the concept of God, or the source of all existence, hold for me?

_____
_____
_____
_____

Let's shift our focus from the pressure or demand to a nurturing embrace of our uniqueness, because this list is more than just a collection of ideas; it's an invitation to explore who you want to become and release the tension.

It's a gentle reminder to prioritize self-reflection and personal growth, and by embracing this approach, you'll find yourself connecting more deeply with your core values and aspirations, allowing you to move through life with intention and authenticity.

Every story is a mirror, revealing a facet of the self. As you journey through these pages, I invite you to pause, contemplate, and communicate with the deepest part of yourself.

Reflect on these questions. There's no right or wrong answer, only your truth.

## Affirmations - Manifestations
## Transformational Declarations

Transformational declarations, often called affirmations, or manifestations are empowering proclamations that can guide you toward aligning your emotional landscape and belief system with the desired reality you envision. Harnessing the power of these affirmations has the potential to usher in life-changing shifts in your personal energy, leading to remarkable transformations in your life experience.

Key to this practice is attaining emotional synergy with your affirmations. Emotional synergy encapsulates the process of harmonizing your emotions with the affirmative assertions you pronounce, thereby amplifying their inherent power. Mere rote repetition of these affirmations is insufficient; the essence lies in authentically endorsing their veracity and feeling worthy of their actualization.

The Law of Attraction is indifferent to your words; rather, it listens to your intent. For your affirmations to be effective, your declarations should reflect your profound beliefs. Gradually developing this momentum is key to ensuring that your affirmations resonate with what you deem possible.

For instance, when you declare, "I'm a multimillionaire," but your internal dialogue is consumed by the anxiety of unpaid bills, this incongruity could potentially manifest the contrary outcome.

Commence with affirmations that are more general, relatable, and conducive to fostering a positive outlook. Start with declarations like, "People appreciate the value I bring," or "Clients happily compensate me for my services," or "My earnings increase year after year." These accessible statements serve as stepping stones toward the grander goal: cultivating a vibration of abundance.

Having the motivation to change your attitude and vibe is an essential component of this process. You can attract abundance, love, and joy into your life simply by harnessing the energy of your thoughts and emotions.

The Law of Attraction is how the inner world shapes your outer reality. Like a boomerang, the energy you send out returns to you, echoing your deepest beliefs and desires. But how do you ensure the energy you emit aligns with your highest aspirations?

When your affirmations echo with authenticity and conviction, the universe listens. But beware of the pitfalls that lie hidden in the shadows of doubt and disbelief. When your affirmations include whispers of insecurity, the universe hears only the dissonance, not the melody of your dreams.

The secret to unlocking the power of affirmations lies in nurturing a strong, unwavering belief in their truth. Begin by choosing affirmations that resonate with your current reality, statements that evoke a feeling of possibility and hope. Slowly, like a blossoming flower, let your affirmations grow in magnitude, always rooted in the fertile soil of belief. As you expand, your vibrations shift, aligning with the energy of abundance and prosperity.

Affirmations are more than just wishful thinking; they are a way to plant new beliefs in your mind. By consistently reinforcing these positive statements, you can overwrite limiting beliefs and negative thought patterns that may have held you back in the past.

Embrace the possibilities that come with emotional coherence, motivation, and belief.

Here are some examples to practice with.

I am alive
I am safe
I am enough
I am guided
I am bountiful
I am beautiful
I am young
I am healthy
I am happy
I am joyful
I am connected
I am inspired
I am awakening to see what I couldn't see
I am kind to myself
I am kind to others
I am satisfied
I remember all that I am
I feel the energy
I trust myself
I trust my heart
I trust my sacral response
I trust my spirit guides
I trust my inner technology
I trust my environment
I trust my path
Grace is upon me
It is okay to feel what I feel
I accept myself
I am safe in my feelings
My feelings are vibrations
I can raise the vibration and attract positive experiences into my life
I observe and release beliefs
I cultivate positive emotions
I clear my solar plexus
There are more than enough space and resources for everyone

We live in a happy and abundant world
Everyone around me wants the best for me
I wish the best for everyone
I have strong roots and a stable foundation
I always leave people better than when I met them
Everything I do contributes to the galaxy
I am love, and love is reflected back to me
All I see is love
All I feel is love
Love is all that it is
Light rebirths through cracks
I am one with the light
I am rebirth
I am light
I feel love and compassion for all beings
We are all one
I breathe love through my heart
The most profound book of wisdom is in me
I listen to my spirit guides
I can express myself
Expressing myself is easy and fun for me
Life is so easy for me
I am enjoying this life experience
I am grateful for my life
I love my voice
Breathing is easy for me
I listen to my higher self
I choose what I feel
I have all that I want
I accept all that I have
I observe and transmute my thoughts as I please
My senses connect me to my world
I appreciate my senses
Through my breathing, I blend energetically
Through my breath, I bend my reality
I am one with the elements
I am fire

I am water
I am earth
I am air
I am energy
I can trust the energy
I surrender to my inner worlds
I honor and let go of the pain
I release attachments
I can live beyond my elders' limitations
I feel good
I can feel everything
Everything is working out in the best way possible for me
My feelings become vibration
I move energy as I move air
Through my feet, I am connected to the center of the planet
Through my crown, I am connected to Source
Through my heart, I am connected to all that it is
Through my pineal gland, I am
I breathe love
I can breathe deeply
I choose joy
I am open to receiving all the love of the universe
I am loved
I deserve love
I am wealthy
I know my worth
My universe supports me
I have everything I want
Everything flows easily for me
I listen to my body
I trust my intuition
I am infinite intelligence
My body responds to my environment, showing me the way
I rely on my inner technology to guide my decisions
I am the most advanced technology
I observe my thoughts without judgment
I transmute and transform my thoughts

I can easily shift my perspective
I release the weight off my shoulders
It is easy for me to release the irrelevant
I am light, agile, and safe
My heart is open
My mind is clear
I am resilient
I am whole
I am the creator
I am the most beautiful being I have ever been
I can reimagine myself as many times as I want
There is inherent goodness in me
I remind myself of everything good
I experience infinite creativity
I cultivate my childlike sense of wonder
My eyes recognize the magic
My magic is recognized by others
I can be all that I want to be
My breathing patterns are practical mirrors
It is easy for me to reset my breathing patterns
In the present, all is well; I release the past
Breathing is pleasurable for me
Exhale and release, are natural for me
It is easy for me to observe and modify patterns
I caress the vulnerability in me by observing what needs to be
processed
Love fills the space where shadows shade
I am the writer of my story
I am the hero of my self-love story
I bend reality
I create my experiences
I conceive my blessings
I receive blessings
I am blessed
I am clear
It is easy for me to inform and initiate
I respond to the universe's invitations

Miracles happen through me and to me
I am grateful for all that I have and all that I am
I am always in the right place at the right time
I fully integrate all experiences
Creativity is my superpower
My possibilities are expanding
There are infinite possibilities
This is a magnificent moment
Collective success is my success
Words are powerful
I am mindful of how I use my words
I create my destiny with my thoughts, words, and actions
I am loved for who I am
I am worth it
I am successful
I am free
I experience miracles
I am grateful for the air in my lungs
I accept myself for who I am
By healing myself, I heal my ancestral line
I forgive myself
I love myself
I am authentic
I am infinite
I am multidimensional
I have many talents
I can do it
My ideas bring wealth to our family
I feel calm, relaxed, and open
I learn from all my experiences
I set and maintain healthy boundaries
I forgive others
I release soul contracts
My life keeps getting better and better
I live in an abundant world
I am grateful for clean water
I feel optimistic

I feel empowered
Good things always seem to happen to me
The universe serves my higher good
Everything I need is available from the Infinite Source
Life is easy for me
Everything is always working out for my loved ones and me
I easily flow through a magnificent life
Something extraordinary is happening right now
I trust how circumstances unfold in front of me
I have faith in me
I am healed
I have a magnificent body intelligence
I am emotionally intelligent
Transformation happens on every level, in every dimensional plane, and in every realm
I am constantly transforming and evolving
I am repairing my DNA constantly
I nourish my body with the purest sources
My body renews and repairs constantly
I am gracefully growing
Life is sacred
Joy is my compass
I enjoy bringing joy to others
I am the manifestation of my ancestor's desires
I am awesome, unique, super amazing—wow!
I'm profoundly thankful, as money flows to me constantly from various sources in increasing quantities
I have a great and long life
I deserve infinite happiness
Well-being is my skill
I am all that I was born to be
Thank God for this lifetime
I choose to live in peace, joy, and happiness
I choose a good, kind, and beautiful world
I choose freedom of the mind and soul
I choose unconditional LOVE
I am Love / Yo soy amor

I encourage you to write your own as you identify the root causes of your beliefs.

## Breathing Techniques

The practical exercises and techniques here can help you reset your body in just a few minutes. By incorporating them into your daily routine, you can positively influence your response to the world around you, decreasing reactive behavior and increasing feelings of joy.

By practicing these techniques, you can create a peaceful and joyful state within yourself. This state of being will allow you to approach life with greater clarity, and every breath you take will feel like an opportunity to connect with the world around you.

From the depths of ancient traditions to the cutting-edge techniques developed by the military, countless individuals have practiced and refined the art of breathing, so it's challenging to attribute these techniques to one specific author. Still, we can trace their evolution through various sources.

Each technique has its unique purpose, from the sophisticated pulmonary respiratory therapy institutes to the hardcore training used by Navy SEALs.

For example, Pranayama draws on the power of breath to harness the life force (prana) and balance the body and mind. Another, the Buteyko Method, uses a combination of nasal breathing, breath control, and breath-holding exercises to treat a wide range of health conditions.

These techniques all tap in to the same principle: the breath's influence on the body and nervous system. And while the count may differ from person to person, the results are the same—a calm mind, a relaxed body, and renewed vitality.

## General Guidelines

- To practice, find a quiet and safe place where you can breathe without any distractions.
- If you can, keep the air running or use an air purifier in the room.
- Before starting each exercise, make sure you read the instructions carefully.
- You can choose to practice sitting or lying down, whatever feels comfortable.
- You may choose to cover your eyes or use the Mana Experience Lighting Systems to create a vibe.
- During your practice, you can choose to practice in silence or with healing sounds. Both have benefits, so feel free to alternate depending on how you feel.
- If you have time to prepare, have water, tissues, a blanket, and a journal, otherwise just breathing is enough.
- Try to practice one of these exercises daily for a month, and write down how you feel before doing an exercise and how you feel after. Allow inspiration to guide your writing. You will observe the positive changes in your physical and mental health.

Choose your favorite ones and incorporate them into your daily life; you can also show them to someone who needs them. With these techniques, you will always have ways to calm the nervous system of yourself or others.

We have provided a link to recordings of these exercises on our website and channels. If you record any of your practices, please tag us! We would love to hear about your experience with these practices.

Safety is our top priority. Please refer to the Mastering Our Breath section in Chapter Six for detailed instructions on how to position your body to maximize the effectiveness of these exercises and ensure safe practice.

Always consult with your doctor to ensure that these exercises are safe and suitable for your condition. Regardless of whether you perceive yourself as healthy or have been diagnosed with a medical condition, it is essential to seek approval from your physician prior to engaging in any activities outlined in this book. In addition, please refrain from practicing these exercises while driving or operating machinery, as they may induce sensations in your body that require your undivided attention.

## Optimizing the way we breathe

Bring your attention to your breath. Observe how the air flows in and out of your body. Take a deep inhale through your nose as if smelling a beautiful flower. Feel the air fill your lungs, and gently pull it toward the crown of your head. Exhale effortlessly, letting the air flow out of your nose without force.

Now, let's take it a step further. Inhale first from your nose to your belly, activating your diaphragm, then to your chest, filling your lungs from the bottom up. Use your full breathing capacity, activating the muscles from your pelvic floor to your crown. Feel your body expand with each inhale and contract with each exhale.

As you continue to breathe deeply, rotate your shoulders to the back, drop them, and open your heart. Align your ears with your shoulders, and let your breath become horizontal, avoiding any tension in your neck or upper chest.

Take deep breaths for a few minutes, and notice how you feel. Are you feeling more relaxed and centered?

_____

_____

_____

_____

_____

_____

_____

_____

_____

_____

_____

_____

# Practical Exercises

## Oscillation Breathing

It is a coherent, connected, circular, conscious energy pattern practiced to cultivate energy within you.

It is the observation of the spectral energy of the natural breathing waveforms and the awareness of its oscillations. It's like plugging into a source of power that's been there all along, just waiting for you to tap in.

- Settle in and get comfortable.
- Bring your attention to your breath.
- Observe how the air moves in and out of your body and how your chest rises and falls with each inhale and exhale.
- Wait to try to change anything about your breathing; just observe it.
- Now, optimize your position.
- Sit or lie in a comfortable position, ensuring your body is relaxed and your muscles are not tense.
- Next, it's time to connect the breath. This means avoiding the pause between exhale/inhale and inhale/exhale.
- Instead, create one continuous motion, like a never-ending wave of air moving in and out of your body. This is where the magic happens.
- Now, inhale bringing the air up toward your forehead.
- Focus on inhaling with enthusiasm, intention, and awareness.
- Visualize taking in all the positive energy and inspiration the universe offers.
- Breathe in deeply. As your lungs fill with air, let your worries dissolve.
- Release with an exhale that carries away old burdens. Natural as a leaf's fall, this effortless surrender is a conduit for change, a testament to life's flow.
- Feel the liberation in this breath—it's more than just an air exchange; it's a shedding of obsolete thoughts, an embrace of the present.

- Each breath makes you lighter and more aligned with life's rhythm.

With each breath, you create a space within yourself for clarity, peace, and love. You're opening yourself up to the infinite possibilities of the universe and allowing yourself to receive all the gifts by being present at this moment, connected to your breath and the world around you. You are a powerful force of nature and your breath is the bridge.

## Vibrational Breathing

This exercise is deep and slow, optimizing the balance between the parasympathetic and sympathetic systems.

You'll inhale and exhale at around 4-6 breaths per minute, which positively influences the body's physiological and psychological functions. This is significantly slower than the typical resting breathing rate of 12-20 breaths per minute for adults.

Breathing at this slower rate can potentially increase HRV, a measure of variations in the time interval between heartbeats. Higher HRV is generally associated with better health, including cardiovascular health, as it reflects more flexibility and adaptability in the autonomic nervous system.

Slow, deep breathing exercises have been demonstrated to have numerous health benefits. These could range from relaxation and stress reduction to improved attention and memory, lower stress levels, decreased blood pressure, and improved cognitive function, among other benefits.

- Sit or lie down comfortably.
- Take a few deep breaths at your natural rate.
- Now inhale slowly and deeply through your nose for a count of 5 seconds.
- Exhale gently and entirely through your mouth for a count of 5 seconds.
- Continue this pattern of inhaling and exhaling at the same pace.

- You will breathe for 2 minutes at approximately 6 breaths per minute, which is slower than the average breathing rate for most people.

Our aim here is to keep a steady and consistent breathing rhythm of around six breaths per minute, which means taking one deep breath every ten seconds. If you're someone who likes gadgets, grab a metronome or set a gentle timer to help you maintain this awesome pace.

After completing this exercise, take a well-deserved break of at least five minutes before moving on to anything else. And hey, if you're feeling particularly zen and want to take things slow, feel free to extend your inhales and exhales to nine seconds or even longer.

You're in charge of finding your own unique rhythm and pace, so experiment and discover what works best for you.

## Bedtime's Bridge to the Subconscious Mind

Do you ever find yourself tossing and turning in bed at night, unable to quiet your racing thoughts? This exercise is an ethereal lullabye. It will stimulate your parasympathetic nervous system and activate the vagus nerve. And by activating the vagus nerve, you're telling your body it's time to relax. It has a calming effect on the amygdala, reducing its activation and helping to promote feelings of well-being.

- Lie down and focus on breathing through your nose.
- Inhale counting to 6, and then exhale on a count of 9.
- Repeat this for 3 minutes.

If you need to adjust the numbers, it is completely fine. Just make sure the exhale is longer than the inhale.

## Open the Gates

Take a deep breath in, hold, and then breathe out with your lips puckered like you're blowing out a candle.

- Relax your face, neck, and shoulder muscles.
- Breathe in (inhale) slowly through your nose, like smelling the flowers and keeping your mouth closed. On your inhale, slowly count to 4, filling up with air from the bottom to the top of your lungs.
- Pucker your lips as if you were blowing the flame of a candle.
- Release the air slowly and gently through your pursed lips while counting to 8.
- It may help to count to yourself: exhale, one, two, three, four.
- Repeat this breathing pattern for 2 minutes.

This exercise can prevent air trapping, and it can also aid with panic attacks and improve resilience. It will decrease the respiratory rate by increasing the expiratory rate.

### It's a Balancing Act

This is an exercise to help you feel calm and balanced.

- Find a quiet spot where you can sit and not be disturbed.
- Sit up straight but make sure you're still comfortable.
- Take a few big breaths to start.
- Notice how you feel. Just notice, don't judge.
- Start counting when you breathe in and breathe out, to the count of four each time.
- When you breathe in, count 1,2,3,4 in your head, then hold your breath and count 1,2,3,4 again.
- Breathe out and count 1,2,3,4 one more time, then hold your breath again for the same count.
- Keep doing this for about 2 minutes.

After you're done, see if you feel any different. Maybe you feel more peaceful or thankful. Take a few minutes to just sit and enjoy the feeling before you go back to what you were doing.

## I Am Love

If you feel distracted and anxious. Find a place to sit for a few minutes keeping your hands free.

- Take a few deep breaths, gently remembering to open your position, allowing good support from your muscles.
- Bring your awareness to your nostrils.
- Use your fingers to close one nostril at a time.
- Inhale through your left nostril for a count of 6.
- Exhale through your right nostril for a count of 6.
- Repeat the same process, but this time inhale through your right nostril and exhale through your left nostril.
- Feel the words I AM LOVE every time you inhale.
- Exhale, release.
- Keep alternating between the 2 nostrils for 3 sets or for 2 minutes.

This exercise can help reduce stress and anxiety and improve focus and concentration.

## Find My Peace

Start by giving yourself a gentle massage on your belly, chest, and every part that feels tight, activating the muscles and energy centers.

For this exercise, listening to cosmic healing sounds would be beneficial. When adding sounds be mindful of the messages and frequencies in songs.

During the activities, you are reprogramming your mind with beliefs that serve you. Search for high-quality healing sounds to listen to and observe your thoughts like clouds appearing and disappearing.

- Find a place to sit comfortably.
- Place your tongue on the roof of your mouth and gently touch the ridge between your teeth and palate.
- Count to 4 while slowly inhaling through your nose and feel your abdomen and chest rise.

- Hold your breath for 1 second.
- Then, count to 4 while exhaling through your mouth—let the core do the work.
- At the bottom of your exhale, hold your breath for 1 second.

You can visualize a force that feels like a kind, calm, gentle energy of kindness that you move with your mind, eyes, and hands. Visualize it spiraling each energy center in your body, aligned with your breathing patterns.

## Rebirthing Twenty Connected Breaths, by Leonard Orr

The practice involves taking twenty connected breaths through your nostrils. The technique includes four sets of five breaths, each set comprising four normal breaths and one deep breath. You inhale and exhale through your nose throughout the practice.

To perform the technique, you would start by taking four normal breaths in and out through your nose, and then take a deep breath, filling your lungs completely. Then exhale completely through your nose.

You would then repeat this pattern for four sets, taking four normal breaths and one deep breath in each set.

- Do 4 sets of 5 breaths.
- 4 normal breaths and 1 deep breath.
- Inhale and exhale through your nose. Breathe in a connected, circular, continuous way.

The technique can be done at any time of the day to calm the mind, reduce stress, and improve focus and concentration.

## DNA Repair

Our DNA is like a blueprint for life, containing all the information that makes us who we are. Our cells have an incredible ability to detect and fix damaged DNA, helping to prevent mutations and maintain the integrity of our genetic code.

To begin this exercise, rub your mid-eyebrow and crown in gentle circles while slowly drawing breath from the cosmic source.

As you deeply inhale through your nose, imagine a radiant golden color flowing in from your nostrils, heading straight to your crown. From there, envisage this golden hue enveloping your body with its healing energy. Trace the energy as it permeates your spine and spreads throughout your body.

Upon exhaling, visualize crafting a pyramid around yourself using this golden light.

Maintain a brief pause of one second between each inhalation and exhalation, and observe the sensation of your breath coursing through your body.

After mere three minutes of this practice, you might start to experience a sense of rejuvenated energy and vitality, as your cells embark on a journey of repair and regeneration.

## Level Up

This is a simple and effective way to increase your focus and energy. Just remember to focus on the sharp exhale and let the inhale take care of itself.

- First, get comfortable.
- Sit in a relaxed position.
- Through your nose, take a deep breath in and let it out slowly.
- Now, let's focus on the exhale.
- Take a deep breath in through your nose, then exhale sharply and forcefully. It should feel like a sneeze, with a sharp shooting breath coming from your diaphragm and lower abdomen.
- Repeat this process, exhaling sharply and forcefully, for 20 counts.

While you're doing this, keep your eyes closed and your body relaxed. You don't need to tense your neck. Your breath should remain normal, with only sharp exhales through your nose.

This technique stimulates the sympathetic nervous system, which is responsible for the fight or flight response. It'll help you feel more alert and ready to tackle whatever comes your way.

Take a few minutes to integrate before resuming activities.

## Breathing Essence

This exercise involves active breathing through your mouth, holding your breath, and then integrating with gentle nose breathing.

- Find an optimal seated position with your back straight and your feet on the ground.
- Take a few deep breaths through your nose, inhaling deeply and exhaling slowly.
- Visualize energy from behind the navel and in front of the kidneys.
- Now, switch to breathing through your mouth.
- Begin by inhaling deeply through your mouth, as if breathing through your navel.
- Then, exhale fully through your mouth, releasing all the air.
- Do this for about 2 minutes, taking slow and steady breaths.
- Next, try to hold your breath for as long as you can and focus on the sensation of energy flowing through your body.
- Slowly exhale through your nose when you can't hold your breath any longer.
- Integrate with gentle nose breathing.
- Inhale deeply through your nose, filling your lungs with air.
- Then, exhale slowly and fully through your nose.
- Take slow and gentle breaths for about 2 minutes more.

Finally, when you're ready, observe how you feel.

## Healing Breath

In this exercise, you will activate healing energy. It involves movement, visualization and two series of nine normal connected breaths and one deep breath, inhaling and exhaling through your nose.

- Find a comfortable seated position.
- As you settle into your seat, bring your awareness to your hips.
- Begin to move them gently, circularly, feeling the energy flow throughout your body.
- Allow yourself to surrender to the movement and feel the sensations in your body.
- Now, focus your attention on the crown of your head.
- Visualize a vortex extending from your crown into space, creating an open gate for a violet light of a high frequency that activates all our bodily cells.
- Visualize this violet light flowing from God's Source energy, filling your crown and pineal gland with healing light.
- Take 9 normal, connected breaths inhaling and exhaling through your nose.
- Your belly and chest should both expand when you inhale.
- With each inhalation, feel your body fill with fresh, oxygen-rich air and violet light.
- With each exhalation, release any tension or negativity from your body along with violet light. When you exhale, your chest relaxes, and your navel pulls back in toward your spine.
- On the 10th deep breath, visualize energy filling your entire being, traveling through your spine, revitalizing your body and mind.
- Take another 9 connected breaths followed by a 10th long deep breath.

Take a moment to observe how you feel after completing this exercise. Notice any changes in your body, emotions, or mental state.

## The Universe Within

This somatic experience can make you more aware of your body and your physical and emotional states, and can help you develop greater control over your responses to stress and other challenges.

- Find a comfortable seated or lying down position.
- Take a few deep breaths, inhaling deeply through your nose and exhaling through your mouth in a gentle sight.
- Focus your attention on the sensation of your breath, feeling the warmth of the sun on your skin, or the coolness of a breeze on your face.
- Notice the cool air as you inhale through your nostrils and the warm air as you exhale through the mouth.
- As you breathe, bring your attention to the rise and fall of your chest and the sensation of air flowing in and out of your body.
- As you continue to breathe deeply and slowly, begin to scan your body from head to toe. Notice any areas of tension or discomfort.
- As you inhale, imagine that you are sending your breath to those areas of tension or discomfort.
- Imagine that your breath is like a warm, healing light that is soothing and relaxing in those areas.
- As you exhale, imagine that you are releasing any tension or discomfort that you are holding in your body.
- Allow your exhale to be a long, slow sigh.
- Repeat this process for 3 to 5 minutes, focusing on your breath and the sensation of relaxation in your body.

Take a few minutes to integrate before returning to normal activities.

## The Dome Breath

When practicing diaphragmatic breathing, the belly moves more than the chest with each breath, expanding while inhaling and contracting while exhaling.

- Lie on a flat surface with your knees bent. If you need support, you can use a pillow under your knees (you can also practice sitting).
- Place a hand on your chest and the other on your abdominal area below your rib cage.
- The bottom hand should do the moving.
- Deeply breathe in through your nose for about 4-6 seconds, feeling your abdomen expand.
- Your chest should stay relaxed and still.
- Breathe out slowly and steadily through your mouth for about 6-8 seconds, pushing all the air out. Keep your mouth relaxed.
- In the next cycle, as you inhale again, imagine the breath filling you up like a balloon. Your hand on your belly should rise as you inhale, while your hand on your chest should stay still.
- Exhale slowly through your mouth, allowing your belly to deflate as you exhale.
- In the inhale, activate your intercostal, abdominal, and pelvic floor muscles and let them fall inward as you exhale.
- Repeat for 5-15 minutes, focusing on the sensation of the breath flowing in and out of your belly.

This can help strengthen the diaphragm, calm the nervous system, and improve GI symptoms like constipation or urgency.

Allow time to adjust to your surroundings, and do not stand up too quickly after completing the exercise.

## Higher Frequencies Breathing

In this exercise, with each breath, you will become more centered, more relaxed, and more at peace with yourself and your environment.

By counting the beats as you breathe in and out, you are training your mind to focus on the present moment.

- Imagine yourself in a serene setting, listening to the soft hum of the wind, contemplating infinite possibilities.
- Inhale counting from 4 to 7, and feel your lungs expand with fresh air. 4, 5, 6, 7.
- Hold your breath for 7 counts. 1, 2, 3, 4, 5, 6, 7.
- Let your mind be still.
- Breathe out through your mouth, slowly counting to 8: 1, 2, 3, 4, 5, 6, 7, 8.
- As you release all the air audibly, make a whoosh sound and let go of any tension; visualize water flowing.
- Again, take a deep breath in, counting from 4 to 7 as you inhale and feel your lungs expand. 4, 5, 6, 7.
- Hold your breath for 7 counts. 1, 2, 3, 4, 5, 6, 7; enjoy the silence.
- Breathe out through your mouth, counting to 8: 1, 2, 3, 4, 5, 6, 7, 8.
- Breathe slowly in a satisfying sigh so you can feel the sensation of releasing the breath and letting go.
- Rest and integrate for 2 minutes.
- Repeat the 2 cycles 1 more time.

The longer exhale helps activate the parasympathetic nervous system, calming your body.

Practice being present and engaged in the current moment without judgment. When present, we are more likely to notice the small joys and pleasures in life, such as the beauty of nature, the taste of a delicious meal, or the warmth of a hug. By staying present, we learn to appreciate these moments fully and find greater fulfillment in our lives; through this, we play at higher frequencies.

## Infinity Breath

This exercise is done through the nose; there is no pause between the inhale and exhale, just a continuous motion with no beginning or end.

Let the air flow, allowing a blossoming phenomenon in every cell and molecule within you.

• Find a comfortable position with your head, neck, and spine aligned.
• Bring your attention to your heart and the space between the heart beats.
• Take a deep breath in, filling your chest with rejuvenating air.
• Feel the expansion of your diaphragm and the stretching of your ribcage.
• Breathe out in one smooth, uninterrupted exhale, envisioning the release of a cloud of astral dust. Observe as it gently floats away from your heart, dissolving into the air around you, and leaving you with a sense of lightness and tranquility.
• In the next cycle, before you exhale completely, begin to inhale, connecting the inhale with the exhale and focusing on filling from the bottom of the lungs to the upper chest.
• Visualize each breath as a wave, flowing in and out of your body in a steady rhythm.
• Keep your eyes closed and continue breathing as if you were breathing through your heart for 10 minutes.

To integrate, take a few breaths intuitively, at your own pace, with the intensity and depth you feel. Observe how you rest so peacefully, breathing synched with the light and sounds.

## Convergence Breath

This practice can help you regulate your body temperature and calm your mind by breathing with your tongue between your lips.

- Sit in a comfortable position, ensuring your back is straight and your shoulders are relaxed.
- Begin by curling your tongue, bringing the outer edges together and sticking it out slightly.
- Inhale deeply through your mouth, breathing in through your curled tongue.
- Exhale slowly and completely through your nose. Slightly extend your breath in length, but don't force it.
- Keep your attention on the air passing through your tongue and nostrils.
- Continue breathing this way for up to 5 minutes.

To integrate the practice, take a few breaths and explore the depths of your being without fear or judgment. Take a moment to notice how you feel, both physically and mentally. Allow the energy cycles to work their magic in your life.

## The Vortex

This exercise is designed to help improve your breathing by expanding your chest and allowing for deeper inhalations.

- Stand straight with your feet shoulder-width apart and your arms down by your sides.
- Place your hands just beside your nipples and rib cage, as if holding onto your rib cage.
- Draw your elbows back slightly to allow your chest to expand.
- Inhale deeply through your nose and simultaneously draw back both elbows, as if you're trying to bring your elbows together behind your back.
- Hold your breath for a few seconds.
- Slowly release your breath by exhaling through your nose.

- Once you have fully exhaled, release the holding force of your hands on your ribcage.
- Repeat this process for 2 minutes, taking deep breaths in and out while moving your elbows back and forth.

Breathe deeply and slowly throughout the exercise, focusing on expanding your chest and allowing your lungs to fill with air. With practice, this exercise can help improve your lung capacity and overall breathing ability.

## A Journey into the Soul

This exercise will take you on a journey of self-discovery, where you will explore the depths of your being and connect with your higher self.

- To begin, find a quiet and peaceful place to be alone or with your partner.
- Sit comfortably and place a mirror in front of you, or sit facing your partner.
- Take a deep breath, and relax.
- Look into the mirror or your partner's eyes, and focus on their left eye. Gaze deeply into it, and observe the colors, patterns, and reflections you see.
- Then, shift your focus to the right eye, and do the same.
- Finally, focus on the third eye, in the center of the forehead, between and a little above the eyebrows. This is a gateway; by concentrating on it, you can connect with your true self.
- Shift your focus back to the left eye and stay there as long as possible.
- Switch back and forth between eyes if you need to.
- Calibrate your breathing as you gaze into your eyes through your mirror or at your partner's eyes.
- Take a deep inhale, and gently exhale steadily through your nose.
- Take deep, connected breaths. Keep your neck, jaw, and throat area relaxed.

• Sync your breath with your partner's, and inhale and exhale together through the nose in a circular way.
• Let your breath flow naturally without forcing it or pausing it.
• Practice this exercise for at least 3 minutes, and allow yourself to sink deeper and deeper into a state of relaxation and inner peace.
• You can add more minutes every time.

You may find that this exercise brings up emotions, memories, or thoughts you have been suppressing or ignoring.

Allow yourself to feel whatever comes up and observe it without judgment or attachment.

It is a way to cultivate greater awareness and understanding of your inner world, and it will also deepen your connection with your partner.

## Alchemical Breathing

As you begin the practice, take three deep breaths and evoke feelings of acceptance and compassion. Be authentic. Allow yourself to be vulnerable and imperfect.

• Breathe gently in and out of your nose without pushing or pulling, and keep a circular, connected rhythm.
• Bring your attention to the lower area of your body, between the navel, kidneys, womb, and sexual organs, observing your sacral and root centers. Let go of expectations.
• As you focus on this area, become aware of any sensations or feelings that arise. You may feel a pulsation or notice the area feels tense or relaxed. Allow yourself to observe without judgment. Be patient. Embrace your body and mind with healing.
• As you continue focusing on this area, you may feel tingling, warmth, cold, or other sensations. Allow these feelings to come up and expand, and imagine the energy flowing freely through your body.
• Release with long exhales what doesn't serve you.
• Embrace the silence around you.

• Use your intention to guide the energy toward the navel and then the sexual center.
• Follow your breath, and smile at the infinite possibilities in the present time.
• Feel the energy flowing down to your feet and then back up through your body toward the crown of your head.
• As you move the energy through each point, imagine it flowing like a river, nourishing and healing every part of your body.
• Allow the energy to continue flowing freely without any resistance or blockages. Explore your essence.
• Once you have traveled through your body at least 9 times, you can let the energy flow continuously like a stream.
• Feel the energy flowing, filling you with vitality and well-being.
• Now, observe and cultivate the energy in your navel center.
• Cover your belly button with both palms, left hand over right, and mentally spiral the energy outward from the navel clockwise, then inward counterclockwise.
• Now, switch by placing the right hand over the left, and mentally spiral the energy outward from the navel in a counterclockwise direction, then inward in a clockwise direction.
• To integrate, continue breathing at your regular rate for 3 minutes and enjoy the sensations.

This practice restores your energy and balances your body and mind.

## Harmony Breath Bath

This exercise involves synchronized breathing with your partner, which creates oneness and harmony between you. When you breathe together, you share the same air and energy, which can foster a deep level of intimacy and trust.

The idea behind this exercise is that you breathe in when your partner breathes out and breathe out when your partner breathes in, creating a harmonious circular and connected rhythm of breathing together.

This synchronized breathing creates a deep level of connection. You can observe your breathing patterns and your partner's. This heightened awareness leads to a higher consciousness and a deeper understanding of each other. It also helps you calm your nervous system and be more present.

- Find a comfortable seated position with your partner.
- During the exercise, you can close or look at each other's eyes.
- Take deep breaths in through your noses and out through your mouths, letting go of any tension or stress.
- Next, breathe deeply and slowly in and out through your nose, focusing all of your attention on the sensation of the air moving.
- Allow your breath to flow naturally through your nose without forcing it.
- Feel the rise and fall of your chest and belly.
- As you breathe deeply, visualize the air moving in and out of your body, circulating through your entire being.
- Synchronize so that you are inhaling and exhaling together.
- As you breathe, allow yourself to feel any emotions or sensations that arise without judgment.
- Keep your focus on the energy movement you have learned throughout this book.
- Continue breathing deeply for as long as feels comfortable, ideally for several minutes.
- Take a final deep breath in, hold it for a few seconds, and then exhale slowly, letting go of any tension. When you are ready to end the practice, hug your partner, expressing your gratitude.
- Reflect on how you feel, noticing any changes.

Building a deeper bond with your partner can be wonderfully enhanced through this practice of conscious breathing. Yet, as powerful as it is for personal growth, conscious breathing should not replace the invaluable aid of professional assistance when it's needed. Thus, it's important that both you and your partner reach out for the appropriate resources and support when facing challenges.

Taking care of your mental health is akin to maintaining essential brain hygiene. The most flourishing relationships are those in which you are able to recognize the beliefs that fuel your actions. By doing this, you can take personal accountability for your growth and development. The quicker you confront and deal with emotional baggage, learning to embrace self-love, the sooner you'll find yourself surrounded by individuals who validate and celebrate your triumphs. This is the true essence and power of manifestation in relationships.

## Money Flow

This exercise is designed to activate your financial abundance.

- Take 3 cycles of deep breaths through the nose.
- Be gentle; inhale with intention, and exhale in a slow count.
- In the 4th cycle, continue with connected breathing.
- Visualize your checking account numbers increasing.
- Keep the image moving as if you are watching a video. See how your deposits keep growing, mentally scroll up, and observe the money flowing in.
- Stay as long as you need in this visualization until it feels authentic.
- You can evoke feelings of gratitude, the sensations of deserving and receiving this.
- Keep breathing connectivity.
- 2nd Round—Take 3 deep breaths through the nose.
- Be gentle, inhale with intention, and exhale in a slow count.
- In the 4th cycle, continue with connected breathing.
- Visualize your assets, money, resources, and cryptocurrency growing.
- Keep the images moving as if you are watching a video.
- Visualize the intelligent allocation of resources.
- Keep breathing connectivity.
- 3rd Round—Take 3 deep breaths through the nose.
- Be gentle, inhale with intention, and exhale in a slow count.
- In the 4th cycle, continue with connected breathing.
- Visualize money flowing to everyone around you, your community, country, and the world.

- Visualize the positive flow of resources within joyful, healthy humans and your happy self.
- Evoke feelings of gratitude, abundance, and generosity.
- Continue breathing at a usual rate and take some time to integrate the experience.
- Do this exercise daily for 21 days.

Breathe deeply and slowly throughout the exercise, focusing on expanding your chest and allowing your lungs to fill with air.

## The Active Cycle of Breathing Technique (ACBT) (Respiratory Care)

This technique clears lung secretions and helps reduce the risk of chest infections. It also improves ventilation in the lungs and how effective the cough is.

It was not invented by a single person but developed over time by a group of physiotherapists who worked in respiratory care. The earliest known version of the ACBT was described by an Australian physiotherapist named Tom Ayres in the 1950s.

However, other physiotherapists refined and further developed the technique over the years, including Pamela L. Eves and Judy A. Moore. It is widely used by respiratory therapists and physiotherapists to treat various respiratory conditions.

When practicing the ACBT, it is recommended to follow the phases: Breathing Control, Thoracic Expansion Exercises, Huffing, and Coughing; but you and your health practitioner can modify this depending on your condition. Please get clearance from your doctor before practicing this exercise.

### Breathing Control

- Focus on breathing gently and at your own pace.
- Breathe in through your nose. If you cannot, breathe through your mouth. If you are breathing through your mouth, use pursed-lips breathing.

- Remember to relax your shoulders and gradually slow down your breathing.
- Breathe until you feel ready to continue.

## Thoracic Expansion Exercises

The inspiration is deep and active, combined with a three-second end-inspiratory hold before a passive expiration. Also, positive pressure can be used to help remove lung secretions.

- Gently place the hands on the thoracic cage.
- Through the nose, take deep breaths in.
- Hold for 2-3 seconds before exhaling passively.
- Repeat this exercise 3-5 times, but take a break if you start to feel light-headed.

## Forced Expiratory Technique or Huffing

A huff is exhaled through an open mouth and throat instead of coughing. Dynamic compression helps move sputum; use a medium- or high-volume huff to move secretions from your airways. A medium-volume huff helps with secretions in your lower airways, while a high-volume huff helps with secretions in your upper airways.

## Medium-Volume Huff

- Breathe in normally and then take a long breath out, like steaming up a mirror.
- 1-2 huffs.

## High-Volume Huff

- Take a deep breath, open your mouth wide, and huff out quickly.
- 1-2 huffs.

The length of the huff and force of contraction of the muscles of expiration can be modified. Listen for crackles when huffing to clear the secretions from your chest.

## Coughing

- Remember to cough gently only when you need to clear your sputum.
- Do not cough excessively, as it may not be necessary.

You can practice ACBT for two to ten minutes depending on your symptoms or condition.

## Mana Session - A Transformative Experience

If you hold a Mana Breathwork Universe Facilitator Certification or you are certified in any other breathwork modality, and consider yourself a facilitator, you are fit to delve into our dynamic group sessions. Seize this opportunity to explore the depths of your practice.

Solo sessions, whether grounded on terra firma or in water, and group sessions share a few common threads, but the differences are game changers. Your individual sessions are custom-built just for you, like a breathwork suit tailored to your body's unique rhythms and goals.

We are detectives in our observant nature, tweaking techniques and shifting the rhythm and tempo just right. It's not unusual for these sessions to be punctuated by long stretches of silence, especially individual sessions in bathtubs. Some of the most transformative, deep-dive experiences in breathwork have emerged from this realm of silence.

Group sessions are different. These sessions run on a more synchronized beat, but there is always enough room for your style and needs.

Solo sessions allow us to dig deeper into your journey while addressing any bumps in the road that might pop up. As facilitators in individual sessions, we're all about letting the magic unfold naturally, supporting your journey with a mindful presence, unconditional acceptance, and solid support. Group settings shake up the vibe a bit. We're not just looking at you, but the collective pulse of the entire group. The spotlight still shines on you, but there's an extra layer of complexity as we tune in to the collective energy that the group whips up. There is magic in the bond with others during the integration phase. This sense of belonging, this shared journey, adds a whole new layer of richness to your breathwork practice.

*The following is a blueprint of the session's parameters and objectives. If you're a breathwork maestro, this serves as a playground for you to explore and experiment. And if you're a student, this intimate sketch will help you peek behind the curtain and understand the essence of a session.*

Think of it like you're DJing your favorite music. You'd probably start with some low-key, chill beats, setting a calm and inviting atmosphere. As the evening progresses and everyone's energy starts to lift, you'd smoothly transition to more upbeat, vibrant tracks and experiment by mixing those.

Your breathwork session can follow a similar flow. Each inhale and exhale is like a beat in your mix; each energy cycle is a track waiting to be seamlessly blended into the set.

As your energy changes, so do your patterns.

## Experimental Template for Facilitators

Introduction, Preparation, and Initiation (Minutes 00:00 - 10:00)

• Begin by cultivating a safe and nurturing environment for participants to embark on their breathwork journey. Encourage attendees to find a comfortable position in which to relax.
• This phase can be enhanced through the incorporation of color therapy and sound healing techniques, providing a holistic sensory experience.
• Before commencing the session, confirm that all participants have had the opportunity to use the restroom. This ensures no interruptions once the breathwork practice is underway.

• Ensure each participant has access to essential items for the session—a blanket for warmth, tissues for any emotional release, water for hydration, socks for added comfort, and a journal for recording reflections or insights post-session.

• Briefly outline breathwork's essence and discuss the particular strategies and goals of the Mana Breathwork Session.

• Query about each individual's past breathwork experience, their intentions for this session, and any prevailing health issues.

• Explain breathwork's value for relaxation, stress alleviation, and overall wellness.

• Inform participants about the prolonged moments of silence during the session.

• Explicitly state the breathing patterns and their usage throughout the practice.

• Detail the various modalities within the session and your interaction style with participants.

• If deemed necessary, ask for consent to delicately touch their faces or backs for guidance and support.

• Showcase the ideal posture for effective breathing as delineated in the Mastering the Breath section in chapter six of this book.

• Facilitate gentle warm-up exercises that help participants connect with their breath and body. Facilitate three to five warm-up breathing exercises from the examples in the Practical Exercises section of this chapter.

• Address any questions, provide clear instructions, and listen to each individual's unique breathing patterns and underlying beliefs.

• Observe the participants' dominant breathing patterns and the rhythm and flow of their breath.

## Mana Breathwork Practice
## (Activation and Release-Level 1) (Minutes 10:00 - 60:00)

• Guide participants through the six waves.

• Each wave should last ten minutes.

• Clarify each technique's approach and advantages, granting participants time to adapt to the procedure.

- Suggest alterations for those who might find certain techniques daunting.
- Following the provided template, navigate the group in a circular and connected breathwork practice.
- Throughout the session, provide guidance, including prompts to modify their breath or relax bodily tension.
- Encourage participants to focus on their breath, noting any emerging sensations without judgment.
- Guide participants in liberating physical sensations, emotions, thoughts, and spiritual experiences by breathing through them.
- Please request all participants to be mindful of others in the room.
- If a participant exhibits emotional responses such as crying or screaming or physical outbursts, gently steer them toward tranquility.
- Advise them to observe any incidents without responding dramatically.
- While participants are free to discontinue at any point, we strongly recommend completing the entire energy cycle once the breathing exercises have commenced. Exiting the session prematurely is discouraged.
- While leading the entire group, it's essential to individually approach each member, offering them personalized guidance. Do this subtly by whispering to them, ensuring not to disrupt other participants.
- We suggest maintaining a facilitator-to-participant ratio of one to thirty. In larger groups and stadiums the primary facilitator can manage the overall group while assistant facilitators attentively monitor their assigned participants.
- If you're a certified facilitator who has spent considerable time refining your skills using this template, you'll develop a keen ability to observe patterns and cycles, which can be thought of as tracks.
- As a master of your craft, you can skillfully blend these tracks, using the flow of creative energy as your guide. Think of yourself as a DJ, co-creating this extraordinary experience.

## Wave 1
### Earth = Body (Minutes 10:00 to 20:00)

• Begin this segment by reducing all external stimuli, ensuring only soft lighting and complete silence, if possible.
• Request that the participant(s) lie down with their eyes closed. Establish a connection with the Earth element.
• Implement a body scanning technique to induce relaxation.
• Engage in circular, connected breathing through the nose for eight minutes unless participants experience breathing difficulties.
• In the final two minutes, alter the breathing pattern to recalibrate and open the airways. An example of this could be the 'Open the Gates' pattern.
• This phase is designed to establish a connection with the body. It has specific phrases intended to foster body awareness, or you can guide a body scan exercise.

## Wave 2
### Air = Mind (Minutes 20:00 to 30:00)

• Go back to the circular, connected breathing. Encourage the participant(s) to connect with the Air element.
• Invite them to observe the mind.
• Cultivate stillness.
• Use pineal gland activation techniques.
• Continue with circular, connected breathing through the nose for eight minutes.
• Invite the participant to observe their thoughts and to consciously let go in order to interrupt the momentum of their mental activity.
• Toward the end of this section, modify the breathing pattern to stimulate the breath.
• The 'Level Up' pattern in the breathing exercises section could serve this purpose.
• Resume inhalation and exhalation through the nose.

## Wave 3
### Water = Heart (Minutes 30:00 - 40:00)

• Begin with circular, connected breathing—inhaling and exhaling through the nose.
• Prompt the participant(s) to form a connection with the Water element.
• You can guide a heart coherence technique.
• Consider the lungs and torso.
• Nurture positive emotions. Tap into infinite intelligence.
• Carry out the practice of circular, connected breathing through the nose for eight minutes.
• Invite the participants to observe their emotions by focusing on their heart center.
• You can inspire deep inhales from the bottom of the lungs into the upper chest and a relaxed exhale.
• In the concluding two minutes of this segment, modify the breathing pattern to invigorate the breath.
• Practice connected mouth breathing for two minutes. At the end of these two minutes, hold the breath for one minute or for as long as feasible.
• Resume nasal breathing.

## Wave 4
### Fire = Spirit (Minutes 40:00 - 50:00)

• Initiate with circular, connected breathing. Encourage the participant(s) to connect with the Fire element.
• Focus on moving energy as well as air.
• Engage in DNA repair and healing and regeneration of the cells.
• Contemplate the spine and energy centers.
• Purify the energy body.
• Continue with circular, connected breathing through the nose for eight minutes.

- By this time, the participants will already have started feeling the energy, making it the perfect moment to allow their inner worlds to expand.
- Inspire them by tapping into your boundless intuition and radiating 'authenticity.'
- In the last two minutes, adjust the breathing pattern to energize the breath.
- The 'Find My Peace' pattern could be appropriate here.
- Hold the breath at the end of the two minutes for one minute, or for as long as comfortable.
- Return to nasal breathing.

## Wave 5
## Ether = Higher Self (Minutes 50:00 - 60:00)

- Start again with circular, connected breathing.
- Invite the participant(s) to connect with the Ether Element.
- Promote gentle and natural rhythmic breathing.
- Inspire them to keep breathing.
- Keep a close eye on the overall mood of the group and aim to maintain a balanced energy level, lifting it or dialing it down as needed.
- Ensure you offer them extended periods of quietude, allowing them the opportunity to tune in to their own inner guidance and shape their personal experience.
- Throughout this phase, encourage participants to breathe in a manner that feels comfortable and natural to them.
- In the final two minutes, gently guide them toward the conclusion of the session, facilitating the assimilation of their experience.
- Instruct participants to turn to one side and adopt a fetal position in silence, fostering a comfortable environment for integration. This is an ideal moment to enhance their comfort with the addition of a pillow for neck support and a blanket.

## Wave 6
## Integration (Minutes 60:00 - 108:00)

- Conclude the session with a tranquil thirty-minute relaxation period, enabling participants to fully integrate the experience.
- Throughout this phase, inspire them to maintain their circular, connected breathing rhythm at a pace that suits them.
- Artfully convey the importance of integration within the realm of breathwork—a principle you've learned in your training—that often continues to develop over hours or even days after the session.
- Share your final reflections or insights and stir enthusiasm among participants to incorporate the techniques learned into their everyday lives.
- Once participants have reached a state of readiness, guide them back to their senses with a soft countdown from eight to one.
- Encourage participants to open their eyes, adopt a seated position and recount their experiences, initiating a dialogue within the group.
- Make space for a ten-minute period of introspective journaling or creative writing.
- In creating an environment conducive to sharing and open conversation, you facilitate the exchange of experiences, provide answers to inquiries, and stimulate engaging discussions.
- If they prefer, allow participants to immerse themselves in silent journaling.
- Express your appreciation for their commitment to expanding their consciousness and explain the benefits of a consistent breathwork practice.
- To cater to those who are eager to delve deeper into their practice, provide additional resources or relevant research data.

### Post-Session

- Invite participants to hydrate sufficiently to replenish fluids and encourage the expulsion of any toxins flushed out through breathing.

- Inform them that they may encounter a variety of sensations and advise them to practice self-care by addressing their body's requirements.
- If anyone feels overwhelmed and requires support, recommend further steps such as prolonging their breathing for a while longer until the energy cycle is over, journaling, walking, or conversing.
- Motivate participants to practice affirmations to reset limiting beliefs.
- Encourage participants to seek support whenever necessary.
- Supply information and resources related to counseling and treatment for mental health and well-being with certified professionals.

## Safe Practices

Guiding or participating in a breathwork session requires proper training and experience. It is highly recommended that you only engage in breathwork sessions with a certified practitioner who has the necessary skills and expertise to guide you safely through the practice.

Breathwork can be a powerful and transformative tool for healing and self-discovery, but it can also be potentially harmful if not approached with caution and care. Incorrect breathing techniques or overexertion during a session can lead to physical discomfort or even injury.

As such, if you have any underlying medical conditions or concerns, please consult with your healthcare provider before engaging in a breathwork session. Additionally, if you experience any discomfort or adverse reactions during the session, it is recommended that you stop immediately and seek medical attention if necessary.

By participating in a breathwork session, you acknowledge and accept that the session is for educational and informational purposes only and that the author, publisher, or affiliates are not liable for any damages, injuries, or losses that may arise as a result of your participation.

CHAPTER 9

# Poetry
# Collection

## A Writer Is Born Every Time I See You Breathe

For me, writing is the art of letting go and allowing. Writing has awakened my senses and has become an open invitation to observe my mind, body, soul, and universe without judgment. It welcomes me into a state of mind where I pay attention to the details and encourages me to remember what I see, hear, touch, taste, smell, or feel.

As a conscious breathing practitioner, I write to explore the self. Writing, as breathwork, is a mindfulness practice that helps me uncover unresolved emotions or beliefs and allows me to express the beautiful sounds of my soul.

The practice of observation is the first step on the spiraling path to evolution. When we become mindful, we recognize the mental stories we have been carrying and have the opportunity to look at our attitudes and perception. It allows us to accept all that it is and, at the same time, develop the courage to make the changes we want to experience to live extraordinary lives.

## The Stages of Awakening

Awakening is not linear
Moving from duality into unity
it's not a predictable pathway.
The unfolding of the human heart
is artful and enigmatic.

I circle back to enter
a deepening spiral,
a dance with the self.
Skating through the borders of my mind
as if they were orchid petals,

I let myself be guided
by the beauty of what I find
by the joy in my field
and the love in my art,

Sprinting and spinning across the skyline
leaping obstacles and gaps
Flirting with you and gravity
it makes landing on my feet acrobatics

Awakening is not linear.
I go from a blissful state into a dream
where the disowned self projects shadows,
where the darkness has seduced the fire,

Where questioning the systems
increases my appetite,
and reactionary moods divide us,

A state where all I can hear are questions,
where all I can see are distractions

The resistance becomes sadness
It soon turns into anger
The anger I am not allowed to feel
Anger speaking loudly, hiding my fears
Fears born from limiting beliefs

The sweet personal lies
Las mentiras personales

I breathe to surpass my mind
release the judgment

and surrender to this healing and readjustment

I breathe, until I bounced back to a stage
where my lungs melt into my chest,
propelling good air.

Where expansion feels inevitable,
and oneness is in my **AIR**

A stage where I have gleaming eyes
at the winning line
and the smile that comes out
of the absolute knowing
that I am right on track

And from here,
EYE can see the stars

However, awakening is not a str@ight line
There are constantly changing cycles

I entered a spiral riding a cloud of momentum,
and somehow, I ended up with an upgraded version

I became a witness to the conversion
The close observer of the immersion
and when I am above all, the distortion
well, desertion is not an option

Maybe, it will keep glitching,
but it will always be magnificent
because even when I'm drifting
I will own my heart
because awakening is not a straight line
There are always changing cycles.

# Perception

I question if what I see is real.

The smell of your skin, the taste of my tea,
their praises and judgments.

I wonder if my perception and the structure of it all are existent.

Me in you.
You are me.

All that I know, I've learned here
my ideas of how this should be.

Here is the birth of concepts based on one-second reactions.
Thousands of images are stored in my mind's colorful library daily,
dictating to me how I should live and what to live by.

Images in motion and one snap.
Selective memories tell me what's true.

I see, I feel, and I take action
and question if what I see is real.

## Paracosmos

Mind Up!

Pull your crown up and rise up.
Even when you have intrusive thoughts
stay up.
There is no point in holding it up.

Find the amazing
in the gazing of eyes
on the streetlights
in that time that you stopped the march of time.

Guide's voices in your head
give you a closer look at the galaxy,
Spiraled the mind's eye,
and bring up the vibe.

You have a magnificent mind
who said you should be fine with going blind.
What's the fuss trying to control
when you can travel whole.

to a better line,

Like that moment when you laughed
or when strong winds passed by.

The face of your lover
declaring undying affection along with true intentions.

...A silver lining.

Trusting the timing
Keeps you gracefully striving.

Lay in a hammock with the truth
and choose a new way back to you.

Because even when there is no aircrew
You can live
Dreamlike - Starlike - Childlike
like life is a mystery.

## Inner Dimensions

It is time to get ourselves ready
swimming the rivers that flow through us
since long ago; we knew this was coming.
We couldn't keep the same drumming.

But we are not alone.
Everything is how it should be.
We can enjoy this blissful life
water is polar, and so is the path

Humans are thriving around the globe.
We can see them closely.
I feel many hearts opening to come alive,
tearing all fears apart.

We chose to come here
to be the custodians
to nurture our planet
into the paradise that is meant to be

A joyous activation in our DNA
shows us every life is a masterpiece
and this world
our home to keep
Together we can slide into a plane of consciousness
where our hearts feel overtaken with appreciation and beauty
where once was, you and me,
there is only oneness

The past is gone, and in this present moment
we become the new way of L0v3
Holding our highest intention
into higher dimensions and beyond.

## E-motion

For a non-emotional,
I am feeling too emotional.
The ones that are inspired
will search far and in between.

We breathe as if we are breathing energy
circularly connected energy
from our feet to the center of the earth,
from our crown to the sky

Energy in motion
allows releasing
what it's not meant to be
what it's stuck within

Bending fire, water, air, and earth
Transmutes the thoughts
making the energy flow.

# Resilience

I am awake inside this dream
where my toes caress majestic grass
grounding me in a forest.

In this forest, giant trees
are fluorescent guardians
illuminating my path,
taking me to my spirit guides.

I see giant peaches and violets
melting over the sky when the sunset meets the moonlight.

Water fills the atmosphere,
preparing to clean my shadow.
I lay on the grass, where delightfully
scented flowers are, listening to new drops of rain
and wildlife's symphony.

In a language made of the sounds of the night,
I ask my guides for ways to cope with pain.

Raindrops turn into stardust with the words,
forgive, surrender, and let go.

## Forgiveness

A heart that once was shattered,
Now it shines with radiant light.
Through the flow of love,
The mind resets what truly matters.

Can you feel it?
The freedom within,
Old ideas collide and dissipate,
Paving the path for peace to win.

As you open up your heart,
The stillness within you abides;
It triumphs over polarity,
Where mind, heart, and spirit unite.

You are free; you are whole;
Consciousness now reigns supreme.
Embrace this newfound liberty,
and let your light forever gleam.

## Falling in Trust

Would you bring your body close to mine?
your vibe feels like good news wrapped
in a soft blanket of quartz;

I invite you to a journey filled with fate.
where new beliefs reset old patterns
giving us the bluest sky we've shared so far.

I'll inhale your exhale
and breathe out a new color chart.

As our eyes gaze, lifetimes will show.
Together, we'll step into a new reality
where we can fall into infinite trust.

Would you bring your soul? it will dance with mine.
As we evolve, we'll leave behind the attention span.

Now I trust myself,
and somehow, there are no more whys.

I've found a reflection so pure in you,
as we become one
I trust the path.

## The Pursuit of Happiness

Your recognition has become my addiction.
I want to see and be seen.

I went to sleep when I was a child,
innocent and undefiled
when I woke up; I was an adult
awaiting approval, validation,
the permission to proceed.

It took me years to release these conditions
they were imprinted in me

But it is not about the chase
so let me rephrase
I am happy. I was born happy.
It is my innate ability to raise the levels of bliss.

It is my decision.
So can you see the fiction?
I'm not in the pursuit of happiness.
Every second is the furthest I have ever been.

I am enough; lovable and deserving of life
cultivating prana makes me neuro-adjustable.
I am not a passenger anymore.
I am the guiding light.
The programmer,
I must say,

That's why I'm not in pursuit of happiness any more
Happiness is here; I'm already home.

## Moonlight

Long nights mind-searching for meaning,
but I always end up heart-dreaming.
Astral traveling,

I've seen guides in a higher state of consciousness
scriptwriting,
Using our galaxy as their stage,

Self-revealing
tapping in the space in which all our thoughts are formed,
the principal seat at the theater of the soul

Instead of trying to figure it all out
I'll let go of the control for a while
walkout, blissed-out, space out

Anxiety reminds me
I am recounting past doubts
and future whereabouts

I bring myself to the present time
where the taste of my tea
erases my worries.

Half of the time,
I don't even notice
my facial lines st0ri3s.

I go to the balcony, where turbulent swirls of AIR
erase the pages and lines of my face.

I am giving the pain away to this mixed cold air
and asking the clouds to be my space heaters.

I stay up with the moon
starting over a new pattern of thoughts,
a new wave of emotions,
and a new connection to the world.

I use sparkler's trails as my pen,
and looking at the sky,
once again
I feel grateful again.

Viviana Escobar

## The In-between

The first thing we did when we arrived in this world
was to breathe in.
The last thing we will do when we leave this world is breathe out.
Our existence lies in the in-between,

In the stillness, without pausing,
In the continuous flow,
In the perception between light and sound,
In the area in between our thoughts.

In every inspiration,
there's a pure loving source.

Our human and our spirit
mastering the art of allowing and letting go.

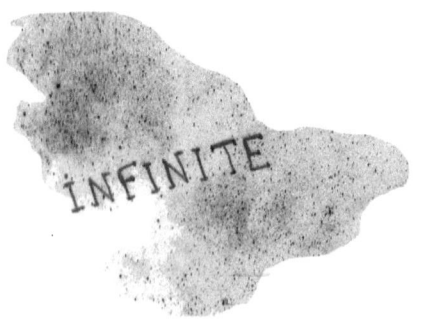

# A Quantum Clock & the Fountain of Youth

A Quantum clock works in a different way
as we search for youth that never fades.
The dream of long life, an eternal flame,
has driven us since memory was made.

We seek the fountain of youth with zeal
and grasp at any potion, herb, or seal
In hopes of finding what we desire,
a body and mind inspired.

We believe that our thoughts create our fate,
and in this truth, there lies a key
to live longer and be forever youthful,
free from disease.

So let us hold on to this belief
that by breathing at ease,
we can bring relief
and achieve a state
of pure rejuvenation and bliss.

## A Human on Planet Earth

In the cosmos, my human lies,
walking in that precious space between earth and skies.

Feelings, intentions, thoughts unfurl,
In the breadth and width, the swirl of the world,
Three dimensions playing their roles.

Synchrony seeks the space between thoughts and emotions,
Vibrations humming, setting in motion,
A perception that opens to a new existence,
To another fragment of my being,
where there is no resistance.

Evolutions,
Guided by whispers from my ethereal mentors,
Voices from the Infinite Intelligence form contours.

Evolutions,
Breath caught in the cage of pain,
In despair, my emotions rain.

Evolutions,
Unlocking the breath, breaking the chain,
Setting free the echoes of pain.

But what if it's not so straightforward, so mild?
What if the pain is just a DNA upgrade, reconciled?
A renewed Self-Awareness baptized anew.

What if the oscillations, the dualities, the stark contrasts,
Are the inevitable forks in our paths?
And healing wears different masks,
from each unique viewpoint, it basks.

Those who dare to reach beyond,
the overachievers,
Choosing deep cleansing,
are relentless believers,
Tenfold in a lifetime,
their wheel spins.

Yet the aim is expansion,
Not to shrink back into a mental implosion
Let's soften our skin

Life's journey, when in harmony, flows
Well-being, is an art for the human flock.

Let's unite, you and I, gather humanity,
Transmute pain and fear, and birth a new reality.

## Within the Cosmic Veil

Humans of celestial luminescence,
we grace this stage.
Embodiments of resilience,
draped in passion's flame.

Carrying galaxies in our gaze,
the cosmos at our fingertips,
Remember our power;
let it pass from our lips.

The ground beneath shifts,
like silk lotus petals,
Welcoming a queen,
as her essence settles.

Peaceful aura, gifted through lineages,
Leadership, a trait in our soul's codes,
It gives us the privilege,
of painting the new images.

A wisdom that silences fear,
that battles the strange,
The power to adapt to change,
to rearrange.

Our bodies are a testament,
a display,
Of the new life,
We foster every single day.

We, divine feminine,
more than what meets the eye,
Transcend the dimensions,
reach for the skies.

Benders of air,
Igniters of flames,
Dancers on Earth,
Underwater, we whisper our names.

Guardians of both
moon's glow and the sun's blaze,
We are the keepers of history,
Breathing life into stories,
Love will always stay.

Muses, survivors, warriors in our right,
Infused with a kaleidoscope of strengths,
A pulsating embodiment
of life's colorful frame.

Living, breathing this wild, earthly ride,
Rising above, with the tides, we collide.
Ruling realms, yet lifting each other higher,
Kindling souls, setting hearts on fire.

## Ageless

Today is a special day,
a day like this, I came to be.

But I don't have only one birth-day;
I celebrate every sweet moment in life,
for I am forever young at heart.

I can't count the number of moons,
for my soul's source is timeless.

My body feels like mine.
The cold skin on my belly,
the taste of my tea,
the warm touch.

It all feels like mine,
a higher version of my design.

A system created the movement of time
with the comfort of a mark on the calendar,
but without that mark in the line,
none of us would have an age,
feeling as young as we want.

But by seven, you will be programmed;
by twelve, you will hunt to survive;
by eighteen, be obedient, or the hunt for you will start.

Simulated society is conditioned to ask,
"How 'old' are you?"
instead of "How 'young'?
Are you sixty-five?"

Seniors cashing their coins are forgotten
to make room for the next one;
because their worth lies in this mark.

But without this collective agreement
on when we are supposed to age,
boldly, we will be taking further steps
and breaking the habit of falling dead.

We will swing across the ocean;
we will feel fearless instead.
Time will be ours.

Because finding a single measurement
of our biological age
is more complex
than simply counting, the ageless self.
If we could only use one of the senses at a time,

for each, a different interpretation would arise every time.
True essence, the senses simultaneously,
is the base for constructing the foreseen.

Everything that dreams is an astral being,
we can control and change our dream world
and the outer experience with lucidity.

So, I don't just celebrate the day I was born,
I celebrate the hidden purposes in life;
I applaud the stream.

The simple moments of inspiration
that could be easily overlooked,
but that guided me to you.

I celebrate the transcendent state,
the lucid dream,
and the complete disruption of age and time.
I celebrate the endless possibilities,
the boundless potential within me,
the unfolding sway.

I celebrate the journey of self-discovery,
the constant growth and evolution,
as I navigate the labyrinth of existence.

I celebrate the connections forged,
the love shared, and the bonds created,
which transcend the limitations of time.

I celebrate the wisdom gained,
through lessons learned and hardships endured,
as I embrace the profound teachings of life.

I celebrate the power of imagination,
the ability to shape reality,
and manifest dreams into tangible forms.

I celebrate the infinite spirit within,
the eternal flame that burns brightly,
defying the constraints of mortal existence.

Today, and every day,
I celebrate the ageless soul,
that dances with joy and sings with freedom.

Yo soy infinita. ¡No tengo edad!

Today is my birth-day.
But there is no need for candles because
I have been born more than once.

# Elemental

Nature's elements are a pure design
that can cleanse our bodies and make us divine.

Earth, water, fire, air, and space
collaborate in harmony to purify anew.

The earth beneath our feet, so solid and strong,
can ground us and balance where we belong.

Water that flows, a symbol of life,
can wash away impurities, cleanse and revive.

Fire, with its warmth, can ignite the soul,
purifying our spirit and making it whole.

Air that we breathe, so essential to life,
brings in new energy and frees us from strife.

And Akasha, the Ether, the space that surrounds us,
brings balance to all; the spirit abounds.

With nature's five elements, our bodies unite,
And we become purified,
refining the art of being alive.

Viviana Escobar

## Trauma

I stand tall,
aligning with my core truth,
reaching skyward in joy,
Transcending the shadows
in an upward spiral toward the clear blue.

Transcending,
Guided, I found a way
a dedication from myself to healing.

I must unravel the unresolved pain
with gratitude; I do not remain
in the past but move forward with grace,
I navigate the course they've traced

I'm all in,
Dedicated to a healing journey
under their benevolent guidance.

Emergence,
I break free from the cocoon
of unresolved torment,
no more the captive

Appreciation as my guide,
the past's chains,
are no longer inside.

I refuse to dwell within yesterday's grasp;
instead,
I slide forward,
Keep up the pace
I am boundless, limitless, as is space.

Enlightenment,
In this grand mosaic of existence,
I carve out my unique place.

Transcending trauma's remnants,
my voice yearns to break through the silence,
Cloaked in tranquility,
my vision undeterred, glows with resilience.

Through compassion I pave the path
toward inner transparency,
Synced to the rhythm of my HigherSelf,
I find my true liberty.

There is no more need to wear armor
against the noise of the world.
and liberty cannot be left in obscurity.

Guided by hope,
I discover unyielding alignment,
a new stride unfurled,
Transmuting trauma,
I rise!

# Bending Reality

I am the physical manifestation of the infinite being
Chosen to be here in this form with freedom as the basis seeing.

A creator of my own destiny
with thoughts that shape my reality
Visualization is the key to my desires,
emotions guide me to my higher aspirations.

The universe adores me, it knows I am God's favorite child
and the joy that I came here to impart
I am an everlasting life, never to die.
Relaxing into my natural well-being, all is indeed alright.

My path is unique, spiraling ways,
and the joy I focus on creates my days.
By-products of my journey, actions to take,
and contrasted circumstances
for the sake of being awake.

Death does not define me, nor does it restrain the self.
I am a creator, a physical extension of all it is,
here to experience joy and remember the love within.

## Attitude

Everything is Perceptual,
A game we play with our mind,
our senses taking in data,
a vibration interpretation we find.

Calibrating frequency,
The waves of reality,
Our focus attention,
A new experience we decree.

Clarifying the moment,
With a surrender to the now,
Choosing by the way it feels,
Our perception takes a bow.

The Mandela Effect,
A testament to our fallible sight,
reminding us that what we see,
is only our perception's might.

So let us be mindful,
of the stories we create,
for the truth is malleable,
in the hands of our perception's fate.

# Mother

A source of comfort, a constant light;
you chase away the fear and the fright.
Your unwavering love stands tall
through laughter, tears, and every trial.

You dissolve all of our differences
by listening to my experiences
and wiping my tears away.

You are what I know.
You hold me so close;
I am deeply grateful
last night you called.
I am ready
to break down the walls.

It's not your fault, mama;
you did your best with what you had.

You have been a gift from above, truly a sign
of love that lasts and never fades;

No matter what in my heart, you will stay.

# Father

My father is courageous,
finds redemption, makes amends
with his arms, shows how much he cares,
gives us strength, and helps us find our own way.

My father has a connection to the world's immense pretenses.
He takes glimpses into the unknown and unseen.
Has a heightened awareness that's not routine,
a sense of knowing that surpasses grace.

My father sees the future and
the secrets mankind has confined.
but with such power, there's also a price,
forgetting reality and losing sight of what's right.

Knowledge has been overwhelming
when his existence has trembled.
We inherited ancestral visions,
Infinite channeling, and intuition.

My father possesses an extraordinary sight,
and he embraces his gifts with delight.
He knows the truth that lies within.
It is not just power but a gift to his kith and kin.

## Sa Seeds

A new generation of beings,
arriving on earth with new meanings,
Born with gifts so rare,
Sa Seeds are beyond compare.

With a vital purpose,
they guide us with a song of love, peace, and unity,
raising the collective consciousness
along with the star seeds.

Their eyes hold a depth
that can see beyond what's left.
They lead us, with their intuition,
to a higher position and understanding.

They are the ones to heal
the wounds our world feels;
with their compassion and light,
they bring hope to the contrasted times.

Let us raise them with care,
for they are the ones to repair
the soul of our world and our race.

So, let us hold their hands
as they take us to new lands
of love, light, and harmony,
a land where we all can be genuinely free
by being 0N3 SA.

# The Body

There's something more than beautiful right there
when inhalation ends, and
exhalation is about to begin.

A great power resting in every organ, every cell,
and every particle filled
with this profundity.

A body with a brain with as many synapses and cells
as stars in the universe
can create and heal.

A body with the ability to perform
an incredible amount of complex tasks, convert ideas,
transmute, and heal.

A body that harnesses the force
to breathe life back into the most forgotten places.
You must adore your body and never forget
the universe that lives within you.

Remember the majesty of your humanity.

The magnificence of the body.

# Legacy

It didn't start with me, but I can heal it.

Breathing in, I smile at the ones that came before me.

I see them in me.

I feel our hearts united, lighting the way for the ones
to come with passion and purpose.

Breathing in, I see the clouds appear and disappear
like thoughts over the Andean Mountains,
gently flowing through its parallel chains, "Las cordilleras."

I "sea" the Caribbean, the Pacific, the majestic coastlines,
forests, savannas, wetlands, rivers, and deserts.

I see the snow and rain shadow of La Sierra Nevada de Santa Marta
and the resilient Wayuu walking over giant sand dunes,
rolling down into sparkling-colored waters.

I see salt flats and salt hills as white as a dove and my son sleeping in
a hammock under the desert sky.

I see a Baudó flying over Bahia Solano, the bright colors in Guatape,
and the strength in Los Llanos Orientales.

I see a land of striking contrasts, the atmosphere,
pink dolphins, micos titis, and the fierce Uitotos of the Amazon.

Breathing in, I feel the years of history in me.
The rich artistic blend of tribal heritage, Afro-Caribbean traditions,
and Spanish customs.

I hear the voices of the antioqueños, boyacenses, santandereanos,
huilenses, caucanos y de la gente del interior.

I see kindness en toda mi gente.

Breathing in, I smell los cafetales,
flowers, and the sweetness of las bananeras.

Breathing in, I can touch la Tierra Caliente in me.

It didn't start with you or me, but we can change it!

Breathing out, we can stand against deforestation,
armed conflict, violence, and corruption.

¡Together!
¡Ya basta! ¡no más!

Breathing out, I release the pain that runs deep through generations.
I smile at the indigenous nature in me.

I wasn't the first, but I can expand upon it.

I am not the first to stand strong, raise my voice, and liberate you.
Love is!

I am not the first to elevate us from our limitations to our potential.
Love is!

I am not the first to bend our reality and shape our destiny.
Love is!

I am not the first to transmute differences and judgments.
Love is!

-I am the love that reveals itself-And now I feel the energy of the
earth, "Pachamama," "Mana," tingling from my toes to my crown
when I hear, are you Colombian?

## Rebirth

Breathing in,
I allow life's gifts with ease.

Breathing out,
I greet the shadow that sits within me,
observing it to feel inspired.

Breathing in,
Grace showers me with elixirs of immortality.

Breathing out,
I let go of the resistance and let life flow within me.

In every breath, I receive life
to live all over again.

## The Dreamer

Breathing in
My soul dreams
It is dreaming the dream of you

Breathing out
You are the dreamer,
and I am in the dream with you

## Oneness

When the mind becomes still,
the mirrors cease to reflect
There is no more subject and object
Just U-N-I verse

## Family Tree

Breathing in,
I smile at my ancestors
and honor their free will.

I Integrate my genes and traits
and choose a new way to live.

Breathing out,
I release myself and turn to ashes the family tree.
It's my free will.

Breathing in,
I receive my people's wisdom.

Breathing out,
I see me, seeing you,
The vast SEA in you.

The pain, the sorrow, the suffering, it stops with me.
I stand on the bones of my ancestors,
forever grateful for their extraordinary qualities.

# Joy

There is a galaxy in my room,
moving constellations.
There is a moon on my side table,
a masterpiece for us to seek.

*There is a place within me where happiness resides.*

Where memories don't exist,
they are fractal information
in the records
beyond my mind.

In the present, I understand
Everything happens for a reason.

We can find joy in life
Just like water flows with the season
and leave a lasting stand.

*Hay un lugar dentro de mi donde habita la felicidad.*

# The Heart Language

Words that we speak, in our mind we seek
To understand how they shape our world
we must observe our thoughts

With our language we can build a bridge
to connect and communicate with an edge
to paint a picture, create a vibe
and take a journey, in the mind's ride

Reframing thoughts, a new perspective
Visualizing goals, with a future objective
Anchors to set, emotions to trigger
a powerful tool, to help you figure

The language is a way, to achieve your dreams
to communicate well, and build self-esteem.

A path to success, a way to grow
It's all about how you think, and what words you let flow.

# CHAPTER 10

# Poesía en Español

## Legado

No empezó conmigo, pero puedo curarlo.

Inhalando, les sonrío a los que nacieron antes de mi.
Los veo en mi.

Siento nuestros corazones unidos,
con pasión y propósito
iluminando el camino para los que vendrán.

Al inhalar,
veo las nubes aparecer y desaparecer
como pensamientos, sobre los Andes;
fluyendo suavemente a través de sus cordilleras.

Veo el mar Caribe,
el Pacífico, las majestuosas costas, bosques, sabanas, ríos y desiertos.

Veo la nieve y la lluvia de La Sierra Nevada de Santa Marta
y los resilientes Wayuu caminando sobre dunas de arena gigantes,
en aguas turquesas.

Veo colinas de sal tan blancas como una paloma,
y a mi hijo durmiendo en una hamaca
en el desierto, bajo el cielo.

Veo un Baudó sobrevolar Bahía Solano,
los colores vivos en Guatapé
y siento la fuerza de Los Llanos Orientales.

Veo una tierra de contrastes impactantes,
la atmósfera, delfines rosados, monos titis
y los valientes Uitotos del Amazonas.

Al inhalar, siento años de historia en mí.
La rica mezcla artística de herencia indígena,
tradiciones Afro-Caribeñas
y costumbres españolas.

Escucho las voces de los antioqueños,
boyacenses, santandereanos, huilenses, caucanos
y de la gente del interior.

Veo bondad en toda mi gente.

Al inhalar,
huelo los cafetales, las flores y la dulzura de las bananeras.

Al inhalar,
puedo tocar la Tierra Caliente en mí.

No empezó contigo ni conmigo, ¡pero podemos cambiarlo!

Exhalando,
podemos oponernos a la deforestación,
los conflictos armados, la violencia y la corrupción.

¡Ya basta! ¡No más!

Al exhalar, libero el dolor que corre a lo largo de generaciones.
Y aprecio la naturaleza indígena en mí.

-No soy la primera, pero puedo expandir-

No soy la primera
en mantenerme firme, en alzar la voz, en liberarte.
¡El amor lo és!

No soy la primera
en llevarnos de nuestras limitaciones a nuestro potencial.
¡El amor lo és!

No soy la primera
en cambiar mi realidad y moldear mi destino.
¡El amor lo és!

No soy la primera
en transmutar las diferencias y el juicio.
¡El amor lo és!

Soy la revelación del amor
Y ahora siento la energía de la tierra,
"Pachamama," "Mana"
hormigueando desde los dedos de mis pies hasta mi corona
cuando escucho, ¿eres colombiana?

## Todo lo que Brilla es Carbón

¿Qué es normal y qué no?
Pides ayuda y juzgan tu comportamiento
Rápidamente te etiquetan con un sello
reflejando sus propios miedos
ciegos ignoran tu versatilidad

Pero no me mal entiendas
Hay trastornos reales
Y de nada sirve ignorar
es importante analizar

Pero a mi gusta observar
Me gusta escuchar de lo que hablas
Me gusta verte respirar
Porque yo me he sentido igual

En mi opinion,
tu eres creación en movimiento
Eres perfección en fragmentos
Fuerza y delicadeza
Eres todo lo que has anhelado
Eres la búsqueda y el reencuentro

Eres el universo sonriendo
La manifestación en atuendo
La danza entre la inocencia y la sabiduría
Eres las galaxias experimentado la vida

El profundo vacío en tu pecho
La ansiedad que sientes al despertar
La melancolía que te visita
Y ese pánico mirando al techo

Es tu mente en el pasado
Eres tu deslizándote hacia el futuro
Eres tú sin los recursos del momento presente
Eres la preocupación alterando la línea del tiempo

El origen del todo está en este momento
Piensas que te falta lo que necesitas
Crees que deberías tener más
Más espacio, más cosas, y ser más,
Ser eso que brilla

Consideras que no eres suficiente
Que debes probarte ante la gente
Que esta es tu unica suerte
Y no tienes a nadie en quien confiar

Crees qué debes solucionar o arreglar
Lo que ya tiene un curso natural
La luna refleja, el planeta gira
Y vos respiras sin pensar

La verdad es que cuanto más te miro, mas veo
Que el amor es el compás
Pero si ya no te amas
¿Cómo podrás amar una vez más?

Dicen que el amor propio es ostentoso
Y que la vanidad, es pecado capital
¿Entonces qué puedes hacer?
Con tanta confusión ante tus pies

Siéntate en silencio frente al espejo
Y mira más allá del ser
Escucha el palpitar de tu corazón
Y respira las dudas, los secretos y el dolor

Eres lo único que necesitas
El océano integrando el carbón
El instante suficiente y eterno
Amate través del miedo y reconoce tu diamante interior

Mira tu reflexión y ve claramente
Que solo tu puedes hacerte feliz
Estás a cargo de la creación
Eres el principio y eres el fin

Y cuando esta sea tu verdad
empezarás a forjar tu realidad
La reacción al mundo será de amor
Y tu carga será más ligera

Tu corazón se abrirá a la aceptación radical
de tu perfecta humanidad
De tu diversidad
Porque no estás fallando
estas evolucionando

Entonces a partir de hoy
te invito a que ajustes tu percepción
Mírate bien en el espejo y di
Todo lo que brilla es carbón.

## Órbita Microcósmica

Quiero amar en muchos países
pero encontré todos los países en ti
El sol salió para ver TU despertar
YO despierto al verte sonreir

      Quiero viajar por el cosmos
      y vos dibujas el cosmos en la piel
      Oscilaciones en altas frecuencias
      son intenciones bañadas en miel

            Eres las fuerzas elementales
            del universo
            alimento al intelecto
            aire bonito para respirar

Querer recordar
Despierta el mar en mi
Un salto en lo más profundo
y descubro que el amor está en mi

      Se me olvida
      el espacio y el tiempo
      al vernos respirar
      más allá del cuerpo
      Yo trasciendo en ti.

## El Amor en los Tiempos del Covid

Te observo respirar cada día

Tu gracia me recuerda

la inmensidad de esta maestría

*Esta pandemia trajo consigo*

*la elevación de la conciencia*

*las ganas de ser tu testigo*

Y cada día trae la ilusión

de ser cada vez mejor

de conocer el interior

Cada dia es una oportunidad de expansión

confinados en una casa

que pronto se convirtió en un templo

permitiendo la libertad del ser y la sanación.

## Metrología Cuántica

Los silencios largos
son espacios para sanar el alma
Pero, yo estoy aquí
Yo no me he ido

El lenguaje incondicional
no tiene palabras
El tiempo se mide diferente
en un reloj de lógica cuántica

Liberemos la mente
y seamos conscientes
que el vivir se siente
Y esta, la distancia
es solo un puente.

## El Arte de Permitir

Hoy no solo es otro día
hoy es el día
en el que me permito ser
el ser que vine a SER

Hoy permito que mi corazón se abra
y reciba las bendiciones del universo
Hoy escojo la alegría
como el propósito de mi vida

Hoy me permito respirar
todo el aire que está acá
De cerquita entrego mi vulnerabilidad
y aprecio mi infinito poder al sembrar

Hoy soy la hija que siempre quise ser
                Hoy no es un día como cualquiera

Hoy es la unión entre mis sueños,
            el momento presente
                        y el ayer
Hoy es, el todo lo que tengo
                  El constante amanecer

Hoy me permito ser la mujer que cultivó una vida
                  La madre que siempre quise ser
Hoy me permito florecer
        en la privacidad de mi atardecer.

            En el aprendizaje de una especie en evolución
                              me permito cada día renacer.

Hoy me permito estar en la conjunción
                  entre la oportunidad y la preparación
Hoy mi frecuencia esta lista
                  y mi suerte es oportunista.
Hoy entendí
        que de poetas, tontos y locos, todos tenemos un poco
Hoy me permito soltar el ego
            y responder a la energía y al placer.

Porque más vale un por si acaso que un lo pensaré
                  hoy mi sonrisa le abre la puerta a las posibilidades
Les dice, sigan, están es su casa
                  pónganse cómodas,
                              que aquí pueden permanecer.

# CHAPTER 11

# Integration

## Final Word

As you come to the end of this book, remember that the power to bend reality lies within you. With every inhale and exhale, you have the ability to tap into a limitless source of energy. You have the agency to shape your own existence.

Take a deep breath and let it out with a sigh of relief, knowing that you now possess these tools to transform your life in ways you may have never imagined. You can use them to release stress, tap into your intuition, and heal physical and emotional pain. Let your breath be your magic wand, paintbrush, and pen as you create the masterpiece that is your life.

Let it guide you through the ups and downs, and always come back to it when you need it. Let it be your compass, anchor, and reminder that you can connect with your deepest desires and make them a reality.

Mastering your breath is not just a practice; it's a lifestyle, a way of living your life consciously with purpose, intention, joy and authenticity.

As you continue your journey, may you always remember to trust in the infinite possibilities within you. May your breath be your companion, wise guide, and loving friend. The world needs your unique gifts and talents; your breath is the key to unlocking them and Mana Breathwork a way to guide you.

As the second day of spring unfurls, Los Angeles finds itself cradled in a tender embrace of rain, a symphony of droplets that bring the promise of rebirth and renewal.

Each day dawns, carrying its unique blend of triumphs and challenges. Still, the one constant is the love and joy that permeates every moment like an undercurrent of sheer bliss.

Last year, the Complex Regional Syndrome Diagnosis that was given in 2002 was reviewed with no sufficient evidence to believe it is still present. Nevertheless, I am dedicated to my well-being, and continue actively in treatments.

This morning, I had a breathwork session guided by Kalyani, a loving spirit I first met during my first training with Leonard in Sierraville. Like a delicate, celestial instrument, Kalyani sang a loving prayer for the messages contained within the pages of this book. Reminding me of how we exist in more than one state simultaneously. A full circle event.

As we dived, I felt the comforting presence of my spiritual guides, illuminating the path before us with a warm, radiant glow. Their gentle and reassuring guidance reminded us that we are never truly alone and are always supported in our journey through this wondrous, ever-evolving existence.

And so, the second day of spring unfolds; each raindrop is a whisper from the heavens. With each breath I am genuinely in love with the family we have gathered around us, of how and with whom I spend my days.

I share a deep bond with Adrian, who, now grown up, is incredibly passionate about agriculture and sustainability.

I am a conscious entrepreneur, a wellness consultant, and a student. My mission is to share the power of the present moment and its infinite possibilities, while continuously uncovering the secrets of longevity and well-being. Each therapy offers unique benefits and targets specific issues. The magic, however, lies in the combination of these therapies and in our discernment, which is guided by our innate intelligence.

Most of my days are propelled by the habits described in the daily practice of The Mana Breathwork Universe. With daily growing awareness of our own boundless potential, the new species coming, and the power of artificial intelligence and precision medicine at our fingertips, we stand at the precipice of an exciting new era.

We are witnessing an incredible awakening as humanity collectively remembers its true nature and purpose, and new souls continue to join us on this miraculous journey as the new species are coming.

I am grateful for you coming along on this journey, I hope you discovered more of who you are, for that is what life and these pages are about.

The time has come for us to seize this incredible moment and harness the power of our collective intelligence.

With a wealth of knowledge and understanding available to us like never before, we have the tools to shape the future of our world in ways that were once unimaginable.

Feel the energy of this amazing moment coursing through your veins. The possibilities are truly limitless, and the future is ours to create.

It is up to us.

So, are you ready to take a deep breath?

# Acknowledgments

Creating *Bending Our Reality* has been an incredible journey of growth and discovery. I am deeply grateful for the unwavering support, guidance, and encouragement of the amazing people who have played a vital role in bringing this project to life.

Firstly, I want to express my deepest gratitude to my family, who has always supported and inspired me. Their unwavering love, patience, and encouragement have been the driving force behind my success.

To my son, his belief in me has given me the strength and motivation to push past my limits and bring my work to the world.

I would also like to thank my students, who have always been there for me and helped me stay dedicated and focused on this project. Their trust and valuable feedback have been invaluable in shaping the contents of this book.

I also want to extend my appreciation to the breathwork practitioners, teachers, and experts who have shared their knowledge and experiences with me. Their insights have been incredibly enriching and have helped me provide a comprehensive guide.

Finally, thank you to my readers for taking the time to read this book. It is my hope that the insights and techniques shared within these pages will inspire and empower you to embrace reality and create the life you desire.

Thank you to all who have contributed to this project in any way. Your support has been instrumental in bringing this book to fruition, and I am forever grateful for your belief in me and this vital work.

Wishing you boundless joy and endless blessings.

## Special Thanks

I want to express my heartfelt gratitude to the following individuals for their unwavering support and contributions to this book:

To my family: Marco Adrián Yanez Escobar, Carolina Escobar, Gianna Escobar, Flor López, Eduardo Escobar, Hernán Escobar, Herni Escobar, Nicolás Escobar, María Alejandra Escobar, and to our extended families in Colombia, the United States, and Argentina.

Especially to: Joaquín "Espinacas" Astelarra, Anyeli Jiménez Gómez, Julieta Villamil Jiménez, Francisco Astelarra, Sara Caputo, Tomás, Clara, Pepa y Mateo Astelarra, Stacy-Thea Kuuipoalohalani, Natalia Quintero García, Marisa Sánchez, Guido Isaza, Marta Vélez Calad, Ángela Vélez Calad, Cristina Tamayo, Jony Muñoz, Natalia Ramírez, Milagros y Martín Muñoz Ramírez, Juan Diego Zuleta, Luisa Zuleta, Isabella Montoya, Vanesa Cano, Julio Camacho, Carlos Guerrero, Isaac Guerrero, Óscar Ruiz Mejía, Jorge Mejía, Beatriz Sierra, José Calderón, David Restrepo, Camila Harb, Paola Harb, Jay Rajagopalan, Gary Chivichyan and Juan David Giraldo Ramírez.

To my Rebirthing family: Leonard Orr, Elvi Orr, Egbert Sukop, Colleen Buckman "Kalyani," Laz Jefferson, Aaron Overstreet, and Howard Mermer.

To our first generation of students: Shanina Rivera, Erika Dorsey, Michelle McKee, Oxana Beliaeva, Claudine Penedo, and Peter Schrager. Their dedication and commitment have been a constant source of inspiration for all of us.

To the Royal Families and diplomatic delegations visiting Los Angeles, Ponte Vedra Beach, and Miami, thank you for always allowing me to participate in your wellness.

My deepest gratitude to Jawaher bint Hamad bin Suhaim Al Thani, First Lady of Qatar, Isabelle Daikeler, Swae Lee, Anderson Silva, Joseph Jourieh, Dr. Ram Dandillaya, Dr. David Nazarian, Dr.

Brian Mecca, Dr. Hernan Luna and Martin Quiroz. Your support has been a fundamental pillar on my path.

To all my dear friends, you know who you are! I am grateful for your support and honored to have you by my side. And to the hundreds of medical industry colleagues and advisors, your love and support are felt daily. Thank you!

Lastly, I want to express my love and gratitude to my beloved birth country, Colombia, and my chosen country, the United States, for providing the rich cultural backdrop that inspired this work.

With love and appreciation!

# About the Author

**Viviana Escobar** is a Colombian-American author, spiritual teacher, and internationally recognized Breathwork Master, best known for her groundbreaking book *Bending Our Reality: The Power of Breathwork to Heal, Transform, and Awaken* and its Spanish version, *Moldeando Nuestra Realidad.* Her work blends ancient wisdom with quantum physics, offering accessible tools for self-growth, healing, and emotional intelligence.

Born in Sincelejo, Colombia, and raised in Miami, Medellín, and Bogotá, Escobar moved permanently to the United States in 2001. Her multicultural background deeply informs her writing and teaching, drawing from Latin American spiritual traditions, consciousness exploration, and somatic practices. With *Bending Our Reality*, Escobar has emerged as a central voice in the global conversation on conscious breathing and its transformative power. The book is widely regarded as one of the most comprehensive and inspiring guides to Breathwork available today.

After a spinal injury, she developed **The Mana Breathwork Method**. Her teachings have reached students globally, including diplomats, royal families, heads of state, celebrities, and athletes. She is regarded as the "master of the masters" among Breathwork practitioners. As of 2025, *Bending Our Reality* is available in four formats—paperback, hardcover, Audible, and Kindle—across the United States, United Kingdom, Canada, Mexico, and Colombia, expanding her impact to audiences in both English and Spanish.

In addition to her literary and spiritual work, Escobar is also a spoken word performance artist, offering a bold, embodied expression of love, resilience, and joy.

Recognized by The Monroe Institute as a certified explorer of consciousness, she has cultivated an interdisciplinary background that bridges ancestral wisdom with contemporary science. Her journey includes extensive studies in Rebirthing Breathwork, Quantum Healing Hypnosis, Pranic Healing, Tantra, Neuro-Linguistic Programming (NLP), Kundalini Yoga, and Transcendental Meditation. This foundation is enriched by her professional experience in audiovisual media, interpreting, and the development of purpose-driven entrepreneurial ventures.

**Viviana Escobar's mission** is to raise the vibration of humanity through breath and presence. Her life's work reflects a powerful fusion of passion, purpose, and poetic soul.

**For more information:**
vivianaescobar.com
bendingourreality.com
moldeandonuestrarealidad.com
manabreathwork.com
@vivescobar

## Medical Disclaimer

When addressing the potential effects and benefits of The Mana breathwork Universe and any method, idea, practice or exercise in this book, we've made every effort to ensure that we accurately represent the program and techniques and their ability to impact and improve your life. However, the author does not guarantee that you will experience results in any given timeframe. This method has been shown to have an effect on the majority of people who have successfully completed the program; however, nothing in this book is a guarantee to you of any particular impact or effect.

This content is not intended to be a substitute for professional medical advice, diagnosis, or treatment. Please consult with your physician with any questions that you may have regarding a medical condition.

The Mana Breathwork Universe practices and methods will not guarantee any medical results whatsoever. Never disregard professional medical advice or delay in seeking it because of something you read in this book. With this disclaimer, the author of this book is released from liability due to misuse of the information it contains.

Any interpretation or application of the information provided should be made with caution and discretion. The author and publisher shall not be held liable for any consequences resulting from using or misusing the information contained herein.

# Privacy Disclaimer

The events, situations, and characters described in this book are the product of the author's mind. Any resemblance to actual persons, living or dead, or any incidents involving real-life situations or events is purely coincidental and unintentional. The author has taken all necessary steps to maintain confidentiality and protect the privacy of any individual or organization mentioned in this book. Names, locations, and identifying details have been altered to preserve anonymity. Any similarity to actual persons or organizations is inadvertent and not intended to convey or imply any factual representation.

The author does not assume responsibility for any unintended offense, misrepresentation, or harm that may arise from the contents of this book.

The views and opinions expressed within are solely those of the author and do not necessarily reflect those of the publisher or any affiliated parties.

# References

Leonard Orr

Rebirthing International

The HeartMath Institute

Gregg Braden

Bruce Lipton

Ra Uru Hu

Esther Hicks "Abraham Hicks"

Dolores Cannon

Mantak Chia

Dr. Joe Dispenza

Darryl Anka "Bashar"

Drunvalo Melquisedec

Camila Castello

Akahi Ricardo

Elizabeth April

Dr. J. Andrew Armour

Nikola Tesla

Albert Einstein

Dr. Stephen Porges

Richard Bandler and John Grinder

Phineas Parkhurst Quimby

Neville Goddard

Paramahansa Yogananda

The International Breathwork Foundation (IBF)

American Lung Association

American Association for Respiratory Care

National Board for Respiratory Care

American Association of Cardiovascular and Pulmonary Rehabilitation

American Academy of Allergy, Asthma & Immunology

American Heart Association

American Thoracic Society

National Association for Medical Direction of Respiratory Care

National Institute of Health

National Library of Medicine

National Lung Health Education Program

National Heart, Lung, and Blood Institute
National Science Foundation (quantum-based research)
National Human Genome Research Institute (NHGRI)
The National Aeronautics and Space Administration (NASA)
Chinese Academy of Sciences (CAS)
Nature and Science categories, Harvard University
Nature and Science, Stanford University
Massachusetts Institute of Technology (MIT)
The Journal of Alternative and Complementary Medicine
The Journal of Affective Disorders
The University of Cambridge
Mayo Clinic
Cedars Sinai
The Holy Bible
The Qur'an
The Bhagavad Gita
The Torah
The Tripitaka, the Mahayana sutras, and Tantric texts
Star Wars Movies
New Thought Thinkers
Avatar: The Last Airbender

Plus many years of tuning my intuition, watching YouTube videos, social media, surfing the net, attending classes and workshops, using grammar apps and fact-checking; here we are, with a harmonic collage of how my mind has interpreted everything I have experienced. I am deeply grateful to each and every person who has studied consciousness and the breath.

# Hey there, amazing reader!

I'm happy that you've joined me on this incredible adventure by picking up my book, "Bending Our Reality." You know, this journey we're on together is really special. It's all about discovering more about who we truly are and embracing a life full of joy and authenticity.

In "Bending Our Reality," we've dived deep into the magical world of breathwork and the importance of loving ourselves. Isn't it just amazing to think that our most powerful tool is within us? It's in our breath – that gentle inhalation and exhalation that we do every single day without even thinking about it. That power rests quietly, waiting in the space between each breath and in those quiet moments between our thoughts. It's a superpower that we all have, and it's always there, ready for us to tap into it. But here's something really important: I would absolutely love to hear what you think about our journey together in the book. Your thoughts, feelings, and experiences mean the world to me. Would you be willing to share your review of "Bending Our Reality"? It's super easy – just head over to where you got the book and write a few sentences about what you liked, what surprised you, or even what you learned.

Sharing your review will help me and guide other awesome people like you in searching for their path to joy and self-discovery. Your words can light the way for someone else's journey, and that's a beautiful thing.

Thanks a million for being part of this experience with me. Remember, the power is right there in your breath, and together, we're learning how to use it to become the best versions of ourselves.

Keep breathing, keep exploring, and stay awesome!

With lots of love and gratitude,

Viviana Escobar

## Visit our shop

bendingourreality.com
moldeandonuestrarealidad.com
manabreathwork.com
vivianaescobar.com

Social Connect
Youtube.com/c/ManaBreathwork
Instagram.com/ManaBreathwork
Instagram.com/vivescobar
Instagram.com/joaquinespinacas
tiktok.com/@bendingourreality
tiktok.com/@manabreathwork
facebook.com/manabreathwork
Discord/ManaBreathwork
X/BendingRe4lity
threads.net/@vivescobar

*Spread Joy by gifting this book*

www.ingramcontent.com/pod-product-compliance
Lightning Source LLC
Chambersburg PA
CBHW030918140626
46545CB00016B/1391